When the Going GETS TOUGH

Still More Adventures from a Country Vet
Dr. David Perrin

Illustrations by Wendy Liddle

Dave's Press Inc.

Published by Dave's Press Inc.
1521 Canyon-Lister Road
Creston, British Columbia
Canada V0B 1G2

Cover and book design by Warren Clark
Illustrations by Wendy Liddle
Edited by Betsy Brierley
Proofread by Elizabeth McLean

Printed and bound in Canada

Library and Archives Canada Cataloguing in Publication

Perrin, David, 1948-
When the going gets tough: still more adventures from a country vet / David Perrin; illustrator, Wendy Liddle.

(Adventures of a country vet series)
ISBN 978-0-9866569-0-3

1. Perrin, David, 1948– 2. Veterinarians—British Columbia—Biography. 3. Animals—Anecdotes I Liddle, Wendy II Title III. Series: Perrin, David, 1948- Adventures of a country vet series.
SF613.P47A3 2010   636.089092   C2010-906797-5

Dedicated to my children:

Joan, Marshall, Gordon, and Alicia

my grandson James

and the memory of Doris Currie

Acknowledgements

It has been twelve years since *Don't Turn Your Back in the Barn* was published. It was followed by *Dr. Dave's Stallside Manner*, *Where Does It Hurt?*, *Keep Sweet: Children of Polygamy*, and *Never Say Die*. One would think that with each book, the process would become simpler—that a path would somehow be worn to make the journey easier. Not so. Writing for me is all about discipline—a character trait that I often find wanting. I can't count how often I've been stalled for days on end unable to force myself to attack the keyboard. Time and again, it was emails and letters from you, my readers, that gave me the motivation to carry on. To you I owe a big thank you.

At 11:30 on the morning of June 4, 2009, while driving towards Salmo over the Kootenay Pass, I was involved in a collision with another vehicle. My van left the highway and rolled end over end down a five-hundred-foot embankment. Needless to say, by the time my car came to rest, it was little more than a twisted mass of metal. My neck was broken and I was unable to extricate myself from the rubble. A dozen total strangers risked their own lives cutting me free of the entanglement and carrying me back up to the highway. It was without a doubt the most humbling experience of my life. By the time they had me on the highway at 4:30 that afternoon, I was drenched with sweat—not a drop of it was mine. I'm so grateful to the Salmo and Beasely Fire Department volunteers, the ambulance attendants, and all the passersby who gave of themselves so that I could carry on.

Once again, I was reminded of how important family and friends can be in times of need. My sisters, Audrey O'Hearn and Kay Rizzotti...my children, Joan, Marshall, Gordon, and Alicia...and friends too numerous to list, I love you all.

As with all my other books, my editor Betsy Brierley, my illustrator Wendy Liddle, my designer Warren Clark, and my proofreader Elizabeth McLean extended themselves beyond my expectations. I couldn't have asked them for more.

A special thanks to Rob McLeod of the Creston Veterinary Clinic for allowing me to share his story about a raccoon named Coonie.

Contents

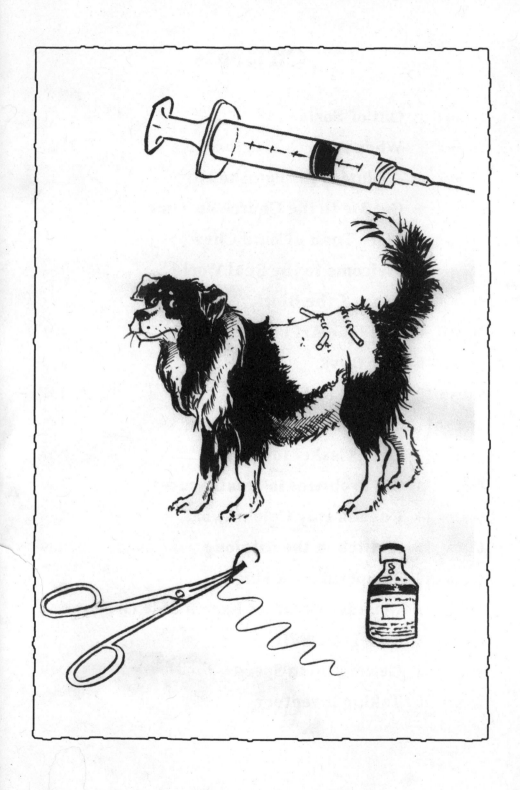

Chapter 1

Out of Sorts

"Just a second, Mrs. Randall. Let me ask Dr. Perrin what he thinks."

My assistant Margaret set the phone down and made her way to the waiting room where I was sitting with Lug's head in my lap. It was the end of the day, and he had been stuck in the car for most of the afternoon while I was doing surgery for the repair of a twisted stomach on a dairy cow. Now that he had my undivided attention, he was determined to take advantage of it.

"Dave...Mrs. Randall's really concerned about Shep. She had him in to see Jim this afternoon. She insists the dog isn't well, but Jim couldn't find anything wrong with him."

"What did you think? Were you there?"

Margaret hesitated a moment and considered her answer carefully. "It seems to me that Jim's been a bit out of sorts lately...it was just before he was leaving for lunch, and I know he wasn't happy when Shep growled at him."

I had noticed that Jim had lost a lot of his zeal lately, and more and more farmers had been requesting that I attend their animals rather than the "new guy." That was strange, because with his gift of the gab, his initial acceptance several months ago had been exceptional.

"Have you got Shep's record handy?"

Margaret dug through a mess of cards that were scattered on top of the filing cabinet.

"Here it is," she said, passing it to me.

The Randalls had been good clients. I had vaccinated Shep as a pup and neutered him about a year ago when he took to wandering beyond the limits of their acreage in Wynndel, the small community north of Creston. Mrs. Randall had always struck me as a no-nonsense type of woman with a good head on her shoulders, and I'd never known her to make a big deal out of nothing.

I glanced over the notations that Jim had made this morning. I couldn't miss the big *HANDLE WITH CAUTION* across the top of the file. The way the letters were scrawled with red ink suggested he was angry when he wrote it.

"Jim vaccinated him today," Margaret informed me. "Mrs. Randall told us he was overdue for his shots, and that if he was okay, we should bring him up to date."

"Maybe he's had a reaction."

She looked at me impassively.

"From what I can see in Jim's notes, everything seemed pretty normal," I added.

My assistant pursed her lips, and I could see that she was struggling with something.

"What's the matter, Margaret?"

"I'm not sure he took enough time with the dog."

"What do you mean, enough time?"

Margaret cringed at the tone of my voice. "Jim was planning something, and he was kind of anxious to get going. When Shep turned and growled at him, he..."

I could tell by her countenance that she was uncomfortable telling me more. It had never been part of her nature to be a tattle-tale.

"Have her bring him in."

With a sudden look of relief, Margaret quickly returned to the telephone. "Bring Shep in, Mrs. Randall. No...no...we won't charge you for examining him again. Dr. Perrin just wants to assure you that it's nothing serious."

There was an uncomfortable silence after Margaret hung up.

"What was Jim up to?" I asked.

"I don't know, Dave. He didn't say."

She was silent for a long time as, one by one, she placed the records in the file holders. After finishing the last of them, she closed the top drawer of the cabinet and turned to me. "He's not been himself the last couple of weeks...Doris and I have both noticed it."

"Maybe he's not getting enough sleep, what with the new baby and all."

"Maybe...but when they stayed with me for the first few weeks, Mary and I got to be good friends—I really like her. I stop by their house every now and then to say hello. The poor girl's lonely without having any friends of her own...she never gets to go anywhere unless Jim takes her." Margaret sighed, then plunked herself down on the bench across from me. "It's like she's caged up in that little house all by herself looking after Cynthia—Jim seems to have lots of other things on the go."

I sat like a lump absorbing her words and petting Lug. As I massaged his ears, he groaned and leaned his head into me.

Man! How unprepared I had been to start this practice. It had been hard enough learning how to deal with clients and have a half decent chance of keeping them happy; now I had to orchestrate a staff of individuals all with their own agendas. I should have been forced to take a master's degree in psychology before seeing my first client and a PhD before hiring my first employee. Why did it all have to be so complicated?

The moment the door opened, my German shepherd grudgingly turned away from me and slunk to the back room. He knew the rule about staying out of the way when there were clients in the front office. For a dog that had been dumped on me as a stray, Lug had turned out to be the best companion I could have asked for. Constantly on my heels at home, he travelled everywhere with me. He knew all my secrets and had accompanied me through many ups and downs in the last couple of years.

Mrs. Randall nodded at me and pulled her rotund collie-shepherd cross the last few feet over the threshold. Grabbing hold of his tail to keep from catching it, she closed the door to cut off his retreat.

"So what's he been doing, Estell?" Margaret asked.

"Nothing...that's the problem. I couldn't get him to budge after we got home from here. He wasn't interested in food...never touched his water. He even growled at the girls when they tried to pet him—that's not like him. He can often be a bit grumpy with strangers, but never someone in the family. The girls normally tumble all over him." She gave Shep a concerned look, then turned to me. "He's just not right."

I settled onto the bench abreast the trembling dog and checked the record again. Although he was within arm's length, I made no effort to make contact with him.

"When did you notice a change in his behaviour, Mrs. Randall?"

"He was fine two days ago," she said pensively. "My sister brought her daughter and their Dobie over...the kids were running all over the property playing tag and tobogganing, and he was right out there with them."

"How does he get along with the Doberman?"

"Oh, great...Jeremiah and Shep have been friends since they were puppies."

"Has Shep ever done anything like this before?"

"No...never, and we've had him since he was eight weeks old."

"And he's not been limping?"

Mrs. Randall shook her head. "He just moves in slow motion, if he moves at all."

"Sometimes back pain makes them act that way," I offered. "Maybe with all that running around the other day, he's injured a disc."

Shep's mistress gave me a questioning look. "Maybe."

"I see his temperature was normal this morning," I mused, verifying the information on the card.

"His temperature?"

"Yes, Dr. Steelman recorded his temperature as 38.5, which is normal."

"But he never took his temperature," she insisted. "After Shep growled at the young man, he hardly laid a hand on him…except to give him his needle, of course."

I looked at Margaret, who raised her eyebrows and quickly left the room. She returned shortly with a thermometer in her hand. "I'll get it now, Dave."

I glanced back at the record, at Jim's notes about normal pulse and respiration. He could have guessed at the respiration from a distance, but the pulse?

When Margaret lifted the dog's tail and inserted the thermometer, he grumbled and turned his head as far as his stocky body would allow.

"You're okay, Shep," his owner assured him, pressing his head into her thigh. "We're going to find out what's wrong with you."

I retreated to the exam room, grabbed some gauze from the glass bandage canister, and unravelled three feet from a roll. Returning to our patient, I knelt beside him and tied his mouth tightly closed with a loop above, a loop below, then a tie behind his head.

"We just want to keep you honest, old boy," I said, giving him a few strokes on the top of his shaggy head.

When Margaret removed the thermometer, I rolled up his lip and examined his gums. They were pink, and the moment I released pressure on them, their colour returned immediately. Margaret's expression was noncommittal when she handed me the thermometer. She watched my face as I rotated and read it—39.8 degrees Celsius.

"He's definitely running a fever," I said to an expectant Mrs. Randall.

"I knew he wasn't right," she replied with conviction.

"Can you have a seat here and hold Shep's head close to you?"

I knelt next to the dog and applied my stethoscope to his left side; his heart sounds were normal. I moved the stethoscope head high on his left side and listened, then did the same on the right. Mrs. Randall was focused on my face as I removed the apparatus from my ears and stuffed it back into my pocket.

"His chest sounds are good," I assured her.

I shifted my attention to the dog's abdomen and slowly worked my way through a rather pendulous tummy. Although he flinched slightly when I palpated deeply towards the region of his kidneys, I wasn't convinced that this was the source of his pain. It was when I moved my hand to the dog's spine that he twirled his head in an attempt to get at me.

"No, Shep! Behave!" Mrs. Randall blurted nervously.

Because I had been suspecting a disc problem, I had intentionally left my examination of his spine to the last. The school of hard knocks had taught me early in my career that valuable information was often missed by immediately looking at what I considered the most likely source of a problem.

"So you think it's his back?" My client kept her eyes on my hands as I carefully compressed the spine over his thorax.

The dog tensed when I continued the process in the lumbar region. It was there that I found the source of Shep's discomfort. The moment I contacted it he winced and began to squirm in his owner's arms. Deep beneath the thick matted hair over his back was an encrusted scab. I pulled my hand back. The index finger was wet and covered with serous fluid. I sniffed my finger—it had an offensive odour.

"What did you find?" Mrs. Randall asked.

"A wound…"

"From what?"

I raised my eyebrows. "It appears he and Jeremiah got a bit carried away."

By the time I was finished with Shep, he looked like he'd had a run-in with a porcupine barber. A two-foot square had been shaved bald in the middle of his back, and two rows of bristly white nylon sutures ran six inches apart for three inches on one side of his spine and for almost five on the other. I had also placed drains in several strategic locations to remove the fluids that were likely to accumulate.

I didn't know what to say to Mrs. Randall as I handed her the antibiotics and she turned to leave. "I'm sorry you had to make an extra trip," I said lamely.

Patches of leftover snow crunched and squeaked under my feet as I picked my way along the trail through the pine trees to my hay shed. It had been sunny for most of the day, but there was a nip in the air tonight. Lug trotted along at my heels with the ever-present stick jammed crosswise in his mouth. It was good to finally get away from the office—this plot of dirt always seemed able to ground me in some small way.

The latest train of events was troubling; maybe I should have just kept plodding along the best I could on my own instead of hiring Jim. The last thing I needed was someone to babysit. It wasn't as if I had never missed a diagnosis myself, but in this case, not even looking for Shep's wounds bordered on gross negligence.

I believed Mrs. Randall's assertion that Jim hadn't examined her pet at all. He couldn't have, because if he had even run his hand down the dog's back, he'd have gotten the same instant reaction I got. Would I have to watch over Jim's shoulder on all his cases now? After all, when a client came to the Creston Vet Clinic, I had an obligation to make sure that they got the quality of service they deserved.

I was almost to the corral when my flashlight picked up a flash of white—Petunia had seen me coming. Although Lug grumbled when she trotted over, she paid him not the slightest heed. Grabbing hold of my coat sleeve, she inhaled it and commenced sucking immediately.

Keeping Petunia out of my living room had been the main reason I had constructed a rail fence between the house and the creek. Late in the summer, when my parents had been down for a weekend, the errant Holstein had snuck in while Mom was out in the yard. Mother was less than happy when she got back to the kitchen and found Petunia plucking the makings of a salad from where she left them on the pantry. Not only was the poor woman upset about the mess she had to clean up, but she couldn't get the calf to leave until Father came to the rescue a half hour later.

"That's enough, Petunia!" I yanked my sleeve from her mouth.

Although she'd been weaned for months now, she was still certain that I was her mom and the constant bearer of treats. I had grown accustomed to her playful antics and usually carried a few chunks of apple or carrots for her to munch on.

"Sorry, girl, but you're out of luck today."

She trotted along behind me until I reached the corral and ducked through the slats of the feeder.

"Dinner's served, girls! Come, boss! Come, boss! Come, boss!"

Pulling some bales from the stack, I lugged them to the trough, broke them open, and spread them along the feeder. With the light directed out into the yard, I watched as one by one the cows sauntered to the corral, stepped up onto the concrete pad, and stuck their heads through the spaces in the bunk. When they were all present and accounted for, I clicked off the light, sank onto a bale, and stared out into the night.

Lug came to me and nuzzled my hand. I patted him and pushed him to the hay-covered floor of the shed. There was something satisfying about sitting here in the dark, listening to the cows munch down their hay. Why couldn't things be this simple at the office?

I sat motionless, focusing on my breath, and doing my best to clear the thoughts that were rumbling through my mind. I kept reaffirming that this, too, would pass. The time I had spent at Yasodhara Ashram a few years back had served me well, and whenever a situation looked too complicated for me to handle, I resorted to meditation. Concentrating on the flow of the air at the tip of my nostrils, I watched silently as thoughts of despair, loss, and jealousy drifted in front of me. As I persisted, they passed and floated away. All that remained was the distant sound of hay being crunched by dentine and enamel.

Finally, there was a persistent image that wouldn't leave me— Swami Radha, the ashram's guru, was sitting next to me. Her heavy German accent hung on every word that echoed through my mind. "Look into the mirror and say thank you," she affirmed. "For you were the creator of your present reality. To you goes the credit, to you goes the blame...for all that you have created." The words would not go away. I opened my eyes and stared at the silhouettes of cattle as they tossed their heads and dug deep into the void of the trough.

After my time at the ashram, I had been convinced that every thought was a prayer, that with my immediate thoughts I was creating my reality in the future. If I was right, then, what had I done to attract these problems with Jim? Hell, for that matter, what had I done to attract the situation with Cory and Marcie?

Cory had been my best friend and roommate at veterinary college in Saskatoon, and Marcie and I never even knew each other's names. Who'd have thought that a few years could change everyone's destiny so drastically? I wouldn't have believed I'd fall head over heels for Marcie, and I certainly wouldn't have predicted the way I now felt about Cory. No matter how hard I worked at driving my resentment out of my mind, I still couldn't let go of one question. After falling in love with Marcie, why did he bring her back here? Was he so determined to one-up me that he wanted to display her as some sort of trophy? Now the two of them were my competition for clients, along with Dr. Keith Marling, who'd had an established veterinary practice in the valley for almost thirty years.

I got up and stomped my feet to get the circulation going. Removing my gloves, I rubbed my hands back and forth together. I wanted to simply discard the notion that my own thoughts had something to do with Marcie and Cory's coming together—it was so much easier to assure myself that it wasn't something I had done. After all, I couldn't have been there at the college when Marcie took up with Cory, and I sure wasn't there this afternoon when Jim examined Shep.

I shook my head in frustration, switched on my light, and approached the feeder. The moment I drew near, Super Bitch, the black white-faced cow who had earned her name by tearing apart the chute every time we handled her, tore backwards and glared at me suspiciously. I crawled through the uprights in her vacant position and headed towards the house.

As I trudged through the trees, I deliberated the possibility that I had somehow orchestrated this mess. No...no, it couldn't have been my doing. If my thoughts attracted veterinarians who were destined to let me down, how could you explain my lay staff? Doris, Marg, and Margaret went above and beyond the call of duty every moment of every day. Granted, there were a few things I'd like to change about the way they did things, but I couldn't ask for more dependable, capable people. I'd trust any one of them with my life.

The last time I rolled over to check my watch it was two in the morning. Some time after that, I mercifully drifted off to sleep. When the alarm went off at seven, I gave it a dirty look and lay there staring into the darkness. Lug stirred, pressed a cold nose to my cheek, then apparently drifted off again. For fifteen minutes I contemplated my plan of action. I couldn't just let this thing with Jim be swept under the carpet, but damn...I hated confrontation.

When I arrived at the office a few minutes after eight, my three trusted assistants were huddled around the counter. Although the moment I opened the door they became silent, I knew I had interrupted an intense conversation.

Marg picked up her pen and started making notations in her ledger book; Margaret and Doris headed for the back. When I got to the treatment area, Doris already had the door of the autoclave open and was unloading bundles neatly wrapped in green linen. By the sound of stainless steel bowls rattling in the kennel room, Margaret was busily working with the patients.

"What does the morning look like, Doris?"

"You have a couple of dog spays and a cat neuter, then some appointments after eleven."

"And Jim?"

"He doesn't have anything till ten-thirty, but he has a couple of patients in the back."

I nodded and stepped into the kennel room to check out my surgery patients. "Have you temped everyone?" I asked Margaret.

"Except for Heidi." She pointed to the St. Bernard–cross dog that huddled in the back of her kennel. "She doesn't look very friendly, so I left her for last."

"Hey there, Heidi." I slowly opened her kennel door. "Come see…there's a girl. Come, girl."

Cringing towards the back of the confined space, the dog continued to watch me carefully. I grabbed a woven leather leash, made a loop, and tossed it over her head.

"Come on, girl…let's go for a walk." I pulled gently on the lead. Heidi reluctantly took a step onto the concrete floor and followed me to the treatment area. I knelt before her and extended my hand. Her tail wiggled ever so slightly. Working my hand to the nape of her neck, I gradually moved up to scratch her ears, then slipped a choke chain over her neck and headed to the back door with her on my heels.

I wandered around in the alley for ten minutes, thinking about how to sort this mess out. I was determined to get the confrontation with Jim over this morning—I couldn't stand to fret about it a moment longer. I entered the clinic ready to deal with the issue. Tying Heidi's leash to the pipe foundation for the exam table, I went to the lock cabinet and drew up atropine and Demerol to prepare the dog for surgery.

Doris had put all of the sterilized packs away on the shelves and was in the process of reloading the autoclave.

"Has Jim arrived yet?" I asked apprehensively.

She shook her head and quietly continued with the task at hand.

I had a listen to Heidi's chest, premedicated the second spay, then paced back and forth from the front of the office to the back, anticipating Jim's arrival. By quarter to nine, I gave up and returned to Heidi.

"Let's get this show on the road, Doris."

I rousted our heavily sedated patient enough to get one arm around her chest and circled the other around her butt. With a concerted effort, I lifted her, staggered to the surgery, and planted her on the tabletop.

"She's a big one," Doris noted casually.

"Yeah," I gasped. "I noticed."

I was half an hour into my surgery before Jim's characteristic Texas drawl reverberated from the front office. The early part of their conversation was muffled, but I heard him respond to Margaret with, "You're kiddin'!"

I tensed as he walked by the surgery door on his way to the kennel room.

Doris peered knowingly at me over her mask. "Practise your deep breathing exercises."

I finished suturing the midline incision and extended my gloved hand towards her. She peeled back the liner from a package of suture material. I grabbed it, took a bite into the fatty tissue on either side of my incision, and tied the first knot. I was halfway along the line when Jim opened the door and poked his head through.

"You may have to cover my first few appointments, Doc." He was already dressed in coveralls. "Dan Hurford gave me a ring at home about a couple of cows he wants me to look at."

"We need to talk, Jim...I won't be long finishing up here."

"If it's about the Randall dog, Margaret's already filled me in. Sounds like I kind of screwed up with the miserable mutt."

"Sounds like..." I agreed blandly.

He opened his mouth as if to respond, then hesitated. After watching me for a minute, he shrugged. "Well, Doc, it's been nice chatting...I've gotta go."

"Hold on for a bit," I insisted.

"I don't want to keep Dan waiting."

Before I could protest further, the door slid closed and he was gone. Doris looked at me and raised her eyebrows. I sighed, took a deep breath, and continued suturing.

A lot had happened in the ten months since Jim Steelman had joined my practice. The thrust to take on another vet had started one morning the previous spring when Margaret was scolding me for not taking care of myself...

Chapter 2

When Push Comes to Shove

"Dave, you look terrible," said Margaret on a rainy day in April.

"If it's any consolation, I probably feel worse than I look." I flopped onto the bench in the clinic waiting room as she ranted on.

"You can't keep going like this...you're a wreck."

My back was killing me and every time I moved, it felt like someone was driving a knife down the back of my right leg. I leaned my head against the fish tank, closed my eyes, and ran my tongue over the gum line of my lower jaw. My wisdom tooth had been playing hide and seek for the past year and a half. Several times, the pressure and discomfort increased until I was certain that wisdom was about to overwhelm me; on each occasion, its arrival fizzled. This time the tooth had been bugging me for weeks.

"Did you get any sleep last night?"

"Not much...I drifted off around two, but Alf Wiens called with a milk fever at five."

Margaret shook her finger at me and continued her lecture. "Doris and Marg and I had a confab while you were at herd health yesterday, and we decided it's time for you to get some help."

"You did, did you?" I replied without opening my eyes or moving a muscle I didn't have to.

I was always suspicious when those three "had a confab" about me. It usually meant some decision was being made that would mean more work for me. Granted, I couldn't do without the three

women who organized my professional life. Doris Currie had been with me since day one in Creston, and now, six years later, she virtually ran the clinic. Margaret Berg lived on a farm in West Creston and had come on side more than three years ago. She assisted with reception, surgery, and with restraint of the animals. Margaret Rogers was my long-suffering bookkeeper. We called her Marg to minimize the confusion around two Margarets in the office.

My assistant was pushing her point. "Do you realize it's over a year since you brought Cory in to help you out here? You were tired then—and you know how much water's gone under the bridge since he went off on his own."

"I know, Margaret…I'm painfully aware of all the water." I sighed, opened my eyes, and slowly leaned forward. Moving my right leg back and forth, I sought a position that would alleviate some of the pain. "I've been telling myself the same thing…but every time I'm almost convinced I should hire someone, I come right back to worrying about whether there's enough work for another vet in Creston. There are four of us here already."

"Well, you're the vet we're concerned about, and you sure have more than enough to keep busy. What with your building your house and all, we have a hard time fitting everyone into your day. It's definitely time you hired someone to help you."

She stepped over to the counter and scooped up a copy of *Canadian Vet Journal*. "Marg skimmed through the classifieds and thought you should take a gander at this one. She found the notice when we were talking about how you should send in an ad to hire a new graduate."

I smiled wanly as I read the highlighted section—my mothers were looking after their boy again.

"This guy's a twenty-six-year-old American looking for a position in western Canada," Margaret said with conviction. "It says he graduated from Texas…that must mean he's had experience working with cattle and horses."

I chuckled, then gasped as an agonizing pain shot down my right leg. "To listen to you, a person would think that everyone who came from Texas was a cowboy—it's been a long time since Roy Rogers rode the range."

Margaret raised her eyebrows and gave me an indignant look. "Well, you suit yourself...but we think you should write to him and see if he's interested."

"You may be right." I leaned back again. "Maybe I'll give him a call after I get done the office appointments."

"Is that girl coming to do the locum when you go to John's wedding?" Margaret fished.

"Yup, she called back to confirm last night."

"Do you think she'll be able to manage things on her own?"

"I'm sure Trudy's a very capable vet."

"So she graduated from Saskatoon, too?"

"She was a few years behind me."

I closed my eyes again and ignored the knife that kept grinding on my sciatic nerve. Life had a way of playing amazing tricks on folks. Cory and Trudy Leishman had dated for the last few years we were at the veterinary college. Back then Marcie was still married to one of her classmates.

My mind was whirling, and before I knew it I was lost in the same back alleys that I always found myself in whenever my thoughts turned to Cory. How many times had I written out all my hostilities towards him and burned them as a symbolic gesture of release?

"Do you want me to iron your suit?" I tore myself back to the present as Margaret pressed her question. "Knowing you, you don't even know where it is."

"I do so...it's hanging in my closet under a garbage bag..."

"Are you sure? The last time I was out to your place, you never even had a closet."

Margaret was right. I had only worn my suit once since I had been in Creston, and that had been at Dud Rogers' funeral. I'd need it for John and Lydia's wedding a month from now in Calgary, so there was time. I had it in the closet when I lived upstairs above the clinic...Where was it now? I shifted my leg and instantly regretted it.

"You should go see the chiropractor," Margaret suggested, wagging her head. "You can't keep working like this. Mary Mulligan's good—she got me up and going in no time the last time I threw my back out lifting bales."

I gritted my teeth and hefted my six-foot-eleven hulk off the bench. "When am I supposed to do that? By the look of the book, I'll be busy till six."

"I can see if I can reschedule some of the appointments. I could give Wayne Adams a call and see if you could go to his place tomorrow instead of tonight. I set up the appointment at the end of the day so you could just head home when you were done."

I sighed and stared out the window. Rain was coming down so hard that I could barely make out the outline of the Creston Hotel across the street. It had been cold and rainy for weeks, and I was dying to see the sun again. At times like this I could understand how people in the medical profession got hooked on mood-altering drugs. Today, I needed a good boost to my mental outlook, and I sure could use something to dull the knife that kept jabbing me in the hip.

Margaret had the appointment book in her hand when the front door opened and a soggy young RCMP officer I hadn't seen before stepped through.

"Do you have time to look at a dog that's been hit by a car?" he asked. "We just picked it up off the side of the road."

Before he had finished asking, his partner strode into the office with his arms full of dog.

"Can you help us out here, Dave?" The big corporal I knew only as Boomer smiled as he pushed past his fresh-faced partner and headed towards the exam table. "It never fails," he grumbled. "Someone ran over the poor thing and left her for dead, out there in this downpour."

I followed behind the young officer. When he hesitated and stopped outside the exam room I stumbled around him.

"This is Rod, Dave." Boomer pointed a bloody finger in the constable's direction. "He joined us last week."

I had never really asked Boomer how he got his nickname, but

I was sure that his forceful way of handling situations and his commanding voice had been contributing factors. I smiled at him and nodded in his direction.

"Dave helps us out with a lot of these critters," Boomer went on. "Don't know what we'd do with them otherwise."

I maneuvered past the dripping corporal and knelt gingerly beside the table.

"You too, eh?" Boomer nodded knowingly. "Why do us big guys pay for our size with back pain? Just went through a couple of weeks of hell myself."

I braced myself to begin examining my patient.

"Sciatic pain, too?" he asked.

I nodded. "Right side."

"Damn...same as me."

"Has she made any effort to stand?" I asked, running my hand over the dog's sodden coat.

"She pretty much just lay there when I packed her to the cruiser. 'Course I tied her mouth up like you showed me before I picked her up." He gestured to the cotton gauze that was tied around her jaw and secured behind her head. "She's obviously someone's dog...she looks well cared for."

He was right: although her hair was sopping wet and covered with chunks of gravel and grime, it appeared as if her long fine coat had been recently groomed.

"Do you need a hand there, Dave?" Margaret asked as she and the young officer moved closer.

The animal lay on her sternum exactly as Boomer had placed her, her eyes closed, and her jaw resting fully on the surface of the stainless steel table.

"She full collie?" Boomer asked.

"Most likely a collie-sheltie cross, by the dainty look of her face," I guessed. I lifted the dog's lip and pressed on her gums. The membranes were blanched and changed little as I watched them. "She's shocky," I muttered. "You better get an IV ready for her, Margaret...she's going to need fluids."

I ran my hands over both front legs, flexing joints and pinching toes for signs of response. "Where's the blood coming from?" I asked Boomer.

"One of her back legs. There was quite a bit under her out there on the highway, too."

I laid the dog on her side and palpated her top leg. There were no obvious fractures and all the joints moved freely. It was when I lifted the leg on closer inspection that I found the source of the bleeding.

"Oh my God!" Rod took one look at the leg, brought his hand to his mouth, and ran for the door.

"I got the feeling he was a bit shy of blood when we were out on the highway," Boomer noted wryly.

"Land sakes!" Margaret said, coming around the corner dragging the IV stand. "What did you do to that poor boy? He looked like he was about to toss his cookies."

"He didn't like this," I said, pointing to the inner thigh. A huge flap of skin was rolled up like a scroll above the dog's stifle. The entire area above it to the level of her nipples had been stripped away to leave bare flesh.

As luck would have it, we got the IV started on our patient as the first office appointments arrived. Within a few hours, her perfusion improved and Margaret was able to schedule enough time for us to patch her up.

By the time I placed the last suture, my back was screaming in pain. I headed to the lab and sank into a chair while Margaret got our patient into the kennel and cleaned up the mess. The moment my butt hit the seat, Lug was there with his head on my lap.

"I know you don't want to hear this, but you better get a move on," Margaret prompted. "I promised Wayne Adams you'd be out there right after he started putting the cows through. He has a heifer that won't milk on one teat, and he thinks you might be able to do something. He starts at four and he's going to keep her in the holding pen till you get there."

I took a deep breath and buried my hand deep into the scruff of Lug's neck. Slowly slipping my fingers through his hair, I worked my way up to his ears. He groaned with pleasure and leaned into me as I rubbed the floppy one.

"You ready to go home, old boy?"

His good ear perked and his eyes lit up. He twirled anxiously in a circle and whined excitedly.

"Margaret, can you grab me a pair of coveralls?"

I stretched the toe of my right foot to the heel of my left shoe and flicked it off, trying to keep my legs as straight as possible. Breathing into the pain that emanated from my contrary hip, I repeated the process with the right shoe.

"My lands, Dave, how're you going to do anything for Wayne once you get to the dairy?" She stood in the door with her hands on her hips, shaking her head. Kneeling down in front of me, she picked up my left foot and slid it into the coverall leg. She repeated the procedure with the right. "Can you stand up?"

I grabbed hold of the counter and pulled myself upright. By the time I had gotten my arms threaded into the sleeves, Margaret had returned with my boots. Putting them side by side on the floor in front of me, she stood back and clucked her concern as I manipulated first one then the other onto my feet.

Lug sat up on the passenger seat of our seven-year-old Volkswagen station wagon taking in the familiar surroundings as we headed past the golf course towards the sheer face of the Skimmerhorn Mountains. He knew we were heading in the direction of home and was not missing a thing. He growled as he spotted a pair of rain-drenched golfers wandering along the rough in search of a ball.

"That's enough, you big goof."

Deep down, I agreed with him. With my hectic life, I couldn't imagine wasting time looking for a little white ball on a nice day, never mind one like this.

Peering attentively out the back window, he watched the suspicious creatures until we rounded the corner towards the Lister school. By the time I turned down Sinclair Road, I was dreading the fact that I'd soon have to move again. Right at this moment, even pushing the gas pedal was more than I wanted to do. I grimaced as I shifted my leg and turned into the Adams' driveway.

Lug growled at their golden cocker and smeared the glass of the passenger window with slobber as his nose slid back and forth across it.

"Sit down and behave!" I hollered with more rancour than he was accustomed to. "Get on the floor!" With a dejected look he sank to the mat to rest his chin on his paws.

The familiar droning of the vacuum pumps and the smell of cow manure welcomed me as I opened the car door. Not giving myself the opportunity to think of a reason to sit for a moment, I grabbed my instrument tray and a bottle of surgical scrub from the back of the vehicle and limped my way through the milk house around the big stainless steel holding tank. Wayne had opened the front gate on one side of the herringbone parlour to release the six cows he had finished processing. I opened the door and waved at him.

"I'll bring her in now!" he shouted as the recently milked cows sauntered into the yard. Locking the front gate, he climbed out of the pit and made his way to the back door. Several cows tried to push their way in when he opened it, but he waved his arms to chase them back.

"Can you stand here till I bring her up? Her number's 386." Wayne elbowed his way through the crowd of black and white cows, patting several on the butt to move them out of his way. "Try and get her in the second stall, so she has a cow in front of her. This is only her second milking and she might get a bit rowdy."

When he reached a heifer at the far end of the holding corral, he tapped her head and turned her in my direction.

"Come on, girl…up you get."

Cows parted as the heifer pushed her way along the wall to the front of the line. "Let that old crow in first!" he yelled as a big beast with a pendulous udder tried to squeeze past me.

The cow lumbered forward as I stepped back and was quickly

followed by a much smaller animal with 386 displayed prominently on her yellow ear tag. Wayne chased in an additional four animals, then closed the gate behind the last one. Hopping into the pit, he set the dials for the automatic feeders in the parlour and started washing down the heifer's udder. Wayne's wife, Eileen, removed the last milking machine from the cows on her side of the parlour, then opened the gate for them to leave.

"This one's got such a nice bag," Wayne said wiping her down with a paper towel. "It'd be a shame if she ended up as a three-titter. She milked out completely on the other three teats this morning, but I couldn't get more'n a few drops out of her left front."

He watched impatiently as I made my way down the stairs. "Jeez, Perrin, you're moving more like an old woman every time I see you."

I made no comment as I hobbled towards him.

"Look at this," he said, squeezing the front teat closest to him. "I get a few drops out of her, then it stops like someone shut off the tap."

I set down my instrument tray. Grasping the teat between my forefinger and thumb, I massaged away from the base, squeezed the swollen teat with my other hand, and sent a shot of milk through the grate at her feet.

"That's good. At least she's got a normal teat sphincter...sometimes there's no orifice at all."

"So why can't I get the milk out?"

"There's probably an island of mammary tissue that broke free in the final stages of the udder's development. It's too big to come through without encouragement and just sits there like a ball valve keeping the milk from coming out."

I grabbed the container of soap from my back pocket and scrubbed the teat, then fished a pair of alligator forceps from the instrument tray.

"Do you think you could put a tail jack on her for me? I'm not moving very quickly today."

Wayne grasped hold of the railing and hoisted himself up to the level of the cow. Lifting her tail over her back, he applied steady pressure forward. This was a tried and true method of restraint. With a bit of luck, it would keep the critter's mind off what I was doing and prevent me from getting kicked.

I tipped the bottom of the teat towards me and slid the stainless steel forceps through the orifice and up inside the teat. Opening the instrument's jaw, I squeezed the teat to force milk down. When I closed the instrument, I squeezed again and applied traction. The heifer lifted her foot and danced back and forth as I pulled out. Clasped in the alligator's jaw was a rounded glob of pale tissue about the size of a pea. I milked the teat, sending stream after stream into the gutter at her feet.

"That's it..." I smugly rinsed my instrument and placed it back in the tray. I was halfway across the pit to the exit when Wayne spoke up.

"I got a calf I should get you to check while I've got you. I'm afraid she's pretty much a write-off now, but seeing's you're here... I've been treating her sore knee for weeks with antibiotics but I don't think she's a darn bit better than when I first started."

He turned to his wife. "Can you handle things here for a bit, Eileen...I'm going to get Dave to look at 422."

Eileen nodded and glanced my way with sympathy. I took a deep breath, groaned under my breath, and shuffled after him to the calf barn. All I wanted to do was get home, crawl into bed, and pull the covers over my head.

"This calf hasn't been thrifty from day one," Wayne insisted as we approached the last pen in the calf barn. "I started treating her with penicillin when she was three weeks old, but her knee kept swelling up. When that didn't work, I tried tetracycline. I started her on chloramphenicol yesterday...all she does now is lay around. This morning I had to feed her lying down."

He lifted the piece of plywood from the front of the pen and rousted the calf from her bed of straw.

"See how swollen her foot and knee are? I was about ready to take her out and do her in this afternoon..." The lean dairyman stood watching me with his hands on his hips. "Got any bright ideas?"

I gingerly knelt next to the calf and ran my hands down her right front leg. The carpus was swollen half again the size of the left and felt hot. The fetlock joint was swollen, too. The calf flinched the moment I pressed my thumb on either joint. I ran my hand down the other legs, then checked the navel. The umbilicus was swollen with a hard core of granulation tissue in the centre.

"It looks like the arthritis resulted from an infected navel."

I pulled out my thermometer and lifted the calf's tail to insert it. The moment I did, a pain shot up my right hip. Groaning, I sank to the straw beside the calf.

"I don't think either one of ya's gonna make it," Wayne mused.

With both me and the critter lying on the straw in the alleyway, I compressed the calf's abdomen between my hands and began palpating.

"What're you looking for?" Wayne asked.

"Just trying to feel the vessels that run from the umbilicus—one goes to the liver, the other to the dorsal aorta. When the vein's infected we can get an abscess in the liver. When the artery's infected, we get a shower of bacteria that can go almost anywhere in the body. Sometimes an animal will crash from an overwhelming infection—sometimes a meningitis, sometimes a septic arthritis like this."

"What're the odds of her coming around? She's outa one of my best cows, but she's really stretching my patience."

I removed my thermometer, wiped it clean with straw, and rolled over on my side to read it. "Her temperature's almost 40 degrees Celsius. The vessels in her abdomen are definitely enlarged. I'd give her a try for a few more days with the chloramphenicol to see if it takes the temperature down. A lot depends on what's going on in her tummy. As bad as her joints are, they may be the least of her problems. I've autopsied calves that died from navel infections and found liver abscesses the size of a softball. As far as the joints…the best results I've had is irrigating them with sterile saline to remove as much debris as possible, then injecting massive levels of anti-biotics into the joint space."

Wayne shook his head pensively. "I'll give her a couple more days on the chloramphenicol and see what happens. If she doesn't improve, I'll let you know. For now, you better get home to bed."

I grabbed hold of the calf pen and pulled myself to a sitting position. He was right. And that's exactly where I was heading.

Lug was doing his circle dance on the seat as I headed down Canyon-Lister Road towards the farm. By the time I turned into the yard he was beside himself, bobbing back and forth from one window to the next to see what was going on.

The moment I opened the door, he bounded over me in a rush to check out his home turf. I shut off the engine and sat like a lump watching Lug tear around the yard. As if determined to make sure no stranger had trespassed in his absence, he sniffed every bush and board in sight. Stopping here and there, he lifted his leg to mark his territory.

How I wished I could borrow a bit of his zest for life and a lot of his energy. Glancing longingly towards the house, I stumbled down the path through the trees in search of the cattle. Although the rain had let up to a drizzle, it was still uncomfortably cold for April. Of the dozen calves I was expecting, eleven were already on the ground and doing well—only one more heifer remained.

Lug ran ahead of me down the hill towards the creek. He hadn't gone fifty feet before he rooted out a stick that met with his liking. Grabbing the end of a branch, he yanked it free from a mound of dirt. With expectation in his eyes, he bounded towards me and deposited it at my feet.

"Not now, boy."

His disappointment was obvious when I passed it by. Undeterred, he picked it up and followed along beside me. Dashing across the engorged creek at the bottom of the draw, he waited as I carefully stepped onto a boulder and swung my leg across the channel. He whined with excitement as I caught up with him, then backed across the thick layer of pine needles, dragging his stick behind him with his front feet. "Whooo, whooo, whooo," he wailed, vying for my attention.

I ignored his display and headed along the packed trail to the top of the hill into the heavily forested area where the cattle usually bedded down. The moment the cows caught sight of me, they started bawling. I paused and peered as they meandered through the trees towards the hay shed. Six, seven, eight under the big pines, three more over there next to the feeder...damn, there was one missing.

I was almost upon her before I saw her. The black white-faced heifer lay all by herself at the east end of the enclosure right next to the roadway. She turned her head in my direction as I approached. While Lug strutted back and forth in front of her with his stick in his mouth, she rose uncomfortably to her feet and tossed her head in his direction. Her vulva was swollen; a long string of mucous dangled from her vaginal lips. I groaned—she'd definitely be calving tonight. My fantasy of a night's sleep was smouldering and close to being shot down in flames.

I was spent by the time I limped back to the house. Dragging bales to the feeder had been a final insult to my aching back.

Construction on my log house had all but ground to a halt. After the initial blitz where hired help had made rapid gains, I was resolved to doing the remainder myself. Just after Christmas, Marg Rogers had cornered me in the darkroom. She ranted that after years of scrimping and struggling to show a profit on their family farm, she thought she had seen it all. She grasped a stack of bills in her gnarled hand and declared I had pushed her creative financing to the limits. Staring up into my eyes with a stern look on her face, she gave me the option of finding someone who could stretch a dollar better than she, or quit spending until she could catch up.

The truth of the matter was that every new addition here at the farm came at the expense of something at the office. It didn't help that Kootenay Meats, a business I had started with a dairyman friend, was now on the rocks. Apparently, the town of Creston was just not big enough to support our elaborate facility in addition to the two other supermarkets. It all sounded good when we tackled the project; after all, it didn't make sense to ship the beef and pork produced in the valley to Alberta for processing. The area needed its own facility.

The fact that the fellow we hired to manage the butcher shop in town had made a valiant effort to corner the Canadian market on turkeys over the Christmas season didn't help. That had been the tipping point. Even now, four months later, every freezer was crammed to the ceiling with the frozen birds.

There never seemed to be a shortage of challenges. Although it was amazing how well the old dump of a building I was in functioned as a clinic, things had to improve. The girls were nagging me constantly about finding a new location. If I was going to hire that new vet, I'd certainly be in need of a bigger facility.

Lug charged past me as I opened the basement door. I clicked on the light and followed him into the cavernous room. There were still no interior walls and only two lonely light bulbs dangling from pigtailed wires to light the entire area. The last project Sam Hoodikoff—the carpenter I'd hired—had done before moving on was a set of stairs to connect the three stories. My good friend and realtor, Gordon Veitch, had drawn up an elaborate wiring diagram for each floor, but before I could begin drilling studs for the placement of wires in the basement, I'd have to frame the walls.

I had made a bit of progress over the winter, but I was nowhere near where I thought I'd be by now. I did manage to shake half the roof before the snow flew; the other half I covered with rolled roofing out of desperation. Stacks of drywall lay all over the house, and each day I kept promising myself to put up more. I was so sick of seeing pink insulation and plastic. Last week I had made a commitment to screw at least one sheet of drywall in place every night; that was before my back flared.

By the time I lumbered my way to the second floor, Lug was rooting his bowl in the darkness in hopes of getting my attention.

The stairs exited into the area that would one day be the kitchen, but the only thing that suggested the room had anything to do with the preparation of food was the presence of an antiquated refrigerator and an old pantry I had picked up at an auction sale.

I skirted the open hole and fumbled along the far wall for a light switch. As much as I liked to eat, it was strange that this was the one room in the house that I had trouble visualizing. As Gordon and his wife Ruth pointed out, the way I positioned the windows left little room for the eventual placement of cupboards.

Tonight, cupboards were the least of my worries. Flicking back the latch that the previous owner had screwed on to lock his beer fridge, I opened the creaky door. The bedraggled head of lettuce I had left too close to the freezer was frozen solid. I fished out the remains of a cauliflower and half a raw onion, then opened the bread bag to inspect the few slices that remained. The cauliflower was covered in black spots, but the onion looked salvageable. After examining the bread for signs of mould, I declared it safe to consume.

I sighed, chucked the cauliflower and lettuce into the garbage can, and shuffled to the pantry. After opening all the doors I found a lonely can of tuna. It appeared that tuna-salad sandwich without the salad had made its way to the top of this evening's menu.

"You'll make out better than me tonight," I lamented to Lug, scooping up a bowl full of dry dog food.

After throwing my sandwich together, I picked my way up the stairs with Lug on my heels. A shiver ran up my spine as I got to the top floor. I hadn't realized how the cold had soaked into my bones. Only my bedroom and the upstairs bathroom had functional heating. The remainder of the house had been kept at just above freezing throughout the winter with the single baseboard heater next to the water tank in the basement.

I struggled to get my boots and coveralls off, then fell into bed. I lay there staring at the nail holes in the ceiling and chomping away at my dry but delicious tuna sandwich.

I was rudely awakened by ringing and reached for the alarm clock to shut it up. It wasn't until I chased it a couple of feet across the floor that I realized it hadn't gone off yet. It was the incessant ringing of the telephone that had ended my respite from pain. I clicked on my bedside lamp and rolled onto the plywood floor. Dragging myself with my hands, I got to the phone.

"Hello," I croaked.

"Dave, I'm sorry to bother you at this time of night, but I've got problems with a heifer calving." It was John Partington's voice. "Jean and I have been trying to get the calf straightened out for the last half hour. One front leg is back and I can't seem to get it. The calf's feet are huge and there's not much room to work in."

"Okay," I groaned, struggling to bend my legs. "I'll get there as soon as I can."

I pulled myself to where I had discarded my coveralls, and struggled to get one foot started. No matter how hard I tried, I couldn't reach my arms far enough or bend a leg enough to accomplish the simple task. I lay in a heap. How in hell was I supposed to calve out a cow when I couldn't even put my coveralls on? I closed my eyes and sobbed in frustration. Lug rushed to my side and licked my cheek in consolation. Hugging him tightly to me, I lay sandwiched between his soft warm fur and the cold hard floor.

Ten minutes later I started my car and headed along Canyon-Lister Road towards Riverview. As I turned down the gravel drive to the Partington dairy, I was somewhat more composed, but still dressed in the same clothes I went to bed in.

I pulled up to the side of the barn and pried myself from the vehicle. Lug was perched on the passenger seat scouting the yard for his arch-enemy. The Partingtons had an intact Dalmatian male that loved to torment my poor shepherd. Whenever I was here for herd health appointments, the dog would circle the station wagon while Lug barked madly on the other side of the glass. The fact that Tye peed on our car tires was bad enough, but he was constantly flitting behind me and lifting his leg on my boots as well. Whenever that happened, Lug sniffed me persistently and shot looks of accusation in my direction. To him, Tye's laying claim to his master was the ultimate insult.

John met me before I entered the milk house. Thankfully, his dog was nowhere to be seen. "Jean's gone to bed so she can get up and start milking at five." He shook his head woefully. "I've got a bad feeling about this…I'm afraid it's going to end up being a Caesarian."

He watched apprehensively as I dragged myself through the door.

"Are you all right?"

"No…to be honest, I'm not. My back is killing me."

"Aren't you going to put on your coveralls?"

"No…couldn't get them on."

John kept glancing in my direction as he filled a five-gallon bucket with warm water.

"You ready?" he asked.

When I nodded, he led the way through the barn to the calving stall. I followed dutifully behind him like a schoolboy being led to the principal's office. The heifer was stretched out on her side. A solid black leg and a white face with black ears protruded from her vagina. She was bearing down hard in an attempt to expel the interloper.

"I almost thought I could feel her other leg when I had her up," John informed me, "but the moment I got my arm in her, she dropped like a stone." He rubbed his forearm. "She almost took me with her."

A tirade of barking erupted from the other side of the barn wall. The angry dialogue between Lug and Tye was on.

"Let's see if we can get her up again," I suggested, trying to ignore the canine carryings on. The thought of flopping down on the stall floor to out-muscle this heifer in a pushing competition was not immediately appealing.

"Come on, girl…get up," John urged.

Untying the halter shank, he tapped her on the nose. The heifer bellowed in protest and rolled onto her brisket. All she wanted was for us to go away and leave her to her misery. John persistently dug his knees into her ribs and slapped her on the opposite side in an attempt to force her to her feet. Sticking out her tongue, the animal bawled in protest.

"Just let her stay there, John."

I limped my way back to the car. Tye was prancing around the front of the vehicle, and Lug was jumping from the passenger seat to the driver's seat to keep him in sight.

"Get to the house!" I yelled at the Dalmatian. "And you!" I hollered at Lug. "Lie down and shut up!"

Lug's good ear folded and he slunk to the floor as I flipped up the rear door. I opened my kit bag and began stuffing my pockets. I looked woefully at my calving jack, then hefted it and trudged back to the barn. After dropping the jack in the alley, I grabbed hold of the pen wall and slowly lowered myself to my knees, bearing as much weight as possible with my arms.

John stared at me in dismay. "Are you going to be able to do anything with her when you're in this shape? Maybe I should call Cory."

I clenched my teeth as pain radiated down my leg, and crawled next to the heifer. I withdrew my bottle of surgical soap from a back pocket and began scrubbing her tailhead. I worked my fingernails back and forth to remove as much debris as possible, then began to shave her hair. Flexing the tail up and down to locate the joint between the first and second coccygeal vertebrae, I shaved further back. As I barbered, the heifer continued to strain. She emitted a low gurgling bellow and sank onto her side.

"Do you want me to try getting her up again?" John asked.

I shook my head and finished my scrub. To get my bearings, I lifted the cow's tail one more time, directed a needle into the intervertebral space, and steadily injected a local anesthetic. I closed my eyes, focused on the pain in my lower back, and visualized the injection numbing my discomfort along with hers.

When I opened my eyes, John was staring at me. I wagged the tail back and forth—it was numb, a dead weight in my hand. For several more minutes, I sat observing the heifer as her breathing slowed and her straining stopped. For the first time, I directed my attention to her calf.

"Do you think it's still alive?" John asked as I stuck my fingers in the baby's mouth. "It was still moving when I called you."

I nodded when the calf resisted my intervention and its jaw clamped shut. "It is at the moment."

I picked straw from the calf's head and leg and worked soap as far into the vagina as I could reach, then scrubbed my arms and began working lubricant around the calf's neck.

My anxious client hovered as I flopped on my side and positioned myself behind the heifer. "Do you want me to do something?" he asked.

"If you could hold the tail up and out of the way it'd be a big help."

John held the tail to the pen wall, and I started manipulating the calf's head back into the heifer. I maintained a constant pressure on the nose until it disappeared from sight. The mother gave an occasional half-hearted grunt, but for the most part just lay panting.

"Will you have to push it all the way back?"

I grunted. "Far enough to be able to get my arm through the pelvis to fish for the other leg."

Once the calf's chest cleared the pelvis, I held it there with my right hand and pushed my left arm through to follow the elusive missing leg to the elbow. I groaned as the heifer strained and clamped my upper arm between the calf's chest and her pelvis. When the contraction subsided, I gripped the elbow and brought it as high as I could. Pushing on the calf's head with my right hand, I followed the leg down with my fingers until I could grasp the hoof. I heaved upward and dragged the foot through the pelvis and out the vagina.

"Thank God." John sounded gleeful. "I might get some sleep after all."

As I lay there peacefully savouring the moment, we were treated to another cacophony of canine discord.

"Damned dogs," John muttered.

"Can you pass me the chains?" I was trying my best to ignore the din. Slipping a looped chain well above the calf's fetlock, I placed a half hitch below and held it up to John. "Put your hook on this and give it a bit of a pull."

With moderate pressure, the calf was soon out to the chest, and I decided to continue on without the puller. Placing my feet on the heifer's rump I pulled along with John. In a matter of seconds, the calf lay stretched out on the straw beside me. I quickly stuck a straw up its nose, and it gasped its first breath. By the time I could force myself to move again, the critter was holding up its head.

John lifted a back leg and smiled. "Darned if it isn't a heifer."

I grabbed hold of a rail on the pen wall and hoisted myself erect. In the dairy I washed most of the blood off my body and cleaned up my equipment.

"Let me get that," John said as I struggled to pick up the calving jack.

At the car we were greeted by Tye. I watched him warily as he pranced back and forth between us. John tried opening the back hatch to put the calving jack away, then looked over at me.

"It's locked."

"I'll get the key." I hobbled to the driver's side.

I stared in disbelief at the handle as it elevated ineffectually in my hand—the door was locked.

On the driver's seat Lug was going crazy with anticipation. Suddenly, he lunged toward the glass and started barking ferociously. I glared at him as he continued his tirade, scratching desperately at the window for access to the outside world.

I felt the strange warming sensation in my boot before John yelled.

"Look out, Dave! Tye!"

Pain filled me with regret the moment I tried to lift my leg to kick at the dog. It was the middle of the night, my boot was full of dog pee, my car was locked, and I was staring at the keys dangling from the ignition.

We made the trip back to my farm in silence. John glanced

sadly at his watch as I pried myself out of his pickup; no respectable dairyman should be caught with his eyes open this time of the night. I limped to the house and searched for my spare key. Thankfully, at this stage of my occupancy there were few places to stash such things, and I found the ring of keys next to the alarm clock in my bedroom. It was two-thirty.

Lug was subdued when we finally returned with the spare key. John had locked Tye in the barn in our absence, and Lug had lots of time to settle down before my return. He hopped from the passenger seat to the driver's seat when the door opened and nuzzled expectantly at my hand. He instinctively knew he was in trouble.

"Get over, you big boob."

I plunked my butt on the seat and lifted my right leg into the car with my hands. All I wanted to do was get to bed and lose consciousness—if this was the world of reality, get me away from it. Maybe it really was time to contact that graduate vet from Texas.

Lug started sniffing me immediately. "Get away, mutt! I've had enough of you for one day."

Like a disciplined child, he sulked all the way home. Several times, he stooped to sniff me and got a rap on the nose for his efforts.

At the farm I pulled alongside the tree line at the place I had last seen the heifer. Lug hopped over me as I dragged myself from the car, and within moments he was tearing off through the woods. Although the rain had stopped, a heavy layer of mist hung beneath the trees. I grabbed my flashlight and carefully worked my way across the roadside ditch to the barbed-wire fence. I stood for several minutes staring at the five strands of wire that separated me from where I wanted to be and finally mustered the courage to lift my long legs over the top wire.

I shone the light through the trees in search of the heifer. She was standing almost exactly where I had last seen her and licking aggressively at an object on the ground.

Hallelujah—she had already delivered! Lug rushed to join me

as I made my way through the trees for a closer look. I pushed him away when he insisted on stuffing his nose into my boot.

"Sit!" I hissed. "And stay here out of the way."

I crept from tree to tree towards the heifer, not wanting to upset her or interfere with the mothering of her baby. I was almost upon her when I realized something was wrong. The black blob at the end of my beam of light was immobile. I grabbed clumsily at the sac that enshrouded the calf's head. I felt for a heartbeat…nothing. The calf was dead.

Chapter 3

A Glutton
for Punishment

"Do you think she'll ever be a worthwhile calf, Dave?" Margaret inquired.

"I sure hope so," I replied. "The swelling's come down a lot and today she spent more time standing."

"You're such a glutton for punishment," Doris interjected. "The last thing you needed was something else to look after."

She leaned her weight on the calf's neck and turned away as I drove a 16-gauge needle into the lower part of the carpal joint. Pressing on the swollen area above the heifer's ankle, I flexed it slightly.

"There's no crap draining out today."

The first time I had popped a needle in, I drew out more than twenty millilitres of turbid yellow fluid that had tiny white flakes floating through it. The calf flinched as I directed a second needle into the top of the joint and slowly injected twenty millilitres of saline.

"It's clear today, Dave," Margaret announced excitedly from her position at the end of the calf's leg.

"It is, isn't it?" The fluid dripped from the hub of the bottom needle looking almost as it had going in the top.

"How many more times are you going to do this?" Doris asked.

"I don't think I'll flush it again, but we should inject it for a few more days. Her temperature was down to normal this morning."

I drew ten millilitres of saline into a 12-millilitre syringe and injected it into the little vial I scooped from the counter. Shaking the concoction until the white crystals dissolved completely, I drew up half the material, pulled the needle from the bottom of the joint, and instilled two and a half million units of crystalline penicillin through the remaining one.

"Do you still think you'll get that heifer to accept her?" Margaret inquired.

"After all I've been through with the pair of them, I sure hope so."

I rubbed my shin and pulled up my pant leg to display a multi-coloured bruise.

"Oh, wow, she landed a good one this morning," Margaret observed cheerfully.

After my heifer had lost her calf, I resigned myself to the fact that she'd just dry up and go for slaughter. When Wayne Adams called to ask if I wanted to take his calf with the sore leg, I came up with the idea of making my own cow into a surrogate mother. With that in mind, I stuck the calfless heifer in the barn. Every morning now, before heading to the office, I trekked through the woods to milk her. Not only did it keep her milk production going, it also provided sustenance for this critter while we were treating her here at the clinic.

Doris gave me a smug look. "You've got so much time now that you don't have pigs to feed that you've started your own dairy." She smirked as I lowered my pant leg. "Besides, you needed a new booboo to get you to forget about your sore back."

She was right, sometimes getting a new problem made me focus less on the old one. Over the last week, the pain from my sciatica had diminished substantially. The wisdom tooth was something else, though—it was turning into a constant aggravation. I couldn't seem to leave it alone. As if to refresh my memory, I ran my tongue over the lower right side to check the gaping hole. Maybe it really was time to do something about it. This was the fourth or fifth occasion the tooth had broken through, and although this time it was taking longer to seal over again, it still didn't appear ready to come all the way out.

Doris petted the calf as I applied a pad over the shaved carpus and wrapped it for additional support.

"What are you going to call her, Dave?" she asked.

"What about Petunia?" Margaret suggested. "She reminds me of a calf I had back home on the prairies."

"Just look at those lashes," Doris went on with a hint of envy. "Why do calves and lambs have such perfect eyelashes?"

Finishing the bandage, I hefted the calf and maneuvered her through the door into the kennel room. I hated the inconvenience of this old building. Although we constantly referred to it as "the clinic," it was still nothing more than a ramshackle building that was literally sinking into the surrounding earth. Only last week, I had rebuilt the entry to the office because people were constantly tripping when stepping back onto the sidewalk. I especially disliked going to this part of the structure, because it was merely a lean-to with ceilings so low that I couldn't stand erect. Margaret rushed in front of me to open the doors.

"Hurry, Margaret," I urged as the calf began flailing her legs. "She's heavy." My assistant struggled with the first door as it stuck on the sill, tugging mightily on the knob.

"This door's such a pain," she gasped, wrenching on the handle one more time. There was a sudden grating sound followed by the thud of something hitting the floor on the other side of the door. "Oh damn, not again…"

Margaret stood staring at the sabre portion of the door handle that she still clutched in her hand. I glowered at the piece of junk; the brass knob with its long notched tongue had become an all too familiar sight. How many times had I tried to tighten that old screw enough to keep it from letting go? I settled the calf on top of the washing machine while Margaret searched out the crowbar to pry the door open.

"I thought you fixed it last week," she griped as she twisted the knob with one hand and wedged the point of the bar between the door and the jamb.

"So did I," I replied grudgingly.

As the antiquated panel door creaked open, I worked the calf's long legs through the narrow passageway and deposited her in the pen.

"Look how she's using that leg today."

It was a treat to see the calf stand erect on all four legs. When she first came in, all she wanted to do was lie in a heap. She literally had to be forced to stand; when she did, she never used the swollen leg for support. I could see why Wayne had given up on her, what with the time constraints of caring for his other animals and the likelihood that this one wasn't going to be viable.

"Do you want me to feed Petunia?" Margaret asked expectantly. "I know it sounds silly, Dave, but I still love feeding calves. It was always my favourite chore when we were back on the farm in Saskatchewan."

"Sure...you go ahead...I'll go check the sensitivity of the culture."

Margaret headed to the front with a look of satisfaction—she was definitely a farm girl at heart.

This old building was really starting to get to me; there were so many inadequacies, with literally everything falling apart. I had anticipated getting out of here within a few months of moving in, and I was still here, years later. After replacing the door handle, I went to the lab.

The first time I had drained the fluid from the calf's joint, I had smeared a drop of the exudate on a blood agar plate. Because the calf had been on antibiotics for such a long time, I wasn't sure that anything would grow. As it turned out, after a few days in the incubator, the surface of the agar had been dotted with little round blebs. Each of those whitish dots represented a colony of bacteria that had sprung up from separate bugs that had been in the fluid. Because each of them looked identical to the others, I had selected one and smeared it onto another blood agar plate. By putting discs impregnated with different antibiotics onto the surface of the agar, I was able to get a notion of which drugs would be the best ones to use to combat the infection.

The moment I opened the incubator I had fashioned from Dad's old camp cooler, I was greeted by the musty smell of the fermenting growth medium. I lifted the blood agar plate from the plastic lid and held it up to the light. The surface glistened with a white sheen over almost the entire surface. The only exception was a tiny zone of inhibition where no bugs grew around the penicillin disc and much larger circles around both gentomycin and nitrofurazone. Gentomycin was a very costly drug that we used sparingly in veterinary medicine; nitrofurazone was used most frequently for topical applications.

That explained why Wayne hadn't gotten a response from using the antibiotics he was giving intramuscularly. The fact that I was depositing a much higher concentration of penicillin directly into the joint was obviously the difference in the response to treatment.

"It's Dr. Catherall's office on the phone!" Doris hollered from the front. "They can fit you in tomorrow to replace that filling he was worried about…and Claudia says he'll let you know what he thinks about your wisdom tooth."

"Okay…but make sure I'm working here at the office before I go. Last time I ended up farrowing a sow just before my appointment and I didn't get a chance to shower. Dentists aren't exactly known for their strong stomachs, you know. Poor guy almost needed a clothespin on his nose to work on me."

"That shouldn't be a problem if you don't get called out early. They want you there first thing."

I collapsed in the chair, taped the culture plate shut, and threw it in the garbage. Leaning my head back against the rest, I closed my eyes and took a deep breath. With the hectic life I had been living lately, I was gaining more and more appreciation for quiet moments that I could have to myself.

"What arrangements have you made with Trudy?" Doris called.

"She can't get here until Friday."

"I thought you said you had to leave on Thursday."

"John doesn't need me there until the rehearsal on Friday afternoon, but when he called last week, he made a big deal about my not being late and asked me to come a day early."

"He knows what this place is like," Doris said perceptively. "The poor kid spent so much time waiting on you in years gone by."

I smiled. She was right. I had adopted John and his brother Brian as my little brothers after their mother had abandoned them here in Creston. Although I tried to take them fishing and camping, there had been numerous occasions when plans were put on a back burner because the rigours of everyday practice intervened.

It was going on four years now since Brian had been killed in a car accident—what a heartbreak it was to watch John select a coffin for his sixteen-year-old brother. Because he had never heard from his mother again and was not interested in finding her, that left me as his only remaining family. I was to be best man at his upcoming wedding.

"I tried to get Trudy to start Thursday morning, but she was already committed to another job. She promised to arrive as early as possible on Friday afternoon."

A lot had happened this week. Over the weekend, I got in touch with the new graduate from Texas, Jim Steelman, about coming to work for us, and things sounded promising. Although he wasn't the cowboy Margaret was expecting, he had worked in a large animal practice during his final year of veterinary college and was interested in living in a rural setting where he could hike and fish and raise a family away from the turmoil of the big city. The fact that he was married, and that he and his wife were expecting their first child, made him sound like someone likely to settle in for the long term.

I had given him a rundown on the practice and my aspirations, and he acted as if this were exactly the type of job he was looking for. Although he'd gotten other offers from practices in Alberta and British Columbia, he had yet to commit and promised to give consideration to my offer.

When he called back the following day, it was obvious he'd done some homework. He asked about Kootenay Lake and Kokanee Glacier, and had spoken to friends who had skied Red Mountain in Rossland and stayed at the Alpine Resort in Fernie. He certainly had the gift of the gab and made a good first impression on me.

Because I was seriously considering hiring him, I had decided to look for an additional vehicle—my Volkswagen was still hanging in there, but the miles were beginning to mount up. After making the rounds of the car lots in Creston, I decided on a new 1979 Ford pickup truck with a canopy over the box. It would be available by the end of next week.

"They want you there at eight!" Doris hollered again. I presumed she was referring to the dentist appointment—poor woman was getting paranoid about keeping me on schedule.

I closed my eyes and took in another deep breath. I cringed at the thought of doing something with my errant wisdom tooth. Every time I even considered having it removed, I was reminded of the story Father told about having his out. He swore he had to hold onto the arms of the chair to keep the dentist from dragging him across the room.

It was quarter to six the next morning when I rolled out of bed and headed to the log barn. It had rained overnight, and the smell of decaying pine needles was heavy in my nostrils as I made my way through the woods. Lug rousted two calves from their beds as we approached the draw, and they sped away from us kicking and bucking as they ran. I set my bucket on the ground by the barn and slid open the door. Lug quickly rushed over to check it out; over the past week, he had come to appreciate the bounties of my milking a cow.

I stepped into the barn and sighed. Two of the three 2x4 sliding rails that had been placed to keep the heifer in her pen were broken and the fragments lay in the alleyway. The door at the other side of the barn was ajar.

"Damn!"

By the time I got a rope on the heifer and had her tied to a tree it was seven o'clock. After a half dozen trips back and forth through the forest, I had finally trapped her in a right-angle corner of the fence at the far end of the pasture. A lucky toss of my lariat snagged her just as she was contemplating a jump over the four-wire barrier. Getting her snubbed down was one thing, milking her was another. I didn't have a second rope to wrap around her haunches to stem her kicks, and I suspected her little taste of freedom had made her even more resistant to handling. The very touching of her teats led to her hind legs flailing like a trip hammer.

It was a direct hit to my already bruised shin that sealed the heifer's fate. After I quit dancing and cursing, I released the honda on my lariat and watched her charge off through the trees. As I limped back to the house, one thought consoled me: that obnoxious creature would be much easier to handle when she was all wrapped up in little packages and resting in my deep freeze.

I was only five minutes late when I tripped up the stairs to the dental office. I took them two at a time and was out of breath as I pulled the door behind me and stumbled to the reception desk.

"Go right on in, Dave, they're ready for you," Claudia said with a smile. "Did you have another early call-out?"

"Not this morning…just had an ornery critter of my own to deal with."

The dental assistant, Denise Ludwar, greeted me and pointed to the room on her left. "We're all ready for you…unless, of course, you want the local anesthetic this time."

I shook my head as I struggled to catch my breath and settle into the chair.

"He'll be right with you," Denise said, trying to make idle talk. "I don't know how you can stand having your teeth drilled without freezing."

"You should try it some time," I joked.

She gave me a look of incredulity.

Dr. Catherall heard us as he entered the room. "Are you sure you won't let me freeze it today?"

"No, let's just do it."

The last dentist I had seen before coming to Creston must have jabbed me four or five times in an attempt to freeze one of my lower molars. By the time he started drilling, the only part of my mouth that wasn't frozen was the tooth he was working on. He went ahead anyway, and I discovered that the worst part of getting a filling was waiting for the freezing to wear off.

"Okay," Dr. Catherall said resolutely. "Open wide."

Within twenty minutes the work was done and I was ready to leave.

"So you think I should get that wisdom tooth extracted?" I asked.

"Let's get it over with," Dr. Catherall insisted. "Claudia checked, and we have a cancellation next Monday at eight."

"That's during my precious week off," I responded lamely. "I've got a lot planned."

"It'll only take an hour or so and after that you'll be able to do whatever you have planned...Really, it's no big deal." He was always so positive. Like me, he was usually dealing with reluctant patients, so "positive" was the only way for a dentist to go.

"Well, okay," I mumbled.

Friday morning arrived before I knew it. It felt strange to start the day with no appointments to rush off to, and to look forward to real time off. Doris, Margaret, and I had worked late on Thursday night to get everything caught up, so I could leave with a clear conscience. I was sure that if I left town by nine I'd get to Calgary with lots of time to spare.

John's wedding was to be in a Catholic church somewhere in the north of the city, and he was more than a little worried about everything going smoothly. He had called yesterday after a session with the priest. The cleric had really laid down the law to the poor boy; apparently, he was upset because John and Lydia hadn't attended all the classes they were supposed to. The priest informed John, in no uncertain terms, that the practice would start at three-thirty sharp and that he expected everyone there by three-fifteen. I had packed my suitcase the night before to make sure that I didn't end up forgetting something.

I left the house shortly before seven and drove leisurely to the office with Lug peering first one way then the other the entire trip. Although the only time he had seen me pack my suitcase before was on our move to the farm, he seemed to sense that something was amiss. My plan was to leave him at the office with Doris until Dad picked him up later to return to the farm.

Although Doris was insistent I stay away from the clinic on Friday, circumstances intervened on Thursday evening. After a long string of office appointments, Dick Douma called to implore me to look at a sick calf. He had caught wind of my going away from Herb Hurford at a dairyman's meeting and didn't want to deal with a strange vet. As it turned out, Margaret had barely started ironing my suit when I left, and I was too tired to return to town for it last night.

Lug circled impatiently as I unlocked the clinic door and let him in. "Go to the darkroom and wait for Doris," I told him, grabbing my suit and heading back to the car. I draped the nicely pressed garment over the seat and returned to lock the door.

I was inserting the key into the knob when the telephone rang. For a moment I stood motionless trying to ignore it, then charged inside. It could be Margaret or Doris calling for last-minute instructions. I maneuvered around Lug who was there waiting with his tail wagging, happy that I had finally realized I'd left him behind.

"Sorry, buddy." I grabbed the receiver on the fourth ring before the answering service picked up. "Hello."

"Dave, this is Diane from Hanson Farms. I just got a call from one of the milkers that a cow has prolapsed. Morris is off somewhere and Ken is away…Can you come right away?"

I stood in a paralyzed state with my mouth hanging open for an uncomfortably long time.

"Hello? Dave…are you still there?"

"Yeah," I responded hesitantly. "Tell them I'll be there shortly."

I ran to the kennel room and threw on a pair of coveralls before grabbing my rubber calving suit from the shelf over the dryer. Prolapsed uteruses were a bloody affair, and although I'd never found a foolproof garment to protect me, this one was the best I had.

My mind was whirling as I rushed out the front door. Being late for John's practice would be bad enough; listening to Doris lecture me for not taking her advice would be even tougher. Surely, if I got on top of things, I'd get this done with time to spare, and she'd never even have to know.

I was halfway to the car when I remembered I had taken most of my kit boxes inside the previous night and would need materials from them for this call. Rushing back to the office, I fumbled with the door yet again. Lug looked up at me as brightly as ever but flopped dejectedly when I hollered, "No!" Throwing the rubber pants on the waiting room bench, I rushed to the lab and sorted through boxes, plucking out the materials I'd need. I trundled out the door, closing it in my poor dog's face.

I made the trip across the West Creston flats in record time and pulled off onto the gravel road to Hanson Farms, thankful that no one from highway patrol had wet the bed and started work early.

I had fantasized finding a heifer that had simply given an extra push while calving and turned her uterus inside out. I groaned when I saw my patient. Stretched out on her side was a 1600-pound Holstein cow. Behind her, covered with straw, was a knobby pink mound the size of a washtub. Curled up in the far corner of the pen was a husky black and white calf, still wet and covered with slime.

I threw a bottle of calcium into my bucket and rushed to the milk house to fill it with hot water. When I poked my head into the parlour, I was disappointed not to see Mark, the herdsman I usually worked with. Instead, there were two new milkers I hadn't seen before.

"Is Morris or Mark around?" I asked expectantly.

A slender fellow with a moustache shook his head. "Both Mark and Ken are away till Monday, and Morris is out somewhere working on the irrigation."

I grabbed my bucket of water and retraced my steps, stopping at the car to retrieve the alcohol container and my rubber calving suit. I cursed under my breath when I realized the suit was back in the office on the bench, exactly where I'd left it.

Grumbling my way to the calving pen, I stooped to insert a thermometer in the cow's rectum. When a prolapse occurred in a beef cow, it was almost always the result of her straining excessively after a difficult calving. It also happened on occasion when a cow calved on a severe downhill slope, and gravity helped turn the organ inside out.

The same things also played a role with younger dairy animals. With older ones, however, there was almost always the complicating factor of a metabolic deficiency called milk fever. The sudden rush of milk production induced by parturition causes a depletion of blood calcium to the point where muscles can no longer contract. The cow becomes unable to stand, her bladder distends, her bowels and uterus lose tone and function. Because the heart is a muscular organ, it slows dramatically and decreases its pumping action. Blood perfusion throughout the body diminishes, and the critter's temperature drops. If left untreated, the condition is fatal.

I grabbed the cow's ear; it was as cold as if an ice pack had just been removed. I touched the cornea of her open eye. The lid closed ever so slowly, but the cow made no effort to shift her head and get away from me. I plucked my stethoscope from my back pocket and knelt beside her for a listen. The beat of her heart was distant and faint.

I pulled the cap from the bottle of calcium and slipped on the rubber administration kit. As an afterthought, I plucked out the thermometer and checked it. A little over 36 Celsius—a full two and a half degrees lower than normal.

Wetting down the cow's jugular furrow with alcohol, I drove a 14-gauge, two-inch needle into the vein. Blood gushed from the needle and continued to run down the cow's neck as I threaded the long shaft further down the vessel. I tipped the bottle of calcium, cleared the line of air, and hooked onto the needle hub. Holding the bottle in the air with one hand, I positioned the stethoscope on her chest with the other.

Thankfully, the lub-dub, lub-dub grew strong and remained steady throughout the administration. Within fifteen minutes, the last of the fluid had drained down the rubber tube, and I pulled out the needle.

Rushing back to the car, I tossed the bloody apparatus on the floor mat, grabbed a syringe, and filled it with lidocaine. I glanced at my watch and breathed a sigh of relief—it was only eight-fifteen. With a bit of luck, I'd be in the shower by nine and on the road by nine-fifteen. That would put me in Calgary by two-thirty, with lots of time to get to the church and keep everyone happy.

I hurriedly shaved and scrubbed the cow's tailhead, then administered an epidural injection to freeze her back end and prevent her from straining. Taking a deep breath, I stared at the pink mass lying behind the cow, trying to visualize its all being miraculously stuffed back inside her body. Luckily, the fetal membranes were still attached and most of the debris was clinging to them.

I cut open a plastic garbage bag and laboriously worked it between the uterus and the underlying bed of straw. For the next fifteen minutes, I worked at stripping the afterbirth. Grasping one cotyledon after the other, I teased the remnants of the calf's membranes away from the mother's womb, exposing one oozing pink knob after the other. By the time the afterbirth was stripped away, most of the debris had gone with it. Finally, I picked away a few persistent pieces of straw that clung to the mucosa and washed the knobby pink surface repeatedly with soap and water.

Ten minutes after starting to manipulate the sloppy mass back into the cow, I began to fret. I knew from experience how formidable the task would be. Unlike a heifer that had simply ejected her uterus, this cow had stuffed her bladder and coils of intestine inside the package for good measure.

Lying on my side, I kneaded the mass continuously in an attempt to chase the extraneous organs back into the abdomen. Every time it appeared as if I was making progress in deflating one horn, I discovered that the other horn was bulging by the same amount. Usually, when working on a cow like this, I had help—at least one pair of extra hands to create a wall and help consolidate whatever gains I was able to make.

I considered hopping in the car to search for Morris, but the thought of wasting half an hour more made me hesitate. With an air of determination, I hefted the uterus as high as possible. Working my legs under the warm, soggy mass, I struggled to gain elevation in the hope of turning gravity into an ally rather than an enemy.

Within minutes, I could see I was making headway. With both hands held in fists to prevent them from puncturing the uterine wall, I continued to lift with my knees and knead downwards towards the vulva in an effort to drive the errant abdominal contents back where they belonged.

Encouraged by my progress, I struggled on, oblivious to the fact that my coveralls were rapidly soaking in moisture and taking on the same hue as the organ they supported. When I gently eased forward on the round structure that I suspected to be the bladder, I was rewarded with a gush of urine. I held fast as the warm, sweet-smelling elixir oozed its way down my legs to the bottom of my boots. I closed my eyes and focused on my breath as the pungent smell flowed through my nostrils. I kept telling myself that it was only water, and I had been wet before.

Continuing my efforts, I pushed at one horn, then prodded at the other, gaining some with one thrust, losing some with another. Finally, all that remained was a pink sac that could fit in a large plastic grocery bag. I spread my fingers wide and steeled myself for the final push. Victory was close, and I could almost taste it. Soon, I'd be on my way to Calgary!

I shifted the cow's tail to the side and began my final assault. I had about a third of the mass back in when the beast made her first attempt to stand.

"Noooo!" I groaned, trying to keep a steady pressure on the now enlarging mass. The cow gave a pathetic moo as she crumpled to her brisket a few feet away. I crawled after her over the soaked straw bedding, determined not to lose further ground. "Just stay put for a few minutes longer," I pleaded.

I had almost gotten the last of the uterus stuffed back in when she attempted to stand again. This time she got all the way up, took a stumble in the direction of her calf, and came crashing down on her opposite side. As if in defiance, she groaned and gave a big push.

"No, no, noooooo!" I wailed as the tide of pink spewed forth once more.

When I could think rationally again, I told myself that other people in the world were dealing with bomb threats. I could deal with this cow.

Three-quarters of an hour later I had achieved my objective and placed a heavy cotton suture to keep the uterus from coming back out. After administering antibiotics, I dug in the pocket of my soggy coveralls in search of my watch—good grief, it was almost ten o'clock.

I waddled to the car with blood-soaked clothing and coveralls clinging tenaciously to my body. My underwear was glued to the crack of my butt; my boots squished with each and every step. I carefully moved my pressed wedding suit farther toward the passenger side, cut open a garbage bag to cover my seat, and after leaving instructions with the milkers, headed back to Creston.

I was fretting as I made my way down Nicks Island Road. I had been so determined to make it to the wedding rehearsal on time and not let John down yet again. Here I was, filthy dirty and more than an hour past my safe departure time.

I turned east onto Highway 3 and pushed the accelerator to the floor. Maybe if I got my act in gear, I could at least show up at the church for part of the ordeal. I tore across the Kootenay River bridge, totally focused on how good it would feel to shed these soggy clothes and step into the shower. I was trying to remember if I had another pair of clean jeans that I hadn't packed when I heard the siren. I glared at the coloured flashing lights in my rear-view mirror for several long seconds before putting my foot on the brake.

"Crap!"

I sat transfixed by the view in the mirror as the cruiser pulled up behind me and the door opened. It was Rod, the rookie officer who had been with Boomer a few weeks before at the office. He stood up, adjusted his tunic, and sauntered in my direction, tapping his ticket book on his leg as he approached.

I unfolded myself from my vehicle and took a step in his direction. He stopped in his tracks and stared at me in disbelief. I could only imagine what was going through his mind as he eyed my blood-drenched clothing. I lifted my arm to wave at him but thought better of it when I saw how crusted blood was gluing down the hair on my arms.

I was about to open my mouth with an explanation when the officer turned on his heel and blurted, "Oh, my God, it's you… you're disgusting! Get outta here."

Chapter 4

Get Me to the Church on Time

Driving in the big city with four lanes of traffic all rushing side by each was one of my phobias, so I was thankful John's directions to the church were easy to follow. Before I arrived on the outskirts of Calgary, I had myself convinced I'd somehow get lost and end up even later than I was already. I was sweating when I turned off Glenmore onto a roundabout to 18th Street SE. I was sure that I had already missed it. When I turned down 76th Avenue SE I was almost starting to relax. There was 20th Street and there up ahead was the one I was looking for—20A Street. How could I go wrong? St. Bernadette Church was at 7103.

Following the street through a residential district, I soon came upon a two-storey white building separated from the roadway by a half-acre plot of lawn. The way John had described it, I was expecting an old-fashioned church with a steeple as high as the building was wide. If it weren't for the upright pillars along the front to break the monotony and a statue of the Virgin Mary over the entrance, this structure would have looked more like a community hall than a place of worship.

I pulled into the parking lot and hurried to a pair of large wooden doors in the middle of a side wall. I glanced at my watch—twenty-five minutes past four. All eyes focused on me as the door swung open.

"That's him now!" John exclaimed cheerfully. Abandoning his

position at the front of the church, he ran up to greet me.

"Sorry I'm late," I blurted.

"I knew it would be crazy for you to try and get away," John whispered, "but the priest's not very happy with us at the moment. I didn't do all the Pre-Cana sessions like I was supposed to, and he was even talking about delaying the service. We told him we had all the invitations sent out and everything, so he's grudgingly going ahead with it. He made me promise to catch up with all the sessions after we're married."

John paused and looked very serious. "When Father Kelly started, he said he had to be finished and out of here by four-thirty." He checked his watch. "That's now."

"Let's do this one last time!" the stocky priest ordered.

John and I rushed to the front of the church, anxious to placate him. Giving me a particular look of disdain, the priest grabbed my arm and led me to a position a few steps away from the front row of seats in the chapel.

"Now, after the bride comes down the aisle," he said tersely, "you have to be ready to give John the ring." He turned to John and with a hint of sarcasm said, "You will have the ring, won't you?"

"I got it right here," John asserted, patting his jacket pocket.

Bellowing like a drill sergeant, Father Kelly put us through our paces, insisting that we pay attention to our cues, and demanding that John and Lydia memorize their vows tonight. By the way he conducted himself, it was obvious that he had put legions of fledglings through the exact same paces.

Both John and Lydia looked completely frazzled by the time the rehearsal was finished and the priest ended the session. As Father Kelly hastily retreated into the bowels of the church, the wedding party quietly filed out to the parking lot. Lydia and her mother had her father, Lou, by either arm. John explained to me as we walked behind that he had been blinded as a result of an accident.

"Sorry to get things off on such a bad start," I said.

"Oh well," Lydia replied, sighing. "There were bound to be a few hiccups...now that this is out of the way, what else can go wrong?"

We hung around in the parking lot for a few minutes while Lydia introduced me to her parents, the bridesmaid, Kim, and her husband, Pete. John explained that Lydia and Kim worked together in a store that had something to do with tennis racquets.

I followed John as he dropped Lydia's parents at their home, then drove to a restaurant somewhere in the south of the city. We had a leisurely meal with Lydia, Kim, and Pete. For the most part, the guys ate in silence and listened to the girls chatter their way through every detail of the upcoming event. John, Pete, and I drove back to the house while Lydia and Kim went in search of the final touches to complete their bridal outfits. Lydia still wasn't happy with the hat and veil, thinking that the one she had just didn't match her dress.

I followed John to a bungalow in a new development on Lynnview Ridge, not far from where we'd had supper. We were met at the door by an exuberant collie-Lab cross that danced excitedly in greeting.

"This is Josie," John said, as she circled round and round him. "She's the reason we're property owners. Lydia brought her home because she was hanging around downtown near the store where she works—that was when we were renters in a fourplex. A couple weeks after we adopted her, the landlord came to collect the rent, and Josie met him at the door wagging her tail…We got kicked out with two weeks' notice. We weren't supposed to have pets."

John led Josie to the fenced yard at the back of the property, then rejoined us. "It was just as well we got evicted, because the monthly payment on our first house turned out to be less than what we were paying for rent."

Pete grabbed a beer from the fridge and sat down at the table while John gave me a tour of the house.

"This place is brand new…the first one was definitely a fixer-upper," John said, remembering all the work. "I knocked out walls, installed a forced-air furnace with new ducting, put in a gas water heater, laid new ceramic tiles through the kitchen and dining area, carpeted all the bedrooms, and finished the basement."

"You've become quite the handyman," I complimented.

"Get my journeyman papers as a sheet metal worker in a couple more months, too," he said with a proud smile.

"It's amazing what you've done in such a short time, John…You sure haven't let much grass grow under your feet."

The boy blushed and stared at the floor. "Yeah, things turned out pretty good. When this subdivision opened up, we checked it out for the heck of it, not thinking we'd ever do anything. As it turned out, we bought this place and sold our other one to Pete and Kim. We just moved our stuff over here last week. This is one of those airtight houses…supposedly built in a plastic bubble. They say it's gonna be cheap to heat."

After John showed me around the house, we cracked a few beer and watched *M*A*S*H* and *Candid Camera* episodes until the girls returned from their shopping spree. Lydia was positively giddy as she walked through the door.

"Look what I found!" she cried, flinging open a very exclusive hatbox. "I love it, I love it, I love it!" She planted the hat firmly on her head and stood back to admire herself in the living room mirror. "I had almost given up finding the perfect one," she went on, "until we went into the Bridal Boutique and I found this."

She stroked her fingers over the dozen shiny brown feathers that sat on the brim of her bangs, then traced them along as they swooped to the side. She lowered the veil and glanced seductively at John.

"That looks real good," the boy said with a goofy smile.

It was midnight before Kim and Lydia came out of the bedroom. They were finally happy with their outfits and had hashed and rehashed their plans for the hairdresser in the morning and the reception at the Lake Bonavista Lodge, which I gathered was somewhere at the edge of the city. I yawned and rested my head back against a cushion on the chesterfield.

"Looks like you're ready for bed," John said with a smile. "That one over there's your room if you're ready to crash." He pointed down the hall to the first room on the right.

While Kim and Pete said their goodbyes, I brought my suitcase and suit in from the car. I was tired and relishing the thought of a good night's sleep. The early morning start, the struggle with the cow, the drive, and the beer had all taken their toll.

I washed up, then headed to bed. My mind was whirling as I was drifting off to sleep. It was amazing to see what John had created for himself in a few short years here in Calgary. Were some people simply destined to be shining stars? Heck, when his family had lived here before moving to Creston, he had dug through dumpsters to feed himself, his younger brother, and his alcoholic mother.

With a start like that, he could easily have gone the other way; after all, some kids who came from that sort of background were nothing but trouble. From the very beginning, John had always been a hard worker. Before graduating high school and leaving Creston, he had bought his own car, a wardrobe of stylish clothes, and still had money in the bank. He had been super conscientious with all of his jobs, and the folks at the Co-op grocery store had been sad to see him go. It was great to see him creating such a vibrant life of his own.

I had dozed off when I heard Lydia's shriek from somewhere outside the window. "Josie, no! Josie, come back here right now! Josie, no! Josieeeeeee!" There was a brief moment of silence, then the shrieking began again. "John! Johnnnn! Get out here quick... Josie's been sprayed by a skunk!"

I lay in bed listening to the commotion on the other side of the wall. "Get away from me, Josie! Get down! Oh, go away...you stink! Noooooo! John...she rubbed herself all over me! John, do something with her!"

It wasn't more than a few minutes before I began to smell the pungent odour—so much for resistance to air flow in John's plastic-bubble house. I lay there under the covers trying to convince myself that John and Lydia could handle the situation. The smell that was creeping through the walls told me I was already close enough to the action.

"What are we going to do with her, John?" I could hear by the tone of Lydia's voice that she was totally freaked by this latest turn of events.

"Dunno, let me try and bathe her with the garden hose."

I slowly stirred and set my feet on the floor—sleeping was no longer an option. When I got to the front door, Lydia was on her way into the house. The moment I got abreast of her, my eyes began watering.

"I took Josie out for a pee and she ran into a skunk…she rubbed her face all over me!" she blurted tearfully. "I can't stand the smell…I can hardly even breathe."

"You better shed your clothes right here, or you'll never get the smell out of the house."

"Why did this have to happen now?" she groaned. "I don't want to smell like a skunk on my wedding day."

"Have you got any tomato juice?"

"I don't think so…I might have a jar of clamato juice."

"Drop your clothes here on the doorstep and try not to touch them. Wash up good and soak your hands in clamato juice…you can try using vinegar and a bit of lemon, too. I'll go see if I can help John."

I found him and Josie in the backyard. "Get some rubber gloves or plastic bags on your hands, John, or you'll be smelling just like her."

He shut off the garden hose and stood back from his bedraggled pet. Josie lay shivering on the lawn; every few seconds she pawed at her eyes or tried rubbing them on the grass.

"Hold her head steady for a moment," I said, removing the nozzle from the hose and turning the flow way down. "We need to see if we can give her eyes some relief."

While John held a squirming Josie, I kept a steady flow of water running over first one eye, then the other. Leaving John with his woebegone pet, I ran to my car and rummaged through one of my kit bags. I came up with a tube of ophthalmic ointment.

"We better go find a store that's open late and get some rubber gloves and tomato juice," I said after treating Josie's eyes. "I've got a product called Skunk-off back at the office, but that doesn't do us much good right now. Wash your hands up well, or your car will reek like skunk, too."

One would never know that John had scrubbed away at the sink for some time before heading to the car. The moment the doors closed, my eyes began watering. Without saying anything to him, I rolled down the window.

We finally found a convenience store that was open several miles from their house. John approached the middle-aged woman behind the checkout counter. "Do you have tomato juice?"

"Dog got skunked, huh?" The plump teller wrinkled her nose and motioned with an outstretched arm towards one of the aisles. "Try looking on the second shelf, you should find some there."

We left the store with three large cans of Campbell's tomato juice, a container of vinegar, a bottle of lemon juice, and a couple pairs of rubber gloves. It was after one o'clock when we returned to the house. Josie was in the backyard barking incessantly.

"She's so spoiled," John grimaced. "She's not used to being outside for more than a few minutes at a time."

"I can see that."

"How do we do this?" John asked, apprehensively peering over the gate at the dancing dog.

"Let's get our gloves on so we don't smell any worse than we do now, then get her over under the yard light so we can see what we're doing."

By the time we finished working Josie over it was after two. We soaked the hair around her face and ears with tomato juice, then shampooed it into the long shaggy coat of her neck and chest where she seemed to take the brunt of the blast from the skunk. After that, we worked in vinegar and lemon juice.

"We've got her all marinated and ready to throw on the barbecue," I joked.

"Lydia would probably go along with that right about now,"

John admitted grudgingly. "Do you really think she smells any better?"

"Either we killed off some of the smell, or else our olfactory senses have surrendered."

We stepped outside the gate and watched Josie from a distance. The moment she was on her own, she rubbed her face on the grass, then began pawing at her red, watering eyes.

"Do you have a plastic bucket of any kind around?" I asked.

"Let me see if I can find one in the basement." John took off and within a few minutes returned with a pink plastic scrub bucket.

"Hey, Josie, this is for you. It's even the right colour…Do you have a knife, and some gauze or string?"

John gave me a puzzled look, then disappeared into the house.

"Josie, quit that!" I hollered as she pawed madly at her eyes.

A few moments later John returned with all the requested ingredients. Grabbing the edge of the metal bucket handle, I twisted it off, then worked the other side free. John watched in disbelief as I plunged the knife through the bottom of the bucket and began carving out a circular hole.

"What in the world are you doing?" he asked.

"Protecting Josie's eyes."

By the time I was finished, the frustrated dog was staring dejectedly through a pink tunnel. Now, every time she tried to paw at her eyes or rub them on the grass, the bucket got in the way.

Half an hour later we were sitting at the table, downing a beer. Josie hadn't shut up since we had closed the gate in her face. Now, her frenzied barking had turned into one mournful howl after the other.

"It's going to be great to try and sleep through this."

John looked at me glumly from across the table, picked up his beer, and chugged it down.

"Lydia's not in very good shape," he stated sadly. "She's been in the bathtub since we went to the store, and hasn't stopped scrubbing. She says she just can't get rid of the smell. I'm gonna run back there for another couple cans of tomato juice."

I washed myself in the kitchen sink, resigned to the fact that I was doing little to diminish the obnoxious odour. While John headed off in search of more juice, I returned to my bed. I tried desperately to succumb to my exhaustion and fall asleep, but Josie's incessant barking wouldn't allow it. I was still awake at three when John returned from the store, I was awake at three-thirty as Lydia and John headed off to bed, and I was awake at four-fifteen when the phone rang.

It seemed an eon before John answered. When he did, he spent most of his time listening. Finally, he muttered dejectedly, "Yes, I know…I will…I'm sorry."

I heard him go outside. After that there was silence. I wasn't sure what he had done to shut the dog up, but whatever he did I was certainly grateful.

I woke with a start to a commotion in the living room. Rolling over in bed, I glanced at my watch—it was a few minutes after eight.

"No…nnnoooo…nnnooooooo!" Lydia moaned. "Josie, what have you done now?" There followed an unintelligible session of wailing with the occasional outburst of "No! No! No!"

I pulled on my pants and shirt and headed to the living room where the stench of skunk hung heavy in the air. There on the couch sat Lydia, still dressed in her nightgown. Her head was in her hands and she was weeping softly. Across the room in the corner cowered Josie, still adorned in her pink bonnet. John was wandering about the living room picking up scraps. In his hand, he clutched a chunk of white veil and a metal band. Brown feathers were scattered from one end of the carpet to the other.

John shrugged. "The neighbour called last night and threatened to phone the cops if I didn't shut that damned dog of mine up. What was I to do? She's used to sleeping in the house."

By nine o'clock things had settled down a bit. Lydia had made arrangements for Kim to pick her up for their ten o'clock appointment at the hairdresser. They were leaving early so they could stop at The Bridal Boutique for one more look around before giving up and wearing the original veil that had come with the gown.

John arranged for Pete to come over with Kim. It had been decided the night before that treating John to brunch and a few beers would help bolster his courage and get him through the afternoon.

We got back to John's a few minutes after twelve. We had decided that it was best to leave the house to the women while they primped and got ready. It wouldn't take us guys more than a few minutes to throw on our suits and strangle ourselves with our neckties.

"Oh oh," John said as he pulled up to the house and turned off the key. "I think we're in trouble."

There on the front doorstep sat Lydia and Kim. "Where have you guys been?" Lydia demanded. Her freshly coiffed hair was garnished with snippets of baby's breath. Her eyes were red and puffy.

"We just went out for brunch and a beer," John replied defensively. "We thought you'd be better off having the place to yourselves to get ready."

"We would have," Lydia wailed, "but I forgot my keys!"

It was a mad rush for everyone to get ready on time, but by quarter of two, Kim and I were cramming ourselves into the back of John's '79 Monza. Pete was to follow us to the church in his own vehicle.

"I can still smell that darned skunk," Lydia worried as we approached the church.

"It's all in your head now, Lydia," I lied. "No one else will notice."

Lydia's parents were waiting in the foyer of the church when we arrived. "You look lovely, dear," her mother said as Lydia fidgeted. Taking her blind husband by the arm she led him a few steps forward. "Lydia's even got little flowers in her hair, Lou."

Staring straight ahead, he grasped Lydia by the shoulders and gave her a hug. He wrinkled his nose, then turned his head to the side. "Smells like there must be a skunk around."

Lydia seemed to shrivel. She looked for Kim, then headed for the door of the waiting room. "We're supposed to wait in here."

"Well, John, we'd better take our positions. Have you got the ring?"

He patted his suit pocket, passed me the box, then walked deliberately to the front of the church. Within five minutes, the organ started playing the wedding march and Lydia was walking down the aisle with her father.

The priest seemed more at ease this afternoon. Standing at the pulpit, he watched as the procession unfolded before him. Lydia's mother waited for her husband and helped escort him to his seat while Lydia continued on to stand by John's side.

I plucked the ring from the box and clutched it tightly in my hand. If there was going to be any further problem with this wedding, it wouldn't originate with me.

I closed my eyes as Father Kelly proceeded with the ceremony, thankful that it was going to be the short version. As he began speaking about the merits of marriage, I found myself wondering if I'd ever take the plunge—after all, I was more than ten years older than John.

When I was his age, all I could think of was getting into vet college; marriage was the last thing on my mind. But I had to admit, there had been a moment or two when I caught myself thinking about the possibility with Marcie. Heck, that was ancient history now. I was already married…to my practice. With all the cats, dogs, horses, and cows to attend to, I'd probably never find the time to even date, never mind marry.

Still standing in his pulpit, the priest was waxing about the exchange of vows—how the words were to become the essential element of the sacrament of marriage. After stressing the importance of the declaration of consent, he stepped forward in front of John and Lydia.

Taking a deep breath, he began, "Do you, Lydia…" Father Kelly hesitated as if he had suddenly lost his train of thought. Wrinkling his nose he gave a few quick sniffs, raised his eyebrows, then continued, "Do you, Lydia, come of your own free will to give yourself to John?"

After that he put things in high gear. Before we knew it, John and Lydia were man and wife and everyone was filing out of the church. It wasn't until we were standing beside the decorated wedding car, and the couple was being bombarded with confetti and rice, that Lydia complained. "He never told you to kiss me, John."

John thought for a moment, then said, "Yeah, you're right."

I poked John in the ribs and joked, "With the smell of us, the poor man probably couldn't hold his breath any longer."

John didn't laugh and neither did his new bride. I was sure one day they'd find it funny.

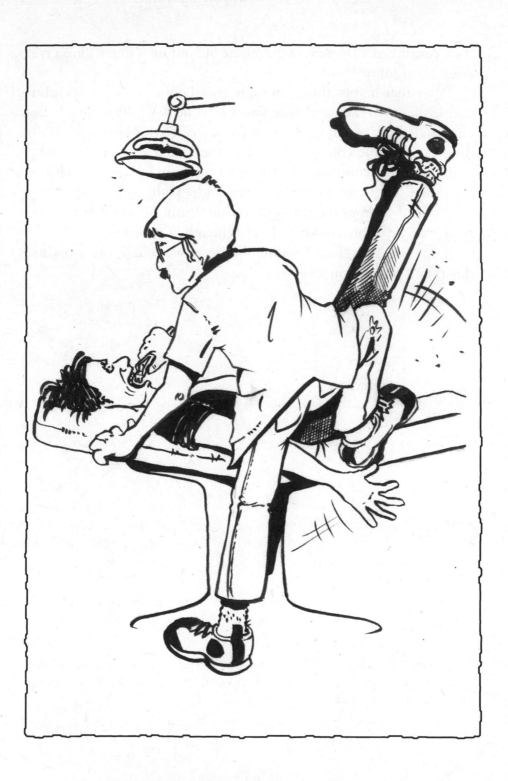

Chapter 5

More Than I Could Chew

As soon as I turned off the freeway towards Okotoks and home, I started to relax. I was even humming along to the upbeat Abba tune playing on the radio.

Calgary was obviously becoming a great place for John, but it sure wasn't a place I'd be happy hanging my hat. I needed open space and fresh air—two things that big cities couldn't offer. Now that the wedding was over, I could start making plans for the rest of my time off—just think, an entire week with nothing to do but putter around on my farm.

Well, that wasn't exactly true. I ran my tongue over the rent in my gum line—darned tooth. Although I had clung to the possibility that the silly thing would suddenly decide to pop through and put an end to the drama, it was time to give up on the hope department. Monday morning had seemed far away when I made the appointment to have the tooth removed, but Monday was now tomorrow.

I thought back to the last molar I had been forced to remove for a patient. Rufus had been a healthy young Rottweiler that had split the crown of the carnassial tooth right in half munching down on a bone. I had dug for hours to separate those four massive roots from the surrounding bone. It would be just my luck to end up like Father, and have to hold onto the chair to keep Dr. Catherall from dragging me across the room.

"Enough!" I groused. He had promised it would be no big deal. I parked my tongue in the middle of my mouth and directed my mind to what I was going to accomplish with this time to myself. Almost every free moment I had during the past few months had been spent working on the stone walls of my house or nailing on cedar shakes. Had I known what I was getting myself into when I first read the how-to book on building a stone house with slip forms, I may well have left the book in the library.

The old structure I had decided to move to my farm in Lister looked fabulous after we had resurfaced the logs, but it was too small for anything other than a bachelor pad. As I had plans of someday settling down to raise a family, I needed to add onto it in one way, shape, or form if it were to remain my permanent home.

The other log buildings I had seen people put additions on simply didn't look right to me. Siding of any kind butting into logs created way too much contrast. For a few days early on, I had toyed with the thought of learning how to use a broadaxe in order to match the hundred-year-old hand-hewn logs from the original house, but I couldn't conceive of a way of butting them together. It was the picture of a little guesthouse on page 10 of the how-to book that got me in trouble—half log and half stone, it was gorgeous.

When I first told Pops about my plans, he was beside himself. He just couldn't understand why I'd waste all that time and effort trying to make things blend, but that was ancient history now. Once he caved in to the notion that I was going to build with stone, he was a tremendous help. Without his efforts, the project would have come to a complete standstill.

As soon as the frost was out of the ground in the middle of March, we began pouring concrete. Almost every week, Dad would drive in from Riondel, fifty miles north on the winding Kootenay Lake road, and work away the best he could while I conducted business at the office. As soon as he had a form nailed into place and braced, we'd fire up the cement mixer. While I strategically placed the rocks one over two and two over one, he would keep me supplied with new stones and sloppy cement to work between them.

Initially, I was convinced I could build the house with rocks that had been gathered from my own property, but as the work proceeded, it became painfully obvious that this wasn't going to happen. To do an artistic job of placing the stones, it was necessary to have variety in their shapes and sizes. Many times Father would stand over my shoulder and shake his head as I rotated a dozen different boulders end for end again and again until the point of one fit perfectly into the notch between two others.

At first he'd walk away in frustration and grumble to himself, but eventually, he started looking for the rock with the long sharp point or the gentle V that would satisfy me. After long sessions of searching for oddball shapes we didn't have, it was his suggestion that we go farther afield. That was the beginning of excursions to other people's rock piles, and long sessions of wandering up and down the banks of the Goat River scrounging for boulders with exaggerated features and at least one flattened side.

Because my veterinary work was so erratic and unpredictable, everything to do with my construction at home became a battle for time—the time to gather rocks, the time to set them and pour concrete, the time to peck away the excess mortar. The fact that doorways and windows made natural breaks meant that the pours could be done in sections. Short sections between windows, or between doors and windows, were ideal to do after work when it only required a few hours to place the stones and concrete, and get everything washed up.

That meant that all I had to do was get up early the next morning, pull down the plywood form, and peck away the excess concrete around the rocks in order to display their best features. I loved that job—it was so rewarding to wield the welding hammer to first peck at, then scrape away the semi-set concrete that hid the beauty of the rock beneath it.

This week would be a catch-up week where I could do all the pours that were too long for me to get done with my limited time off. For weeks Dad and I had been hauling loads of stones from the river with his truck and dumping them in the centre of the courtyard. The first session would definitely be the worst; we'd have to do a continuous line for twenty feet along the base of the house. That pour would form the foundation of the wall for the bedrooms in the basement. There'd also be the base of the wing wall for the courtyard, which could be done in two pours if time became an issue, because there was a door in the middle of it for entry into my root cellar. It would be great to get a good start on those pours early in the week. If that happened, maybe Pops and I could even get out for a bit of fishing.

It was eleven-thirty, still morning, and the June heat was building by the time I pulled into my driveway in Lister. The moment I opened the car door, Lug was there yipping his greeting and licking at my hands.

"Down you get, old man…I missed you, too."

Before I could even get out, he squeezed past me, climbed up on the seat, and sat staring out the window. He watched attentively as I got out, took a few steps away from the car, and stretched.

"Come on…I'm not leaving you again…I'll be here all day."

I grabbed my suitcase and wandered into the house with Lug at my heels. It was already warm and he puffed with every step, his long pink tongue hanging low.

"Where's Grampa?"

The banging of a hammer in the courtyard answered that question.

"How you making out?" I hollered, peering over the edge of the embankment.

Dad leaned on the plywood structure he was working on, wiped his face with his sleeve, and looked up at me.

"Pretty good…I'm working on the last set of forms now."

"Really? You got all of them up already?"

I assessed his progress. The form consisted of 2x4 construction with half-inch plywood nailed to the inside surface. Stakes protruded from the ground every few feet to hold the bottom tightly in place, and at three-foot intervals braces were nailed to keep the top from bowing once the space was filled with concrete.

"Looks good…I'll change and give you a hand."

Within a few minutes, I was in a well-worn pair of jeans and a denim shirt that had already survived a few sessions with sloppy cement.

"Do you think we could get away with pouring this today?" I asked.

"I'm not sure," Dad answered. "I'll be another hour finishing this form…maybe we could tackle some of it."

"We should be able to get at least one of them poured," I insisted. "Maybe I should give Ron Renz a call to see if he can come and help." Ron was an ambitious young guy in his final year of high school who often helped me on weekends.

Within the hour, I was placing the first stones along the base of the wall. The time I had spent selectively gathering triangular rocks with at least one large flat surface really sped up the process, and I soon had them placed across the entire length.

Ron arrived as I dumped the first mixer of cement into the wheelbarrow, and soon he was hefting the five-gallon bucket to fill in behind them. I put on the musty-smelling pair of rubber gloves I had used for the last session and started working the wet mixture behind and under each rock. When a stone wouldn't stand of its own accord, I'd jam another behind it so the face of the prominent one would sit flat to the outside form. It was after four by the time I placed the final stones and Ron slopped the last concrete behind them.

"So that's it?" The way Father said this, I knew he was hoping for an end to the workday.

"I don't know." I looked to Ron. "Do you have anything to do later tonight?"

He shook his head.

"Why don't we have a bite to eat and see if we can get the short piece done?"

Father had stocked the fridge with groceries, and it didn't take long to slap together some ham and lettuce sandwiches.

It was after ten when Father dumped the last load of concrete into the wheelbarrow. The sky was almost completely dark, but the air was still warm from the heat of the day.

"That's it," he asserted resolutely.

"Right here," I said to Ron as he lifted the bucket of concrete and dumped it behind the rock I was holding. "Get me another little one to wedge in here, can you?" I asked, still fighting to keep the oblong-shaped stone from tipping over.

"You're such a glutton for punishment," Father said, shaking his head. "When do you plan on pulling the forms? In this heat, the first pour must be ready to chip already."

I got off my knees and straightened up. My shirt was wet with sweat, and every muscle in my body was aching. I had hefted a lot of rock today, and I was exhausted.

"Put the last of the mix in here, Ron," I said, pointing to the depression behind the big boulder that filled most of the twelve-inch form.

I grabbed the trouble light and picked my way around the form braces to the corner where we first started. I jabbed at the concrete. Father was right; the concrete had set well enough here to allow me to pull the form. I had almost convinced myself to start pecking by the time I had maneuvered my way to the other end. Grabbing a spike from my back pocket, I jabbed at the concrete there. It sank easily into the matrix.

"This end's not set up well enough...if we drop the form now, we may have a few of the last rocks we placed breaking away."

Father nodded and continued hosing down the cement mixer. "That leaves you a lot of chipping to do tomorrow. What time did you say you had to be at the dentist?"

"Eight."

"Good luck," he said sarcastically.

I felt as if my head had just hit the pillow when the alarm went off. Monday was here. I ran my tongue along the gum line one more time, as if expecting something to have changed overnight.

"Damn! What a way to ruin my week off." The last thing I wanted right now was to have needles poked into my mouth and a tooth pried out of my jaw.

Lug lifted his head from the pillow next to me and watched absently as I pulled back the covers, deposited my feet on the floor, and switched on the lamp. I rubbed my bleary eyes and glared out the window. The trees in the front yard were mere silhouettes in the fading darkness. Imagine getting out of bed this early on a day off…I struggled to my feet and stumbled to the fireplace where I had discarded the clothes I had pried off last night. The pants and shirt were still damp, and the concrete that had splattered all over them was now crusty.

I quickly dressed in some clean work clothes and threw on my boots. I was halfway down the stairs before Lug caught up with me. Father was snoring away on the other side of the bare 2x4 studs that defined the bedroom wall. I should have known better than to push him so hard yesterday. He wasn't as resilient now as he was in his younger years. The last thing I needed was for something to happen to him.

I felt overwhelmed as I walked into the courtyard and closed the basement door behind me. What had I been thinking when I kept going last night? Taking a deep breath, I clicked on the trouble light and draped it over one of the braces. I grabbed a welding hammer and pecked at the surface of the concrete—it was certainly set enough now!

With a hammer, I pounded off the first brace and tossed it to the centre of the courtyard. I had two hours to get something accomplished here before it was time to leave. Tossing the hammer on the window ledge, I grabbed a twelve-pound sledge. I flailed away, knocking the braces over one after the other, then reefed on the top of the form and jumped back as it fell towards me. Some of the underlying surface was smooth, but other areas were mottled with huge pockmarks. Grabbing the welding hammer, I aimed a blow at the edge of a defect. Tiny chips of concrete flew, revealing the blue-green rock underneath.

"Oh no," I groaned, whacking the encrusted surface again three or four times in a row. "This is going to take forever."

By the time I had exposed the first two rocks by the basement door, I was panicking. What should have taken only a few minutes with green concrete had taken me twenty. What had I done?

It was seven-thirty when I put down my welding hammer and headed upstairs for a shower. I was frustrated; I had chipped less than four feet of the first pour, and I was going to be lucky to get to my appointment on time. Why couldn't I have stopped with this one piece and chipped it last night?

I scaled the stairs to the dentist's office at a few minutes after eight. Claudia smiled as I glanced at my watch. "You almost made it on time today," she said, getting up from her chair and escorting me to the back.

"Dr. Catherall's got a busy morning scheduled, so he's anxious to get started."

"Ah good, you're here," he said with a hint of relief as Claudia led me to the chair.

"Hopefully, you're going to be taking anesthetics today, Dave," Denise chirped as she tucked an apron under my chin.

"He is!" the dentist said without a moment's hesitation.

Within ten minutes of hitting the chair, my jaw was frozen.

"Can you feel this?" he asked as he poked at my gum line.

"No," I gurgled with my mouth wide open.

While Denise finished prepping my mouth, Dr. Catherall carefully studied my X-ray. "Be all over before you know it," he said confidently.

An hour later, he looked far from confident. Beads of sweat were obvious on his forehead as he continued to focus his attention on that annoying conglomerate of dentine and enamel that had never wanted to see the outside world.

I glanced at Denise as the dentist checked the X-ray film yet again. I knew only too well the expression on his face—I had seen it staring back at me from the mirror more frequently than I cared to admit. It was the look I got when I had inadvertently bitten off a chunk bigger than I could comfortably chew. He wiped his forehead with a paper towel, then peered again at the X-ray film. Changing his gloves, he took a deep breath, fired up his drill, and continued his onslaught.

Claudia appeared from reception to see what to do about the patients who were piling up in the waiting room. In the ensuing hour, she returned a second and third time, only to retreat to the front to rebook the patient for a future date with the dentist.

It was quarter to eleven when he stepped back from the chair and took off his gloves. "I'm sorry, Dave, but I just can't get it. The roots of the tooth are wrapped right around the lingual and inferior alveolar nerves, and I'm afraid that if I drill any more, I'm going to damage one of them."

Denise handed me a paper cup full of water, and I rinsed and spat out a mouthful of blood. "What does that mean?"

I knew how difficult it could be to get healthy roots to let go of neighbouring bone. I always hated performing extractions on young dogs that had somehow fractured a tooth.

"I'll call and see if I can get you in to see an oral surgeon in Spokane," he said defensively.

"Spokane?"

"Yes, I'm sorry…but there's no one closer."

I looked mournfully at Denise as he headed for his private office. "Spokane? I had my whole day planned."

She sighed and shook her head. "Sorry, Dave…this has never happened before."

I crossed the border around noon and headed south towards Bonners Ferry, Idaho. I was tired, my mouth was numb, and every muscle in my body ached. What a great start to my week off!

The last time I had driven this far south to the States was over five years ago, when I first moved to the Creston Valley. At the time, I was worried that with Dr. Marling still in Creston, I might not find enough work to keep me busy. Back then, there was no full-time veterinarian in Bonners Ferry, and farmers down there were interested in having me look after their emergency service.

For weeks I had vacillated back and forth about writing the Idaho State board exams so that I'd be able to legally practise on both sides of the border; finally, I signed up to do them. I started my drive with the vague notion that Boise, Idaho, was somewhere a few miles southeast of Spokane, Washington.

When I stopped at a gas station in Sandpoint to pick up a road map and discovered that the trip to Boise would be a ten-hour drive, I was mortified. Somewhere between Sandpoint and Coeur d'Alene, I pulled off at a rest station to commiserate with myself. I remember gazing across a serene little lake and wondering why I was stacking so much on my plate. After a long session of arguing the merits of what I was doing, I decided to determine my future by the toss of a coin—heads, I'd continue on, tails, I'd return to Creston.

I flipped a quarter, caught it, and plunked it on the hood of my car—the Queen's face was staring up at me. After giving the coin a long hard glare, I threw it into the lake, turned my car around, and headed north.

That episode now seemed so long ago, and the decision so unimportant. Time has a way of turning mountainous obstacles into mere bumps in the road. I rubbed my hand over my numb lip and gently prodded the crevice in my mouth—I hoped I'd feel the same a few years from now when I looked back on this event.

All the way to Spokane, I worried about leaving the chipping of the rock face undone. I had been crazy to pour so much of it in that kind of heat. It had been brutal working on it this morning, and with each passing hour the job would only get more difficult.

I had stopped at the office to let Doris know about the

unfortunate turn of events, and if she couldn't get hold of Father by telephone, she'd have Margaret drive out to tell him. I hated the thought of dumping yet more bull work on his plate.

It was two-thirty before I stepped up to the reception desk at the Spokane Dental Clinic and handed over the envelope containing Dr. Catherall's X-rays.

"We've been expecting you, Dr. Perrin." The woman at the counter gave me a sympathetic look and pointed me to a chair. "It'll be another hour before Dr. Knight will be able to attend to you. In the meantime we can get the paperwork filled out, and you can peruse this informational material. The doctor likes his high-risk patients to be well informed of the potential ramification of the surgery before he'll continue with the procedure."

I nodded and took the booklet, pen, and clipboard she handed me. I sat down and thumbed through the pamphlet on potential post-surgical complications from wisdom tooth extraction. My eyes bugged at the pictures of men and women with lips drooping and long strings of drool hanging from the corners of their mouths.

I was shocked to discover that for every one hundred wisdom teeth extracted, there would be at least some form of nerve damage in one of the patients. Knowing that I possessed the first tooth that my own dentist couldn't extract made me suspect that the odds would be even worse in my case. I instinctively ran my tongue over the gaping hole in my jaw. There wasn't much I could do about it now.

I set the pamphlet on the end table next to me and picked up a copy of *National Geographic Magazine*. Browsing through an article about sea turtles, I tried hard to care about the decline in their population. I was working my way through a debate about whether they were decreasing in numbers because the seagrass they fed on was dying back or because man was interfering by inhabiting beaches where the turtles laid their eggs. I was into the second page of the dissertation when I set it aside.

I returned to the pamphlet on wisdom tooth extraction and

plowed on. It was suggested that complications were far fewer in younger patients, that the roots of wisdom teeth developed and formed through a patient's twenties, making extraction more difficult and nerve damage more likely, and that the incidence was as high as ten per cent after the age of thirty-five. Although I tried to console myself about being just a few weeks past my thirtieth birthday, I ended up finding yet another reason to mourn the passing of my twenties.

Reading through the potential ramifications of nerve damage, I decided that it would be far better if the good doctor happened to nick the inferior alveolar nerve rather than the lingual nerve. Enduring a numb lip and chin sounded far more appealing than having a tongue and inner mouth that were either totally numb or subjected to pains that were burning, dull, achy, or a combination of the above.

My mind shut down totally at the suggestions of frequent drooling and biting of the lip, the inside of the cheek, or the side of the tongue. I hadn't come here to end up with "paralytic disfigurement or trigeminal neuralgia with stabbing electric shocks or intractable shooting pain," and I sure as hell didn't want the sense of taste, the facility of speech, and the sensory pleasure of kissing to be diminished.

"Have you finished filling in the consent form, Dr. Perrin?"

I glanced at the receptionist, then the clipboard, and shook my head.

By the time I got into the surgery, the earlier local anesthetic had worn off and a dull ache permeated my jaw. My mind was numb from considering all the negative possibilities, and all I could think of was getting this whole affair over and done with.

A trim, middle-aged man with greying temples was examining my X-rays on a view-box when I was escorted to the dental chair. He smiled and nodded to me as I settled in.

"You've had quite the morning," he stated matter-of-factly.

Giving him a lopsided smile, I replied, "You don't know the half of it."

"You have a third molar with a very difficult presentation." Turning to point to the image on the view-box, he continued, "And this root is very close to the inferior alveolar nerve. It'll be necessary to dissect around the remaining roots to avoid compressing the underlying nerve."

He checked the clipboard to make certain the release was in order, then donned his gloves. I spent the next half hour with my mouth wide open, staring at the top of a magnification hood and listening to the scream of a high-speed drill.

When the whining finally stopped, the doctor grabbed a pair of thumb forceps from his instrument tray and picked up the root for me to see.

"There you go..."

The moment I was sitting in the car I peered into the rear-view mirror and stared at my face. Opening my mouth, I wiggled my tongue back and forth—it moved where I wanted it to, and I could feel it. I wasn't drooling, and although my lower lip was somewhat droopier than normal, it wasn't that obvious. I poked at my lips and chin with my fingers. The right side of my face was definitely numb, but I'd expect that until the rest of the freezing wore off.

I arrived back in Lister in the early evening, happy to have the ordeal behind me. Lug was there to greet me, jumping and twirling and yipping with joy. I gave him a cursory pat on the head, then headed towards the courtyard.

I took a half dozen steps with Lug still rooting at my hand for attention, then stopped to listen. There it was, the clink, clink, clink of metal striking stone. Poor Father was still at it. Seated on an upturned five-gallon pail, he was swinging a blunt-looking welder's hammer. He was close to finishing off the far side of the first pour.

"How's it going?" I asked hesitantly.

Without moving, he dropped his hammer and turned his head towards me. "God, Dave," he said wearily, "you have no idea. My arms are so sore that I can hardly swing this thing anymore...I took it over and sharpened it a few times, but within a half hour of pounding this damned stuff, it's as blunt as a shovel handle." He stared dejectedly at the wall in front of him and held up his right hand. "Got so many blisters they're starting to run together."

Without another word to him, I rushed upstairs to change into my work clothes. When I returned, he had moved his bucket a foot closer to the root-cellar wall. Swinging wildly with the sledge-hammer, I dislodged the braces of the next form and pulled it off.

"I kept hosing them down with cold water, hoping to keep them from setting up as fast," Dad said. "But I doubt that it worked any miracles."

He was right. The miracle was in waiting—waiting for me to swing my chipping hammer ten thousand times.

I finally turned the trouble light off at two o'clock and headed up to bed. The last seven hours had been a nightmare of self-induced torture. During that time, I had broken the wooden handles of both my welding hammers. After the last one snapped, I resorted to the use of a hammer and coal chisel to whack away at concrete that had hardened to the same texture as the rock it encased.

My jaw was throbbing as I peered at myself in the bathroom mirror. I opened and closed my mouth several times, each time wiggling my tongue from side to side for good measure. With the tip of my index finger, I poked from my lip to the bottom of my chin—the entire right side still felt like the freezing had not worn off.

I'd just have to wait and see what tomorrow would bring…my truck should be arriving any day now, and if Pop and I could get some more forms up, maybe we could do a couple more pours.

I wasn't sure about the fishing.

Chapter 6

Welcome to the Real World

It was Sunday afternoon and I had been poking around the house all morning. The two sheets of drywall I had screwed into place went a long way to defining the limits of my upstairs bathroom. Now, the view from the throne was no longer a panoramic view of the entire upper floor. I stood with my back against the new wall trying to visualize the room when it was finished.

Because it was part of the new addition onto the log portion of the house, the east wall sloped away at an angle as a result of the way it butted into the hip roof. If the west wall was going to be drywall, and the walls around the sauna were going to be cedar... wouldn't it be cool if I could work some stone into the décor?

I was trying to picture how the sloping wall would look covered in stone when the phone rang. Prying myself from my visualization, I rushed to the main bedroom. "Hello."

"Dave, this is Jim Steelman. Mary and I just got into town. Do you want to get together for a bit of a chat?"

"Sure...where are you?"

"At a phone booth down the street from your office."

"In front of the Depot Restaurant?"

There was a pause as he took a moment to get his bearings. "Yup, that's the place."

"Go in and order something to eat...I'll meet you there in fifteen to twenty minutes."

I hurriedly changed from my tattered jeans and washed my hands. I was excited about actually meeting my new employee, but I was also apprehensive. Although he seemed to be an upfront kind of guy, I continually reminded myself that Cory had seemed to be, too.

It would be great to have someone to bounce cases against for a second opinion, and it would be even nicer to have a few days a week where I could do whatever I wanted without worrying about letting my clients down. But would there be enough money? Maybe someone new would appeal to people who weren't presently using my services. Were there enough calls that I couldn't handle now to fill in the days for two of us?

One moment I was convinced there were, the next I was fretting that there was no way a small town like Creston could support five vets. No matter what viewpoint I took on the issue at any moment, there were times during the same day when I was convinced of the exact opposite.

One thing I was sure of…I was tired of working every waking hour and uncertain as to how much longer I could keep putting in the time it took to keep my clients satisfied.

I pulled up in the parking lot behind the restaurant and hurriedly made my way down the street. The place was full and there were several people standing at the door waiting to be seated. Stopping at the till, I looked in both directions in an attempt to locate my new employee.

"They're in the corner booth," said Shirley, one of my favourite waitresses. "Didn't think you could pull one over on us, did you?" she asked playfully. "Seems like a nice young couple…he told us he was in town to meet his new boss."

Not much went unnoticed in this little town. I spotted the couple as soon as I rounded the corner to the front dining area. A well-built, blond man pushed his plate aside and stood when he saw me. He stretched out his hand as I approached.

"Jim," he said, giving my hand a hearty shake. "I assume from your stature that you'd be Dave. Shirley was just filling us in on some of your escapades."

I smiled. It was a good sign if Shirley had warmed to him already. "Good to meet you, Jim."

"This is my wife, Mary."

"Hello, Mary. How was the trip up?"

She sighed and patted her ample abdomen. "It was a beautiful drive up here, but I think I'd have enjoyed it a lot more if I wasn't so uncomfortable." She squirmed and leaned back, seeking a position where her baby would rest more easily.

Jim slid into the seat next to his wife and I settled in across the table. He certainly looked like a man who'd be able to handle himself in large-animal practice. He was husky and well over the six-foot mark; the Texas State T-shirt he wore stretched over muscular arms and a brawny chest.

"This is sure a beautiful part of the world that you've settled in," Mary began.

"It is, isn't it? It doesn't matter where you go in this valley, you have a great view. If you live on the mountain, you have a fantastic view of the flats. If you live on the flatlands, you have a panoramic view of the mountains."

"I'm really looking forward to checking out some of this country on my own," Jim said with a smile. "Mary and I love to hike and get off the beaten trail." He reached out a hand and patted his wife's belly. "It won't be long before she'll be ready to go again."

"Well, there's lots of opportunity for hiking and camping here in the Kootenays. That's one of the main reasons I wanted to come here, too. Trouble is, a one-man practice doesn't leave you enough time to get out and do it."

Jim smiled broadly. "Well, hopefully, that'll change for you, too…now that I'm here to give you a hand. I have to tell you, I'm happy to be saying goodbye to the books and getting out where I can get my hands dirty."

"Sorry to interrupt, Dave, but did you want something to eat?" Shirley was standing at my shoulder, coffee pot in hand.

"I'll take a shot of that poison," I said playfully. "And you can order my usual."

"So that's two eggs sunny, bacon crisp, brown toast?"

"You got it."

She was refilling the other coffee mugs when there was an annoying beep, beep, beep. I took a deep breath, shut the pager off, and smiled at Shirley. When I bought the contraption, I had reasoned that it would give me a lot more personal freedom; I wouldn't have to continually phone in to my answering service leaving behind a trail of numbers where I might be reached. It didn't take more than a few days before I recognized a feeling of constant tension, a dread that it might go off at any minute.

"Do you want me to hold off on your order for a moment?"

"Maybe you better," I said, hurrying to the front counter to use the phone.

June Miller picked up on the second ring. "Creston Vet Clinic." June was still running the taxi service as well as acting as an answering service for me and several other local businesses.

"It's Dave."

"I just got a call from Verna Levett. She's having trouble with a heifer calving. The animal's been pushing for some time now, and Verna says there's still only one leg coming." June hesitated for a moment, then said blandly, "Verna said to tell you to get your ass in gear—that she didn't want to lose the calf."

I chuckled. Good old Verna. Some things had changed significantly since I had started my practice here in Creston, but Verna wasn't one of them. "Tell her she interrupted my Sunday dinner— she'll appreciate that. I'll head over there right away."

I wandered back to the seating area where Shirley was still chatting to Jim. "Looks like I go without today. Got a calving..."

"Do you want me to tag along, Doc?" Jim asked eagerly.

"Sure thing, but we better let Mary get settled first...I've made arrangements for you two to stay with Margaret Berg, one of the ladies who works with me at the office. She'll take great care of you until you can find a place of your own."

"Do you think you can manage without me, hon?" Jim asked his wife.

She stared at him for a few seconds, then nodded uncertainly.

"I can draw you a map," I said, sitting down and scrawling across the surface of a napkin. "Her place is easy to find—you just get back onto Highway 3 and head west until you are right across the flatland. You take the last turn to the left before you go through a rock cut and start climbing to Kootenay Pass."

Within a few minutes Jim and I had donned coveralls and were in my new truck heading east on Highway 3.

"This is Erickson, where most of the fruit in the valley is produced."

"What do they grow here?" Jim asked, gazing out the window at long rows of fruit trees.

"You name it: apples, pears, plums, cherries, peaches, apricots, grapes…Most of our dog poisonings come from here, too."

"That's something I've never seen," Jim mused. "You'll have to bring me up to speed on that…what kind of poison?"

"Mostly strychnine and warfarin, but it can involve almost any spray or rodenticide."

"Not much livestock here?"

"There are lots of horses, still a few backyard cows, but most of our large-animal work is from further out in the country."

We turned south off the highway onto Canyon-Lister Road. "This is the Goat River," I said, slowing to a crawl over the bridge so that Jim could watch the water boil through a boulder-strewn maze on its way into a steep rock cavern.

"We're going to a farm out in Canyon, the little community at the top of this hill. There's quite a bit of fruit grown in this area, too, but out here, almost every property has a few critters somewhere in the backyard."

"Where do you live?"

"I'm in the process of building farther south on this same road, and just past me is a polygamous group. If you get a call for a Blackmore, Oler, or Palmer, that's likely where you'll be heading."

"Polygamy? I thought that only happened in Utah."

"Nope...we have our own homegrown version right here in the Creston Valley."

We drove in silence past the Canyon community hall, the local store, and dozens of ten- and twenty-acre farms.

"You're in for a real treat, today," I said as we started down an incline.

"How so?"

"Your first call in the Creston Valley is to Verna's."

"Who's that?"

"You'll see...she's special. The Big Guy Upstairs definitely broke the mould after He made her. She used to be my neighbour until she downsized her operation and moved a few miles up the road."

I slowed the vehicle halfway down the hill, then turned up a steep drive into Verna's yard. I was impressed...she had done a tremendous amount of work since she'd traded farms with Jack Rodgers. The little knoll was now covered with buildings, and every inch of her drive was topped by asphalt. I only wished Jack had made out as well with the trade. Just after he took over Verna's hog operation next door to me, the price of hogs plummeted and he ended up losing the property.

I avoided a bob-tailed Border collie that rushed over from the house, pulled to a stop on a steep slope in front of the new barn, and set the emergency brake. The dog continued to circle the truck, yapping aggressively.

"Trinity...go lay down and shut up!" came a brusque voice. I opened my door. Verna was waiting impatiently with her hands on her hips next to a hayshed that took off at a right angle to the barn. Her shoulder-length grey-brown hair was windblown; she was dressed in sloppy green sweats and gumboots.

"Damn time you got here, Perry." Her gruff voice had the faintest taint of sarcasm. After six years of dealing with Verna, I still hadn't figured out why she called me Perry. "It must be nice to be a rich, bloody vet and be able to sit around in restaurants all day!"

I smiled at Jim's puzzled expression and opened the back of

my truck. After throwing a bottle of soap, the calving chains, and hooks into my stainless steel bucket, I passed it to Verna.

"We'll need some warm water."

"Who've you got in tow?" she demanded.

"This is Jim Steelman…He's a new vet who's started working with me."

"Fresh meat, are ya?" Verna said, giving him a long hard look.

"Guess so," Jim responded matter-of-factly. "Just graduated from Texas State." He shrugged and gave me a sheepish grin.

"Don't give a rat's ass 'bout where you come from, 's long as you know your way around a cow's back end," she retorted. "Do you think he'll last longer than the last one?" she asked me smugly before grabbing my bucket and heading for her milk house.

I flushed and followed her into the newly finished structure. "Pretty nice digs," I said, trying to change the subject.

"Damned time," she groused. "I'm tired of roughing it…you get to my age, and you like things to be gettin' easier."

"I thought you said you were going to retire when you moved over here."

"I did," she retorted defensively. "I only have five sows and twenty head of cattle."

"That's retirement?"

Verna punished me with a stern look. "You sound like my bloody kids! If I quit my critters, what would I do with myself… curl up my toes and croak?" She filled the bucket to the rim with warm water and set it next to the door.

"Come see my farrowing pen." She strode across the concrete floor and out a door on the opposite side of the room. "Look at the beautiful litter Clara gave me." Stepping over the 2x6 rails of a pen, she squatted next to an enormous recumbent sow. The animal grunted contentedly as Verna rubbed her pink belly. Grabbing a teat, she squirted a spray of milk in my direction and rousted a dozen plump little piglets from beneath a heat lamp. She gazed at the babies fondly as one after the other settled in to nursing. "How the hell could I give them up?" she asked defiantly.

As if suddenly remembering her heifer, she climbed out beside me and ushered me back to the milk house. "Better get you buggers to work. Knowing you, Perry, you punched the time clock the moment you turned in my driveway."

Grabbing the bucket, she headed outside. I followed behind her as she threw open a gate at the side of the barn and led us into a roofed corral where several cows were feeding.

"This heifer's been frickin' around all bloody day," Verna lamented. "I was suspicious she was up to something last night and got up to check her a couple times. I got the boys to put her in here and throw a halter on her after I finished milking this morning. It's over four hours since she broke water. I stuck my arm in her just before I phoned you, and all I could feel comin' was the nose and one foot. I called all over hell's half acre to find one of the boys, but do ya think I could catch up to one of 'em? Frickin' kids don't want a thing to do with my critters."

The red, white-faced heifer was stretched out on her side pushing. She was a good-sized animal of Holstein-Angus heritage. As we watched, she strained.

"See," said Verna. "There's only one foot and you can see the nose."

"Looks like the calf didn't get positioned right when it started into the pelvis," I mused.

"Bloody hell!" Verna cursed. "Big girl like her should've crapped it out like nothing." She grabbed hold of the halter and slipped a rope through the shank. "What do you want to do with her?"

"Best to get her up so we can get her to stop straining."

I knelt beside the critter and slapped her exposed side. When she rolled to her sternum, I dug my knees into her rib cage. As she slowly got to her feet, Jim leaned against the rope and brought her up short. I scrubbed her back end, soaped myself up, held her tail to the side, and slipped my fingers into the heifer.

Although there seemed to be adequate room to maneuver, Verna was right—only the right front leg was present. I slid past the calf's head to the brim of the pelvis and pushed deep on the calf's right side. The leg went straight back as far as I could reach.

"Do you want to check her out, Jim?"

"Sure thing," he said enthusiastically. He quickly stripped his coveralls to his waist, tying the arms around his abdomen like an apron. Pulling his T-shirt over his head, he tossed it onto the top rail of the corral.

He was scrubbing up when the dog resumed her incessant barking. Verna looked uncomfortably towards the yard and turned to investigate the commotion. The moment Jim's hand entered the heifer's vagina, she snapped back to the action at hand. I held the heifer's tail to the side as Jim buried his arm deeper.

"Can you feel the leg?" I asked.

He nodded, then pushed further forward, burying his muscular armpit deep into the cavern.

"Just follow it to the elbow, then flex it until you work your fingers down to the foot."

Jim nodded, worked his arm back a bit, then dove in deeper still. I was so intent on watching his progress I didn't notice that Verna had left. I turned when I heard her voice from a distance. She was arguing with someone on the other side of the gate. I realized with a start that it was a very red-faced Cory.

"Why couldn't you at least have called me?" he asked defensively.

"You snooze, you lose!" Verna barked. Turning on her heel, she stomped back to continue watching the delivery of her calf.

For several minutes I was lost to the proceedings at hand. My face was flushed and each beat of my heart caused my temples to pulse. Why did I always let Cory have that effect on me?

Verna stood stone-faced with her arms folded, scrutinizing Jim's efforts. It didn't seem to bother her that she had summoned both me and Cory at the same time with the intention of dealing with whichever one of us arrived first. I glowered at her, wondering if she felt the least bit guilty about treating Cory that way, about treating me that way. She showed not the slightest indication.

"I got it!" Jim cried enthusiastically.

"Make sure you cup the foot in the palm of your hand when

you bring it up," I prompted. "You don't want the tip to tear the uterus when you turn the corner."

Jim nodded, shifted ever so slightly, and brought his arm out of the heifer. When the animal strained, two yellow-capped feet protruded. Jim slipped the chains on the feet and within a few minutes, a red and white heifer calf lay gasping on the ground.

When we made our way to the milk house to clean up, Jim still had no idea as to what had happened between Cory and our hard-edged client. While I was hosing off our instruments, I mentioned to him that the fellow who had arrived during the calving was our opposition. He raised his eyebrows but said nothing. We were settled in the truck and ready to leave when Verna came over.

"Well, thanks, Perry...till you're better paid," she said in an offhand manner.

"So we're going to have to compete for your business now, Verna?" I asked.

She flushed ever so slightly, then quipped without a trace of a smile, "I just wanted to see who could drive here the fastest."

"You might have neither one of us show up next time."

"Naaah," she said confidently. "That'll never happen...you'd never leave your ol' neighbour hanging."

Chapter 7

King of the Block

Doris and I had gotten nicely started on a dog spay when I heard the door open, and we were treated to a spate of cursing in the waiting room. There followed a volley of loud voices in a language other than English, and the slamming of the door. Doris peeled back the outer protective sheath on a packet of sterile suture material and held it up for me to grab. I placed it on the draped instrument tray and finished my incision through the linea alba, the fibrous structure running down the centre of the ventral abdomen.

"I'll see what that's about," Doris said, opening the folding doors and stepping through to the front office.

I probed deeply into the abdomen with my finger, searching for the uterus. In an older dog like the one I was operating on, it was usually a substantial, tubular organ half again the size of a pencil. I had just located the structure and brought it to the incision when there was a high-pitched screech from a cat followed by Doris's troubled voice.

"Don't let him out—keep the box in place! Dr. Perrin's in surgery and our other doctor is out on a farm call...we can't do anything with your cat until one of them is finished."

I traced the right horn of the uterus to the ovary and elevated it to the incision.

"Skroopchuck, behave!" came a heavily accented voice.

"Keep the lid on! Keep the lid on!" Doris insisted.

Trying to ignore the distraction, I kept a steady traction on the ovary until its ligament ruptured with a pop, and it came up into plain sight where I could start stripping the fatty tissue from the large vessels that supplied it with blood.

The folding doors opened and Doris rushed through to the kennel room. Her forelocks were sticking out from beneath her cap and her mask was dangling under her chin. She grabbed a couple of blankets and hurried back to the waiting room.

"Just cover the box with these and don't let him out," she insisted.

"Settle down, Skroopchuck! Settle down."

I had the ovarian stump ligated by the time Doris returned. She closed the folding doors and leaned against them while she adjusted her cap and mask.

"I've never seen a bigger cat," she swore breathlessly. "They've got him sandwiched between a couple of cardboard boxes, but he keeps getting his head through one of the holes."

"What's wrong with him?" I asked, applying traction to the left horn of the uterus.

"The man says he's been in a fight." Doris tucked her hair back under her cap and adjusted her mask. "He doesn't have an appointment."

"Did you tell him I'll be a while?" Sheba was an older Labrador retriever, and she had several benign tumours that needed to be removed after I was finished with the ovariohysterectomy.

"I told him that, but he insisted he wanted to wait while his wife walked down to Super-Valu to do a bit of shopping."

I had ligated the stump of the uterus and was severing it, when Doris poked her nose through the folding doors to check on our client. It had been quiet for some time, and I presumed that the cat had settled down.

"I'll get the record filled out while you close up. Give me a holler when you're ready for me to scrub up those lumps." It was amazing how many things the woman could handle at once. The job of a veterinary receptionist in a practice like mine required the wearing of many hats that often were stacked one upon the other.

I held the uterine stump with a pair of forceps and watched for signs of blood seeping before releasing it into the abdomen. I had just placed a suture in the distal end of my incision and tied a knot when the folding doors opened and closed, and Doris came rushing back.

"I've never seen anything like it," she gushed disgustedly. "The guy's eating sunflower seeds and spitting the shells all over."

"Are you serious? In the office? On the floor?"

Doris nodded.

"Well, give him a dog dish and ask him to spit them in that."

Doris went to the kennel room and ran to the waiting room with a stainless steel bowl. I had finished closing the abdomen by the time she returned.

"I'm ready for you to scrub the big one," I said, pointing to the fist-sized lump on the Lab's rib cage.

"The nerve of the man," Doris snorted, squirting soap over the mound and scrubbing it with a vengeance. Wiping away the brownish suds with a 3x3 gauze, she slathered on more. "Never in my life," she went on. "Can you imagine someone coming into your house and spitting those darned things all over your floor?"

I smiled as Doris ranted on—it took a lot to get her this worked up. She finished her scrub and impatiently ripped the wrap from a cloth drape.

"Just stay here till I'm finished," I suggested. "After we get done with the cat, we can clean things up with the vacuum cleaner."

Doris fidgeted as I made an incision over the length of the lump and began working my finger around the margin of the fatty mass. Lipomas were the most gratifying of tumours to remove. They were almost always totally encapsulated so they separated easily from the surrounding tissue. Within a few minutes, a glistening glob of fat was sitting on the tabletop, and I was suturing the subcutaneous tissues together to close the dead space created by its removal.

Doris had finished scrubbing the remaining two areas on the

nape of the dog's neck by the time I had completed the closure of the wound.

"These ones are much smaller," she observed.

I had made a two-inch incision over a second lipoma when the cursing began in the adjoining room.

"What now?" Doris groaned.

She disappeared into the front office as I began running my finger around the golf-ball-sized glob of fat.

"No!" Doris screamed. "Keep him under the blanket!"

I couldn't stand the suspense a moment longer. Taking a quick look at the heart monitor to make sure my patient was stable, I sidled to the door to see what the commotion was about. Doris was standing halfway across the office, dancing back and forth and waving her arms in an attempt to ward off the charge of a massive black cat. A rotund grey-haired man was sprawled out on the waiting room floor clinging precariously to the end of the cat's tail.

In a desperate attempt to break free, the cat lunged straight for the wall. He clawed his way up the black velvet wallpaper and vaulted onto the ledge over the fish tank. I stood helplessly with my gloved hands in the air as several African violets tumbled over the edge and spilled onto the floor.

"Skroopchuck!" bellowed the man as the cat repeatedly pummelled himself against the window. "Get back down here!"

Mounting the waiting room bench, our portly client lunged towards Skroopchuck. He grabbed him by the hind legs and pulled the struggling cat towards him. When the cat's flailing feet snagged the rim of the pot containing the hoya plant and threatened to bring it crashing down with him, Doris entered the fray. She grasped the container just before it left the shelf.

"Watch out!" warned the man as the cat screeched and dug his claws into the margins of the shelf.

"Oh my God!" Doris ducked as a stream of urine sprayed like a water pistol from Skroopchuck's rear end. When the owner jumped back to avoid the shower, he stepped into his spit bowl and fell against the wall. The fox and hound picture that had been presented to me at graduation crashed to the floor, and shattered glass flew everywhere. The stainless steel bowl rolled upside down across the carpet, leaving behind it a trail of hulls from the sunflower seeds.

I took a deep breath and gently closed the sliding door with the toe of my shoe. I had a job to finish, and Doris seemed to have this situation well in hand.

By the time I had the second lipoma removed and the skin sutured, an eerie silence had fallen over the office. Other than the rhythmic rattling of the valves in the anesthetic machine and the occasional sounds of passing traffic, I would have thought that Sheba and I were alone in this corner of the galaxy.

I dropped the last of the globs of fat into the surgery bowl and stripped off my gloves. Wiping a drop of blood from one of the dog's incisions, I stripped the drapes from her sides and turned off the dials for nitrous oxide and halothane. I squeezed the re-breathe bag on the anesthetic machine until it was totally empty, then hit the flush valve for a flow of pure oxygen.

I took my time cleaning off the table and depositing the drapes and gown in the washing machine. I was sure that Doris had things under control on the other side of the surgery doors, and I was in no hurry to meet the monstrous black cat that awaited me. I was almost disappointed when Sheba started breathing more rapidly and gagged on her tube.

"There's a girl," I said, unhooking the endotracheal tube and releasing the air from the cuff. I straightened the blanket in the recovery kennel and hefted the old girl from the table. When she gagged and brought her front foot forward, I pulled the tube and stretched out her tongue.

"Oooooooo," she moaned.

I watched her for a few minutes more, then timidly opened the surgery doors. Doris stood at the counter. I noticed that she was no longer wearing the same smock she had on when she was on the receiving end of a golden shower.

"How are we doing here?" I asked nonchalantly.

Doris gave me her how-do-you-think-I'm-doing look. Raising

an eyebrow, she said almost pleasantly, "Mr. Paige has a cat for you to examine."

I peeked into the waiting room where the floor was still a clutter of potting dirt and sunflower seed hulls.

"I was afraid of getting him more riled up if I started the vacuum cleaner," she informed me. "I'm hoping that no one comes through the door before I can get to it." She handed me the card, smiled ever so coyly, and said, "I'll just be watching Sheba if you need any help."

With that, she slipped into the surgery, grinned wickedly, and closed the bifolds in my face. I wandered through the carnage into the waiting area. Sunflower seed shells crunched under my feet and the smell of cat urine was heavy in the air.

"Mr. Paige?" I said as casually as I could manage. "So Skroopchuck has been in a fight?"

"Steve. Call me Steve. He's the boss of the neighbourhood," he said proudly. "But every now and then, the other cats get a few licks in. The last few days, he's been holding up his hind leg and just lying around the house." Steve rubbed his hand over several days' growth of stubble on his chin and shook his head slowly. "He didn't think much of the car ride to town."

"Let's bring him into the exam room and have a look at him." I stepped over to the door and depressed the lock.

Mr. Paige peered apprehensively at the blanket-covered mound on the bench beside him. "You want to bring him in there?"

I nodded.

He folded the grey woollen blanket that Doris had given him farther under the box and pried himself from the seat. Carrying the burden as if it were a bomb that the slightest jar might explode, he took baby steps in my direction. He was almost to the exam table when there was a scratching inside the boxes and the sound of tearing cardboard.

"He's out! He's out!" Mr. Paige shouted.

The cat gave a frightful yowl as I grabbed the blanketed bundle and tightened the enclosure. The boxes fell to the ground as the owner and I struggled to contain Skroopchuck. He screeched again and I felt the hairs on the back of my neck prickle to attention.

"Draw up a millilitre and a half of Ketamine, Doris!" I hollered.

Teeth gnashed through the grey blanket mere inches from Mr. Paige's hand as I tried desperately to grab hold of the cat's scruff.

"Just hold tight on his legs," I gasped. "I've got control of his head."

Sweat began dripping onto the blanket. Mr. Paige's face was flushed and running with perspiration.

"Hurry up, Doris!" I yelled.

I heard the crashing of the bifold doors at the same time as the blanket gave way to the cat's slashing teeth. I held tight to his scruff as he wriggled more and more of his head through the parting fibres of the blanket.

"Here it is!" Doris was still squirting the last bit of air from the syringe as she ran towards us.

I grabbed it with my left hand and plunged the needle into the well-defined mass of Skroopchuck's hindquarters. The cat screamed defiantly as I injected the anesthetic, and his entire head popped through the hole he had created. Glistening white teeth gnashed and fiery green eyes glared hatefully at his captors. The smell of urine and feces was overwhelming. There were several tense minutes before the cat finally began to relax.

"Get me the mineral oil, will you, Doris?"

I placed a drop of oil in each of Skroopchuck's open eyes, then slipped him free of the blanket. Doris cleaned the cat up as well as she could and headed towards the laundry with the blanket.

"Isn't he a beauty?" Steve said, staring at the huge pet that covered half the tabletop.

"He's definitely one of the biggest I've ever seen," I said, clipping away at one of the bite wounds on his back leg. "The only cat I can remember that could hold a candle to him is one from Canyon. Nell Blair has a huge seven-toed orange cat called Septamus that I'm sure is every bit as big."

"Skroopchuck could take him," Steve declared confidently.

"Do you want me to remove these and lighten his load a bit?" I pointed to the two huge marbles under the cat's tail.

"Castrate Skroopie?" Mr. Paige shifted uncomfortably, as if I had suggested I perform the procedure on him. "No way...it wouldn't be fair...not to the king of the block."

"It would settle him down a lot and put an end to stuff like this," I said, indicating the open wounds on his back foot.

Mr. Paige was resolute. "No, I couldn't do that...not to a beautiful boy like Skroopie."

Chapter 8

The Fine Art
of Schmoozing

"You'd think I lived in a dairy barn," I grumbled to Lug as I hurried across the living room.

There was another mournful bawl when I threw open the door. The moment the Holstein calf saw me, she charged over the threshold into the room, pushing Lug aside in the process.

"Easy there, little girl...I know I'm late with your grub, but you have to learn some patience."

I quickly thrust the nipple of the two-quart milk bottle into the calf's mouth and sidestepped towards the exit. Lug squeezed past us and wandered over to lift his leg on the big fir tree in the front yard. Taking tiny steps, one after the other, I induced the calf to follow me far enough outside to close the door behind her.

"You're becoming a darned nuisance, Petunia." I could hardly open the front door these days without having her come charging through.

She had still been on antibiotics when I brought her home from the clinic a month ago, so I put her in the pen in the barn where she'd be easy to handle for her daily injections. Once she was off medication, I let her out, thinking she'd hang with the rest of the cows. The problem was, she couldn't wrap her mind around the concept that she was a cow and that I wasn't her mother.

Initially, I'd fill my bottle with milk replacer and wander through the trees to feed her. She was still limping badly on her front leg

and I could easily outrun her. Last Saturday, though, she decided she could keep up with me, and it was only by taking an evasive route home that I was able to ditch her. Sunday morning I awoke to a doleful wail beneath my bedroom window—she had figured out where I was hiding.

Although I was elated with the way her joints had healed, she'd never win the Miss Moo contest for the most beautiful heifer in Lister. The bones around the affected joints flared markedly, and she'd probably always have a knobby knee and fetlock.

Petunia's antics got more and more aggressive as the bottle emptied and she began sucking air—these days two quarts never seemed to satisfy her. The harder she sucked and yanked on the rubber nipple, the more she frothed and the more frantically she bunted. Attracted by the frothy milk that dripped to the ground at the calf's feet, Lug moved in and started licking at the corner of her mouth.

When I pulled the nipple away and took a step back, Petunia searched desperately for something to suck on. Lug was in the wrong place at the wrong time, and his floppy ear disappeared into her mouth. Shocked and insulted by the invasion of his privacy, he yelped and nipped at the calf's muzzle.

While they were both distracted, I snuck into the house and went upstairs to the bathroom. Staring into the mirror, I slathered my face with shaving cream. I could get used to not having to be at the office every day by eight; here it was quarter to nine, and I had yet to hear a peep from anyone.

Now that I was more confident in Jim's abilities, I was allowing him some leeway. For the first weeks, I stood over his shoulder while he performed surgery, and stayed within earshot when he was dealing with clients. Invariably, my mouth would reflexively twitch wanting to qualify each point he was making; only with a great deal of effort did I keep my silence. Several times, I had actually bitten my tongue to stop from intervening. I kept telling myself if this practice was ever going to support two vets, Jim would have to be his own man.

Things had come to a head with Kootenay Meats, and for weeks I had been dealing with the manager of the Royal Bank to try and extricate myself from the imploding business. Just after getting back from John's wedding, he had presented me with a deal that I decided I couldn't refuse: if I personally bought the Kootenay Meats building up the street at an inflated price, he'd wave further liability on the guarantees I had provided them for a line of credit on the business.

I scraped pensively at my face with the razor. I wasn't looking forward to this afternoon. Marg Rogers and I had agreed to sit down for a heart-to-heart talk about my finances. Although I had a pretty good idea of where I stood at the moment, Marg had a way of focusing on the nitty-gritty. The poor woman: she thought she'd been challenged trying to balance the books of a family farm. Her juggling abilities were about to be stretched to the max during the next few months.

The payments for the new building would begin next week, and somehow, I was going to have to materialize enough capital to renovate, not one, but three units. Because the building was far bigger than I'd need for the veterinary hospital, I had decided to chop it into three 1200-square-foot units.

My realtor friend, Gordon Veitch, had been approached by a government agency seeking space for a small liquor store somewhere in the downtown core. With his help, I had worked my way through most of the hoops for making them one of my new tenants. I had already given my former neighbour, Jack Rodgers, the heads up to start the renovations. If that went ahead, Marg would have at least one opportunity to put aside the red pen and use the black one in the ledger.

I set down my razor and gazed at the blue eyes staring back at me from the mirror. Why did I have so much difficulty being satisfied with what was on my plate? Why did I insist upon pushing the envelope so far beyond my comfort zone?

Father was going to have a conniption when he found out that I had added yet more to my financial burden. It had been hard working with him over the last few weeks and not telling him what I was getting myself into; I knew the knowledge would make him worry more than ever. He and I had definitely come from different eras; I was sure I'd have been less foolhardy if I'd survived the Great Depression as he had.

I ran my hand over my jaw—the right side of my lower lip and chin were still numb. Screwing up my face, I wiggled my lip, wondering if the feeling would ever return. It was a persistent reminder of how important it was to take care of the rest of my teeth. After my surgery, I vowed that on my dying day I'd still have all the teeth I had now. Looking on the bright side of things, a bit of numbness was better than constant drooling.

I opened my mouth and peered into the mirror—the wound was finally closing. Although the good doctor's booklet had mentioned a dry socket as yet another of the potential complications of wisdom tooth extraction, I had paid the possibility little heed until my jaw started aching worse than ever, and my breath took on the odour of a week-old afterbirth. The daily trips to Dr. Catherall to have the wound packed had been just one more of the highlights of my "week off."

I was getting out of the shower when the phone rang. Running, still dripping across the plywood floor, I picked up the receiver on the eighth ring.

"Oh, thank goodness you're still there…Wienses want you to come as soon as possible." Doris sounded stressed. "Hilda says they have another cow down with milk fever. Alf's out giving her a bottle of calcium under the skin, but she's sure it won't be enough."

"Okay, I'll head over there right now."

"Don't get carried away talking over lunch again—you know what you're like at the Wienses. The telephone hasn't stopped ringing since I set foot in the door, and you have a one-fifteen appointment with Sorina Maletta."

"Okay…okay, I'll be there."

"Make sure you are," Doris asserted. "Both you and Jim have a busy afternoon ahead of you."

"Call Alf and tell him to have a warm bottle of calcium waiting for me."

Alf Wiens was wringing his hands at the barn door.

"She is not *gut*," he warned in his heavy German accent. "You better hurry!"

Alf was right. I had to look at 186 closely to see that she was still breathing. She was stretched out flat on her side, and it was a struggle for the two of us to wrestle her upright onto her sternum. I quickly set up my IV administration kit with a bottle of calcium and popped a needle into the cow's vein. Alf watched expectantly as the flutter valve bubbled and calcium began flowing.

"Do you think we get her in time?" he asked. "When I give her that bottle under the skin, nothing happen."

"Probably because her peripheral circulation was so poor that she wasn't able to absorb any of it."

I moved my stethoscope again, hoping to pick up some indication that the cow's heart was still beating. Shaking my head, I placed my hand on top of the bottle Alf was holding to force it lower and slow the flow of calcium. Although I had put a halter on the cow and tied her head to her hind leg, she remained a dead weight. While struggling to hold her up, I continually repositioned the head of my stethoscope, hoping to hear a heartbeat.

I nodded to Alf. There it was—a faint thump, then another.

It was quarter of twelve by the time Alf released the last cow from the parlour. He was all smiles when we finished. I had been teaching him how to perform artificial insemination on his cows, and all but one of the eight we checked for pregnancy were in calf.

Hilda made the last notations in her herd health book, then closed it with resolve. Alf did a lot of the physical work with the cows and the maintenance of the buildings, but Hilda was the recorder, and the herd health book was definitely hers.

"Lunch'll be on the table by the time you get cleaned up," she said, heading out the door.

Alf and I wandered to the calving pen to check on 186. Sitting upright, the cow was tentatively picking at the flake of second-cut hay Alf had left in front of her. I climbed between the rails of the stall and dug my knees into her ribs.

"Yah! Get up girl! Come on!"

Grabbing her tail, I hefted to assist as the cow struggled to her feet and stood trembling before me. "There's a girl." She shifted her weight back and forth from one leg to the other. I allowed the big animal to lean against me until I was sure she had her sea legs. "Looks like she's away, Alf."

The round-faced farmer smiled, then flipped a flake of leafy hay onto the straw-packed floor in front of her.

"What got you into the dairy business, anyway?"

"I grow up on farm in the old country. I always like the cows," he answered tentatively.

"Where in Germany was that?"

"Danzig..." Al hesitated a moment as if dealing with an issue he'd rather not discuss. "Not German anymore."

He could see that I was puzzled, but I got the feeling he had no intention of telling me more.

"Come, Hilda will have lunch," he ordered.

I was hosing off my boots in the milk house when Alf suddenly piped up. "They call Danzig Gdansk now...it is part of Poland."

He had several times mentioned that he had fought on the "other side" in World War II, but he had never offered to tell me more.

"Have you ever been back to see where you grew up?" I asked, trying to keep the conversation going.

"One time," he said with melancholy in his voice. "There is nothing left of our place but the stone chimney. You can see it a mile away. Papa would hate to see his home like that. He had quarter section, nice black loam, with a house and barn."

"That must have been a big place for those days," I suggested.

Alf nodded. "Papa was *gut* farmer. We were Mennonite."

"Really?" I said, egging him to go on. "So he had a dairy there?"

"*Ja*. Fifteen, twenty cows...we milk by hand. He had pigs, chickens, horses. He is growing sugar beets, wheat, and barley, but his big thing is breeding Trakehner horses for the German cavalry."

"What happened to the place?"

Alf paused for a moment and I thought he wasn't going to answer. Finally, he shrugged and simply said, "The war...the Russians come, *Vater* get four hours to take what he can take and get out. The German army burn his place to the ground, then they blow the dykes and flood everything so the Russians can't use it."

The war. It seemed there was always a war somewhere. Then it was World War II; now the Middle East and Afghanistan were in turmoil. We were both in our own thoughts as I pulled off my coveralls and washed my hands. Alf's shoulders slouched when he opened the milk house door and stepped out into the yard.

"Hilda will have lunch ready," he said matter-of-factly.

"What happened to your family when they left?" I asked as I threw my coveralls into the truck.

"Papa, Mama, my sister Lisbeth escape to Belgium. *Vater* died with pneumonia in winter in the refugee camp...Mother and three sisters come to Canada, join my brother Erik on his farm in Saskatchewan."

"You must have had a big family." I trailed behind him to the house.

"We were twelve...I was the last. The closest was my sister, Lisbeth...she is seven years older now than me."

We were standing on the stoop pulling off our boots. "Did you enlist in the army?"

"*Nein*, I am in agriculture school. We are Mennonites and *Vater* never want his boys to go. I was youngest...four brothers already were called up, two of them killed, but...they did call me, too."

"Hurry and wash up, Alfred!" Hilda hollered through the screen door. "Lunch is on the table."

Lunch with the Wienses was always a special occasion. I could never figure out why, when I couldn't keep one tiny block of cheese from moulding, Hilda could serve five or six different selections, all looking like they had just arrived home from the deli. In her case, of course, some of them had already been mouldy when they arrived on the store shelf. I was still not big on Alf's favourite, Limburger. For some reason I couldn't convince myself that anything smelling like rotting feet or mouldy boots could be something I should eat.

"Well, dig in, Dr. Perrin, before you let Alfred talk your ear off."

I sat in my usual chair with my back to the kitchen door, and Hilda passed me a plate with a variety of breads—white, whole wheat, rye, and a heavy European-looking whole grain variety. I selected a piece of the heavy bread and slathered it with butter. Hilda sat down with her back to the kitchen sink, then passed me an oval dish laden with lettuce, tomatoes, radishes, onions, cucumbers, and avocados.

She asked, "Why are we having so many milk fevers, Dave? This is driving me bonkers. We've had to treat every one of the last four cows that calved…and this one was another close call. They keep going like this and you will need to be giving me the amphetamines instead of the cows."

"I know," I agreed. The last milk fever cow I had treated here was still down two days after repeated treatment with calcium. Following a tip that I had picked up from a veterinarian in the Fraser Valley, I loaded her up on an amphetamine called Dexedrine. By the end of the day, she was standing and happily chewing her cud.

"We'll have to make some changes in the dry cow lot. Alf's got them on almost straight alfalfa hay, and that's giving them too much calcium."

Alf settled into the chair at the head of the table and began loading his plate. He scooped up several pieces of sausage and one of head cheese and began spreading a piece of rye bread with butter.

"There was no choice!" he affirmed.

I looked towards him with a start, thinking he was defending his feeding alfalfa hay to the cows.

"When I get called up, I must go."

It took me a second to get back into our previous conversation.

"It was '43," he said decisively. "I start driving a general around Berlin."

I nodded at Alf with the hope that he'd continue his story.

"Why should too much calcium cause milk fever when you treat them with calcium to get them better?" Hilda asked.

I turned to face her. "Because too much calcium, in the dry period before they calve, actually makes their parathyroid gland lazy. If they've got all the calcium they need for daily maintenance, they don't need to mobilize any from their bones. Then they calve and there's a sudden demand for more calcium."

"And then, when things get rough with the war," Alf continued, "I get transfer to antitank unit on Eastern Front."

The moment Alf mentioned the Eastern Front, all I could think about was the television show *Hogan's Heroes* that I had loved as a kid. On that show, every German soldier at Stalag 13 who screwed up got sent to the Eastern Front as punishment.

"That must have been terrible..." I said, looking across the table with concern.

"So is there some way of giving them more calcium right away when they calve, to keep them from crashing?" Hilda asked with a puzzled expression.

I turned to her again. "Definitely...giving them good second-cut hay when they first deliver is important, and giving them an injection of vitamin D eight days before they're due will also make a big difference by increasing their absorption of calcium from the gut. But remember, the cow will not be totally safe until her parathyroid gland is functioning normally."

"It was!" Alf declared with his mouth half full. "Never enough to eat...we never know from one day to next if it is our last."

"We're so spoiled here," I said, chomping into my own sandwich. "Not many people here know what it is to be hungry."

"Ach...the Russians teach me what it is!" Alf asserted. "The day before end of the war in '45 we know it is over...we drop our arms and start back to Germany."

"So explain more of what the parathyroid gland has to do with milk fever," Hilda insisted.

"If you were to cut 186's parathyroid gland out right now and look at it under the microscope, you'd see that all the cells that produce hormone are shrunken down, and the crypts where the parathyroid hormone are stored are virtually empty. On the other hand, if you were to take a healthy cow and remove her gland, you'd see that the hormone-producing cells are plump and full and secreting parathormone into the crypts. When the cow runs low on calcium, she releases parathormone into the bloodstream, and then cells in the bones, called osteoclasts, start munching away at formed bone to break it down and release calcium."

Hilda nodded and thoughtfully took a sip of her coffee.

"I am two years in Russian work camp," Alf said, pouring himself a glass of milk from a pitcher. "When I am released in 1947, I am weighing ninety-five pounds." Alf shook his head slowly when he saw the look on my face. As he sat across the table now, I was sure he outweighed me by ten or twenty pounds. "They capture us in Hungary and march us all the way up to Siberia."

As if reminded of his hunger, he slathered another piece of rye bread with butter and mayonnaise, and buried it with layers of cheese and sliced meats.

I also grabbed a piece of bread and started building another sandwich as if the hunger were contagious. "How did you two meet, anyway?"

"He ran me down in the doorway of the china factory we were both working at!" Hilda bellowed.

Alf laughed out loud and shouted back with his mouth full of sandwich, "After I am finally back in Germany I am taking a job at china-making factory in Schoenwald. I am going out the door after shift and Hilda come rushing in...of course, she doesn't watch where she is going!"

Hilda shook her head and fanned the air in his direction. "And Alfred always does!"

"And you came over here together?"

"No!" Alf said, racing Hilda for the chance to speak next. "I come here in '51. I go to Saskatchewan because my mother and my sisters are with my brother Erik...he get me a job working for Herman Klassen on his farm. I work the summer there, then off to Vancouver, work in the shipyards unloading grain cars."

"I came over here to join him in the spring of 1952," Hilda added.

Before she could finish, Alf blurted, "We are married in Vancouver in June."

Silence ensued and I poured myself a glass of milk. "Did you start dairying at the Coast?"

"I get on longshoremen's union, and get a chance for job in Kitimat. We are one of first to go there when they start the aluminum factory. We stay up there till '62."

"That's when Mr. Wiens's seven-year itch took over," Hilda interrupted. "Alfred can't stand to be in one place for too long." She sighed. "Sometimes, I'm surprised that we're still here."

"We buy a farm in Cloverdale," Alf continued as if Hilda was not sitting at the same table.

"We put all the savings we had left into buying and planting cucumber seedlings..." said Hilda.

Alf's face dropped, and he started loading up his third sandwich.

"There was a late frost, and ttthhhhhh..." Hilda stuck out her tongue and made a gesture with her right hand as if slitting her throat.

Alf continued to attack his sandwich and poured himself another glass of milk.

"If it hadn't been for my working as a practical nurse," Hilda went on, "we would have starved to death."

"We did sell the vegetable farm in '69," Alf offered.

"And that's when you bought here?"

"That's when Alfred decided we were going to buy a dairy farm," Hilda said glumly. "I would have been just as happy to take the $30,000 we had and buy a house down there where I could work and he could get a job in construction."

"So you didn't want to come here?" I asked Hilda. I was surprised, because she was now so attached to her cows. She'd have to be at death's door not to show up for a milking.

She shook her head and was about to speak when Alf interjected. "When I load truck and trailer and I am leaving the yard in Cloverdale, I don't know for sure she's coming until I see the car pull onto the highway."

Hilda gave her husband a look usually reserved for insects as he continued on with his story. "We did buy this place from Farm Credit...it belong to Hobdens before they are into receivership."

"You should have seen the cows we started with," Hilda said, shaking her head. "Half of them were beef crossbreds with horns out to here." She spread her arms as wide as she could.

Alf carried on. "We did buy Ken Fox's herd from Cranbrook at the end of September, and October we ship our first load of milk."

I casually checked my watch, then stood with a start. "Oh my God! It's twenty after one...Doris is going to kill me. She warned me that I had to be back at the office for a one-fifteen appointment."

I quickly said goodbye and headed to the truck. As I sped down the winding road in the direction of the Rykerts border crossing, I was fretting about being late again. A lot of clients with pets wouldn't mind seeing whichever one of us was available, but Sorina was not likely to be one of them. I had been looking after her poodle, Jeeters, since I first arrived in town, and I was sure she'd be upset if she had to bring Jim up to speed on his case history.

I glanced at my watch as I approached the Indian reservation, and the steeple of St. Peter's church came into view. It seemed too much to have to slow to sixty kilometres an hour when I was already ten minutes late, but speeding on this strip of highway was like begging for a ticket. Known locally as the Mission, this was the domain of the Lower Kootenay Indian band, members of the Ktunaxa nation. There was a lot of history in this small community.

It was after one-thirty when I got to the clinic. I pulled off my rubber boots and slipped into my street shoes. With my dirty coveralls under my arm and my boots in my hand, I ran up the bank and down the sidewalk. I burst through the door, expecting to run into an agitated Sorina. Instead, she was cheerfully paying her bill at the counter with Jeeters tucked under her arm.

Jim came around the corner, flashing his charismatic Texas smile. "Hi there, Doc...what's the panic? Everything's under control."

Sorina smiled at me as she headed out the door. "Jeeters and I approve of your new assistant."

In the kennel room I tossed my coveralls into the laundry basket. I didn't know why, but I was feeling strangely disappointed that Sorina had been so completely satisfied with Jim. I headed to the back room and grabbed my smock from its hanger on the darkroom door. Doris popped her head around the corner to reach for a prescription bottle.

"How did it go?" I asked.

She raised her eyebrows, then very deliberately checked her watch. "You found a real gem here...he's great at handling clients." With just a hint of a twinkle in her eyes, she continued, "He's such a schmooze."

Chapter 9

Dog Days

Everything had gone splendidly with Tyrone until I brought out my nail clippers. After that, it was all Doris and his shapely brunette owner could do to keep the little dynamo on the table.

It was after eleven on Saturday morning, and there was no sign that things were ready to wind down soon. I had finished vaccinating the strong-willed Jack Russell terrier, but the trimming of each nail became a battle for supremacy that Tyrone was determined to win. All of us breathed a sigh of relief when he quit tugging long enough for me to snip the final nail of his last foot.

Gary Archer smiled as we all made our way to the front. He had been sitting in the waiting room listening to the kerfuffle. "You mean that little guy created all the commotion?"

Doris rolled her eyes and patted her locks. "It's a good thing I'm going to get my hair done later this afternoon."

Gary's son was in the car with their black Labrador. Doris wasn't big on cleaning blood off the indoor-outdoor carpet in the waiting room, and by the sounds of Gary's description, Blackie was likely to leave a trail of it. He had somehow sliced open one of the pads on a front foot.

"Dave, Brenda Freeman's on the phone, and her dog has had a run-in with a cat." Doris was holding her hand over the mouthpiece of the phone as she talked. "She sounds pretty worried—she says the dog's keeping his eye totally closed and isn't his normal self. She can see blood."

"You better have her bring him…hope you didn't have big plans for your afternoon off."

Doris rolled her eyes and went back to talking to Mrs. Freeman.

I shifted my attention to our next client. "Okay, Gary, let's have a look at Blackie."

The heavyset man got up from the bench and headed out to his car. Doris hung up the phone and continued to fill out Tyrone's vaccination certificate. His owner was an Albertan passing through on her way down the Oregon coast. She had forgotten his vaccination records and had needed to update his rabies shot before crossing the border.

I wiped down the table and got my instrument tray ready; Blackie was probably going to need a few stitches. I was chasing the remains from Tyrone's nail trimmings into the dustpan when there was a sudden explosion of yipping from the front office. I arrived in time to see Tyrone tugging at his leash in an attempt to get to the Archers' portly Lab.

"I'm sorry about that," said the brunette, hefting the feisty mutt to her bosom and rushing out the door. "Tyrone's such a pain sometimes." We could hear the dog's continued yipping from well down the street.

Poor Blackie lay outside on the sidewalk looking woefully into the waiting room.

"The last time he left the farm was when we brought him here to be neutered," Mr. Archer said blandly. "I can understand his not wanting to come back."

After considerable encouragement, Blackie stood and took a quivering step over the threshold. The moment his foot touched the carpet, he put on the brakes and collapsed in a heap.

"Come on, Blackie, we're going to fix your foot." Gary's son walked into the waiting room and clapped his hands on his knees in an effort to convince the dog that this was a place he wanted to be.

"Nothing doing," Gary sighed. "He's terrified about coming into the house at the best of times…You take that end." Motioning to his son, he stooped his big frame and grappled the dog under the armpits.

"Right here on the table," I said, rushing to assist them with my roly-poly patient. As soon as the dog touched the surface of the stainless steel table, he clenched his feet around the corners, determined to hold on for the ride. "Let's see if we can get a peek at that cut."

I worked a few wraps of torn bed sheet from the Lab's foot. Each time I attempted to straighten the foot, Blackie would flex it again and make a desperate attempt to hold on to the table. "Can we get him settled on his side?" I asked after losing yet another battle for access to his foot.

Gary and his son struggled with Blackie to roll him over.

"Ooooooohhhhhh," the big Lab squealed, struggling to stay on his brisket.

"That's enough, Blackie!" Gary hollered as the dog finally settled to the table. Quivering uncontrollably, he lay in a state of unabashed panic. I let him lie there for a minute before removing the rest of the bandage and turning the foot over. The lateral pad had a deep cut running its full length.

"It was still bleeding pretty good when we first found him," Gary noted, lifting his elbow to his forehead to wipe away sweat with his shirtsleeve. "The grass in the backyard was splotched with red."

"I can believe it—the pads of a dog's feet are extremely vascular." I filled the wound with surgical scrub and began picking out debris. "It's clean for the most part."

I filled a three-millilitre syringe with lidocaine and began injecting the margins of the pad. I had placed the first suture when I heard the office door open and another client arrive. I was focused on suturing until I detected an angry tone to the man's voice.

"She's my damned dog, and I'll do what I want with her!"

Gary gave me a sardonic look. "There's never a dull moment in this place, is there?"

"Excuse me for a second, guys."

I stepped around the corner in time to see a stocky, red-headed man shaking his finger in Doris's face. The veins on his forehead stood out as he shouted at her.

"I'm sick and tired of her chewing everything up the moment she's left alone!"

"I'm sorry, but Dr. Perrin doesn't like to put young dogs to sleep when there's nothing wrong with them." Doris engaged the man with her matronly gaze.

I could feel myself glowering as I joined them. The man's pale blue eyes focused on the needle driver I still clenched in my bloody fist, and his demeanour softened considerably. Looking down into the squat man's eyes, I intentionally stood well within his comfort zone.

"I'd appreciate your keeping a civil tongue when you're dealing with my receptionist," I growled.

"I just want my dog put to sleep," he returned defensively.

"And I think I heard Doris tell you I wouldn't do it."

"She's my dog, and I can do with her what I damned please."

"That may well be, but I don't have to be a part of it! What's wrong with her, anyway?"

"She's no damned good. That's what's wrong with her."

"Do you have her with you?"

"She's in the car."

"Bring her in and I'll have a look at her. If she's healthy, and you pay the cost of her euthanasia and disposal, I'll keep her here until we find a home for her."

"I don't want her to go to someone else."

"Then you should go and see if Dr. Marling will put her down for you."

"I should just take her out and shoot her," he mumbled, staring at his feet.

"You could," I replied curtly.

"Okay...I'll leave her with you then..."

With that, he turned on his heel and headed out the door.

"Thanks for taking over, Dave." Doris's face was scarlet. "I hate that scumbag. Just standing next to him makes my skin crawl."

My heart was pounding. "He talks tough, but I bet he wouldn't have the courage to point a gun at her head and pull the trigger himself."

"His dad was like that, too. My Stu had dealings with him the year we bought the orchard—after that he wouldn't let him set foot on the place."

"I should have asked him to leave the office and not come back," I told her. "Every time he comes near me I feel like giving him a rap in the mouth. I bet it's not six months since he brought that beautiful Dobie puppy in and talked me into putting her to sleep…Remember, the one with the broken femur? I begged him to let me do something with it, but he wouldn't pay a cent more than the cost of the euthanasia. The worst of it was, I was sure he had something to do with breaking her leg. I never slept a wink that night fretting about the fact that I had bumped her."

I had washed up and put the needle drivers back in the cold sterilization solution before the door burst open again.

"Get in here, damn it!" The redhead stomped into the waiting room dragging a young golden retriever–cross at the end of a yellow plastic twine. Before I could intercede, he yanked on the rope and dragged the poor critter across the threshold.

"Does she have a name?" I asked matter-of-factly.

"The kids called her Trixie."

"Come here, Trixie," I coaxed. "There's a girl."

The dog's tail twitched ever so slightly. Crawling on her belly towards me, she squirted urine in her wake.

"Damned dog," he cursed, as I stooped to pick her up. "I'll be so glad to see the end of her. What the hell's a guy supposed to do with a dog like her? If she's not chewing something up, she's pissing on the bloody floor."

"Doris, can you finish off with Mr. Rand while I take Trixie to the back?"

Doris passed him the euthanasia form that we modified to state that he had relinquished possession of his dog to Creston Veterinary

Clinic for the purpose of finding her another home. He hastily scratched his name on the form and reached for his chequebook.

"We'd rather have cash," Doris stated bluntly.

Mr. Rand was soon gone, and I returned to the Archers.

"I'm sorry to keep you waiting like that," I apologized. My face was still flushed and my heart pounding as I scrubbed at my hands.

"I hope you don't have many clients like him," Gary said blandly.

"Thank God, no," I replied. "I wouldn't still be at it if I did."

By the time Mrs. Freeman arrived, I had Blackie's foot sutured and bandaged and they were on their way out the door. Doris ushered her right to the back room where she deposited a trembling grey mass on the exam table. Rosco was a portly Shih Tzu with grey-black hair enveloping his face.

"I took him in with me when I went to visit my friend. She insisted that her cats wouldn't bother him, but the moment I put him down on the kitchen floor, one of them took after him in a fury."

She closed her eyes as I knelt beside the table for a closer look.

"It all happened so quickly...the instant she attacked him, I scooped him up."

The woman stood quietly as I moved in to inspect Rosco. Even with his left eye half closed I could see a glistening membrane bulging from the surface.

"It's bad, isn't it?" Brenda stared at me and did her best to avoid looking at her pet.

I nodded. "It is...towards the inner corner there's a glistening bulge that resembles a deployed air bag. The entire surface of the cornea has been sliced through and that bulging structure is Descemet's membrane. It's the only thing keeping the fluid in the anterior chamber from spilling out."

Brenda was fighting back tears as she stroked Rosco. "I knew it was bad when I saw the blood...Is he going to lose the eye?"

I shook my head in uncertainty as I got to my feet. "I've honestly never seen anything quite like this before...there's no doubt that the eye needs to be stitched as soon as possible if it's going to be saved. Is there any chance that you could drive him to Spokane right now? There's a board-certified veterinary ophthalmologist there. Dr. Yakely's one of the best there is. He was a professor at the vet college in Pullman before he started his own practice. If anyone can save Rosco's eye, he can."

"Would he be working on a Saturday afternoon?"

"I'm not sure…but if you can take Rosco down there right now, I'll make a call."

"Can I use your phone?"

"Certainly, go ahead."

I moved closer to the exam table as Brenda retreated to the front. Rosco peered over his shoulder and fully opened his eye as his mistress left. I cringed…the rent had to be half an inch long. How could that shimmering little structure be keeping the contents of the eye from spilling out? It seemed no thicker than the soap bubble that a child might blow. When we had been told in lectures about descemetoceles, I had no idea that the membrane would be so thin, so delicate—that it could extend so far without rupturing.

I closed my eyes and focused on the air flowing through my nostrils. Driving the feeling of negativity from my mind, I repeated, "I can handle this! If it can be done…I can do it."

"There's just no way, Dr. Perrin."

I opened my eyes to see Brenda's staring up at me. "I have to be at work tomorrow, and I can't find someone to drive to Spokane with me now…Can you do something for him?"

I nodded. "If you'll keep him on the table, I'll get the sedative to prepare him for surgery."

I drew up the premix of Demerol and atropine and returned to Rosco. The dog sat stoically as I gave the injection.

"Brenda, before you leave, I want to prepare you for what Rosco will look like after we're finished surgery. As you can see, the wound is close to the middle of the cornea where there are no blood vessels. Rosco's tears normally contain all the ingredients necessary to maintain the cornea and keep it healthy, but this is a major injury that will need more nutrients than tears can supply. Success in healing will likely depend on holding the cornea together until new vessels migrate out to repair it."

As I talked, Brenda focused on me and not her beloved pet. "So how do you get the vessels to migrate?"

"You see this pink structure in the corner of Rosco's eye?"

She reluctantly looked at his eye and nodded as I pointed to the nictitating membrane. "That's an anatomical structure that humans don't have. In the dog it functions as a protective mechanism when the eye is threatened. After I've done what I can to suture the wound, I'm going to do what's called a third eyelid flap. After roughing up the back of the structure to make it bleed, I'll suture it over here so that it covers the entire eye."

Brenda swallowed and passively nodded.

"The flap will encourage the migration of vessels and protect the wound, but it will also mean that we won't know how successful we've been until we release it."

"How long will that be?"

"Probably ten days."

Brenda picked Rosco up and cuddled him for a moment before passing him back to me.

"Doris?" Doris gave me her knowing look when I went to the front desk with Rosco in my arms. "How many appointments do we have left?"

"Two…one's a vaccination, but the other is for Jim Reid. Poco isn't doing well."

"Do you think you can hold the vaccination off till next week and ask Jim to wait at home till we give him a call? We have to do something with Rosco right away."

Doris rolled her eyes and patted her hair. "You know how hard it is to get an appointment with Tom on Saturdays? He'll be impossible if I cancel, and I don't know how I'll get through next week with this hair if I miss today."

"You can wear a surgery cap all week long…that way, no one will notice how rough it looks."

Doris glared at me and started dialling the phone.

It was with a feeling of trepidation that I cranked open the valves on the oxygen and nitrous oxide tanks. I checked the dials after the system pressurized, and took a deep breath. One would expect that this feeling of anxiety would have subsided with six years of practice, but here I was with the same schoolboy mentality: My God, what have I gotten myself into now?

"Have you seen anything like this before?" Doris asked timidly.

"Not in real life." I pointed to the schematic picture in *Canine Ophthalmology,* the text that lay open on the table beside me. "Only here."

"It's going to be one of those, then, is it?"

Doris was all too familiar with open-book sessions where she had to read me the text over and over while I tried to make sense of an author's description of some abstract procedure.

I spun the dial on the halothane vaporizer and turned up the flow of oxygen and nitrous oxide. I carefully slipped the mask over Rosco's nose and stroked the top of his shaggy head.

"We don't want a struggle," I muttered to Doris. "Whatever happens, avoid putting pressure on that eye."

Rosco continued a steady pattern of breathing until he folded onto his side. After a few minutes more, I rolled him onto his tummy. Doris assumed her position holding his upper jaw, and I grabbed his long pink tongue and slipped a tube through his larynx. After it was down his trachea, I inflated the cuff and laid him on his right side. I carefully trimmed back some of the long hair that surrounded the eye and scrubbed around the margins of the lids with surgical soap. Opening the eye fully, I squeezed a big gob of chloramphenicol ophthalmic ointment over the glimmering mass.

"Oh my, that doesn't look good," Doris groaned. "I can see why Mrs. Freeman was so upset."

While I scrubbed up, Doris got the materials prepared for the surgery. I plucked a sterile towel from the suture pack and dried my hands. Doris opened my gloves and held them up for me to grab.

"What suture material will you be using for that?"

"I think I'll go with 6 0 silk."

I placed a cotton drape with a one-inch hole over the dog's head and took a deep breath. How I wished I had some sort of magnification to do this properly. The diagram in the text clearly showed the sutures penetrating only the epithelium and the stroma, without penetrating the endothelium, or inner layer.

"Can you reach under the drape and hold his eyelids open, Doris?"

"You mean I have to watch you do this? Just the thought of your poking needles into his eye gives me the willies."

"I know what you mean."

Picking up my needle drivers, I locked them on the tiny needle and withdrew the suture material from the packet. With a swab, I dabbed tentatively at the transparent bleb protruding from the surface of the eye, removing a rope of mucous that extended across it. Somehow my hand and the instrument in it seemed far too big for the job required.

"I can hardly believe that a layer that thin can keep the contents of the eye from spilling out," I marvelled. Holding my breath, I hesitantly drove the needle through one side of the cornea near the centre of the lesion. I grabbed the tip of the needle and pulled the material all the way through. As I took a bite of the cornea on the other side, I pushed down on the descemetocele, made the first throw of my knot, and drew the tissue together. The transparent bubble miraculously shrank and all but disappeared as the corneal edges came into apposition.

"I can't believe how tough this cornea is, Doris. Somehow, I was afraid the knot would tear through when I tightened it."

"That looks better already," Doris chirped enthusiastically.

"Doesn't it?"

Placing a pair of sutures on either side of the first went far easier than I had anticipated, and before long I was ready to place the third eyelid flap. I grasped the margin of the nictitating membrane with a pair of forceps, and scraped at the epithelium on the underside with a scalpel blade.

"Isn't his eye sore enough already?" Doris sounded disgruntled.

"Hopefully, scraping it like this will cause nutrients to leak out and expose vessels that will migrate to help heal the wound."

Placing a suture through the front margin, I pulled the third eyelid over the globe and sutured it to the farthest corner of the upper lid, anchoring it to a plastic tube.

Doris watched the procedure with disgust. "It's gross to look at a pink blob instead of a dog's eye. What happens if it doesn't heal?"

"Unless he starts bothering it, we won't know until we remove the flap in ten days."

I filled the pocket between the third eyelid and the cornea with more of the ophthalmic preparation, and placed a second suture.

"That about does it...Why don't you give Jim a call while I wake Rosco up?"

When Doris announced the arrival of Jim and Martha Reid, Rosco was sitting up in his kennel peering at the world with one eye through the plastic tunnel of his Elizabethan collar.

"Are you going to give Jim a hand?" Doris hollered. "Martha has such a time managing both Jim and Poco at the same time."

Poco had been one of my first patients when I opened the office here on Canyon Street. From my introduction to the tiny chihuahua, I recognized him as a feisty little devil. When I rolled back his gums to look at his tartar-encrusted teeth, he had done his best to nail me. From then on, every time I handled him, I was careful not to tempt fate by moving too quickly or exposing a finger in a convenient position for him to chomp. Listening to his heart revealed that he had a murmur most audible on his left side. As most valvular lesions in dogs result from a showering of bacteria from bad teeth and infected gums, I started him on antibiotics and recommended doing dental work. Shortly after buying my anesthetic machine, I extracted most of his teeth and cleaned the remaining few.

Three years ago, Poco developed a persistent cough that got worse whenever he became excited. At the time, I started him on Lasix to remove the excess fluid from his lungs, and within a few weeks, Jim swore he was back to normal. Over the last year, his cough returned and he was no longer able to keep up with Martha on her walk around the block. The X-ray that I had taken on Poco's sixteenth birthday had shown a globular heart that filled most of his chest cavity.

Initially, increasing the Lasix had diminished the cough, but as his condition progressed we had added digitalis to try and strengthen the contractility of his increasingly flabby heart. We all knew that we weren't curing anything—only buying him more time. As Jim had put it on his last visit, three of Poco's feet were firmly planted on banana peels, and the other had its toenails dug deeply into the mud of a very slippery slope. If it had been anyone else's dog but Jim's, I would have recommended euthanasia several months ago, but how can you tell a man to end his dog's misery when the man is in no better shape himself?

Martha had both doors on the passenger side of their old Chevy open by the time I arrived on the scene. Kneeling on the back seat, she was about to wrestle the oxygen cart to the ground.

"I'll get that, Martha," I said, stepping around Jim's walker.

She stood back as I grasped hold of the apparatus and hoisted it to the sidewalk. "Oh, thank you, Dave." The slight, grey-haired woman plucked the breathing apparatus from her husband's nose and passed the plastic tube around the upright of the car. Jim sat passively while his wife draped the tubes over his head and re-adjusted the tips in his nostrils. When she was done, she allowed him the opportunity to equilibrate.

"You ready?" she asked.

He grabbed hold of the door and nodded to his wife. Grasping him under his arms, she lifted as Jim pulled himself upright. Taking a few exaggerated breaths through his nose, he steadied himself and took a hesitant step towards his walker.

"Would you like me to carry Poco?" I asked.

Martha knelt on the front seat to pick up the dog. "That might be best," she said, reluctantly depositing the frail old critter in my arms. With Poco struggling and craning his neck to keep his owners in sight, I proceeded to the clinic. Martha closed the car doors and fell in behind Jim, pushing the oxygen cart behind her husband as he shuffled down the street towards the clinic.

I grabbed the stool from the surgery and placed it at the head of the exam table in anticipation of Jim's arrival. Poco's chest was flailing as he dragged in air. Even the bit of struggle he had put up on the way into the clinic had left him exhausted. He was pale and he hacked several times in rapid succession. Struggling on the tabletop, he positioned himself to watch for his owners.

"Can you bring me a towel, Doris?"

Doris arrived at the same time as the Reids. She knowingly folded the towel and set it at the end of the table. Both of us knew from experience how upset Martha got when Poco had to rest his bare tummy on cold stainless steel.

Martha quickly parked the stool under Jim as he shuffled up with his walker. She gave him a worried look. "We have a wheelchair, but do you think I can get him to use it?"

"I'm not helpless!" Jim hissed through pursed lips.

The colour of his lips and the distress in his eyes suggested otherwise. For several minutes we all watched as he struggled to breathe in the oxygenated air through his nostrils. Every once in a while his lips parted and he dragged air through them with an annoying whistle.

"So things aren't going too well with Poco?"

"He's having as much trouble breathing as I am," Jim said in a voice little louder than a whisper. "There are times when I think he needs this damned thing more than I do." He pointed to the apparatus that adorned his face.

"He's coughing a lot more the last few nights," Martha noted. "And now that we've upped the water pills, he has to pee every couple of hours. I put a bunch of papers down in the corner of our bedroom in case he can't wake me up during the night." She raised her eyebrows and shrugged. "I never would have put up with that when I was younger...I tried to talk Jim into letting me put him in the bathroom where it's easier to clean up after him, but he wouldn't hear of it."

Jim sat with his eyes closed in stoic fashion, apparently oblivious to the conversation. His lips were a hideous blue-grey, and each breath he drew was a focused effort.

I grabbed my thermometer, lubed it up, and slid it into Poco's rectum. The dog turned his head and glared at me but made no effort to pull away.

"You remember the first time you tried to do that?" Jim's pale green eyes were focused on his pet. He shook his head abjectly and closed his eyes again. "He 'bout took your hand off."

I smiled. "I remember…he's always been a feisty little beggar."

"Wanting air takes a lot of the zest out of a guy…I know all about it."

I inserted the tips of my stethoscope into my ears and applied the head to Poco's side. There was little change from the last time I had listened to him. The lub-dub, lub-dub, lub-dub of a normal heartbeat was now whoosh, whoosh, whoosh, as blood leaked back through the valves with each contraction of his heart. I moved the head of the stethoscope farther up Poco's side and tried to filter out the overbearing noise from his heart. There was definitely an increase in lung sounds as well.

"Is it worse?" Martha inquired as I set the apparatus aside.

"It's bad."

I grasped Poco firmly under the jaw and lifted his lip with my finger. The grey pallor to his gums was almost as disgusting as the condition of his few remaining teeth.

"Is he eating?"

Martha shook her head. "Nothing to speak of…he'll eat a bit of meat when Jim cuts it up and gives it to him directly from his plate. If we give him the same thing in his own dish, he turns up his nose at it."

"Is there something more you can do for him, Doc?" Jim gasped. "I know he's about ready to pack it in, but I don't want him to go before me."

Tears welled in Martha's eyes and she left the room. I could hear her talking softly to Doris in the waiting room.

Leaning forward on the stool, Jim continued in a hoarse whisper, "I know you're not God, but you've got to keep him going a bit longer…Martha doesn't like it when I talk this way, but I plan on goin' first. I bought two brass urns when I was in Calgary—a big one for me and a little one for Poco. They was just like the one Mom kept Dad in for goin' on thirty years before she passed on… had him perched right up on the mantel of her fireplace where he was nice and warm."

As an afterthought, he mused, "We don't have a mantel in our trailer…Guess Martha'll have to plunk Poc and I side by side on the coffee table."

Jim stopped talking and looked longingly at Poco, as if he had said his piece and was just too tired to carry on. For lack of a response, I reached for my stethoscope. Kneeling beside the table, I closed my eyes and listened to the tumultuous gushing of blood in the little dog's chest, wishing it could tell me what to do.

Chapter 10

Danger in
Them Thar Hills

Bob Rogers and I were downing a coffee in the darkroom, where the coffee pot was located, and discussing a problem he was having with one of his old Hereford cows. Bob was my bookkeeper's son; they lived in separate homes on the same farm on the Creston flats.

"I feel terrible that I let it get so far ahead of me." Bob frowned, leaned back against the sink, and chomped into one of Margaret Berg's chocolate chip cookies. "I noticed a little pink sore on her right eye when I turned 'em out to pasture this spring and now she can hardly keep it open."

"The way you describe it makes me think it's cancer," I replied, taking a sip from my cup. I still couldn't stand the taste of this stuff, but could finally force it down in order to be sociable with my clients.

"Damn, Dave, I hate to lose her. She's been a good old cow…even this year, her calf's fifty to a hundred pounds heavier'n the rest."

"Well, we'll do what we can with it. If it's just on the surface of the eye, we can freeze it with liquid nitrogen…if it looks like it's involving the lacrimal drainage, then we may have to take it out."

"Out?" Bob snorted, almost gagging on his coffee.

"Yeah, sometimes we need to take the eye right out to eliminate the spread of the cancer."

"That sounds gross."

"Working on eyes has always been a touchy thing for me, too, but I'm sort of getting hardened into it…"

Bob shook his head in disgust and set down his cup of coffee as if he'd suddenly lost the desire to finish it.

"...That doesn't mean that I like it, though."

I had always placed removing severely traumatized eyes—with tasks like dehorning—in the category of a procedure I'd rather avoid. But performing the surgery could often extend a cow's productive career for years, and at the very least, allow a farmer to salvage the animal for slaughter purposes.

"Dave, can you speak to Mr. Jacks?" Doris was standing at the darkroom door. "He sounds pretty upset...apparently there's a problem with one of his horses."

Bob set down his cup and headed to the front. "I'll give you a holler as soon as I get the old girl in. With any luck, Willie and I can get her and the calf in the corral later this week."

I waved to Bob and picked up the phone. "Hey there, Joe... what's happening?"

"I'm afraid I've got big trouble with one of my mares."

"What's she doing?"

"Staggering around like she's drunk...she looked a bit wonky when I went out to check her this morning, but she was nothing like this."

"Which mare is it?"

"Tinker, the one I called you about when she was getting ready to foal. Remember how she went on and on for a week after starting to drip milk."

"Okay, I remember...she's the one that foaled the night you slept through checking on her."

"Yeah," he replied sheepishly. "After watching her night after night we slept through the alarm, and when we came out in the morning, the foal was up, dried off, and sucking."

"How long ago was that?"

"The foal'll be three weeks tomorrow," he responded with certainty.

"Tell me exactly what the mare's doing."

"She's staggering all over; acting like she doesn't know where to put her feet. I tried to lead her down to the corral for you to look at her, but ended up leaving her where she was. She can hardly stand up, never mind walk down that hill."

"And the foal looks all right?"

"Yeah, the foal's great. She was bucking and running circles around her mom."

"So you think the baby's getting milk?"

"I watched her suck and she looked like she was getting a belly full."

"And the mare doesn't mind her sucking?"

"Doesn't seem to."

"You can't see any signs of trauma? No bruising of the eyes? No signs of blood?"

"She looks perfectly normal other than not being able to walk."

I paused as I ran through a list of possibilities in my mind. What could produce those neurological symptoms? Early tetanus? Western equine encephalomyelitis? Eclampsia? A stroke? A physical trauma? A tick? Heck, from his description, she might even be foundered.

"Can you come and check her out?"

"Yeah, I'll leave right away."

As I headed towards Arrow Creek, I found myself wishing that Jim had been in the office when this call came in. As it happened, he had just left to see a sick cow in Wynndel. Joe's mare sounded like an unusual case, and I would have liked to debate the possibilities with another vet.

I was lost in thought as I made my way through Erickson. If it was tetanus as a result of a vaginal wound from foaling, wouldn't we have expected to see signs sooner? Not necessarily. *Clostridium tetani,* the organism that caused tetanus, could sometimes lie dormant for months before taking off and starting to produce toxin. It could still be eclampsia, too; a calcium deficiency in horses could cause that sort of behaviour. Horses were like dogs. Calcium deficiencies produced uncontrolled muscle contractions.

By the time I turned up the steep drive to Joe's house, I was convinced that I was about to treat my first case of eclampsia in the mare. A bottle of calcium sat next to me on the truck seat.

As I pulled up to the house, my client was waiting in the drive-way. Joe was tall with chiselled features, a weathered face, and black hair. Although he worked at Crestbrook sawmill, his heart was in this little acreage on the side of the mountain.

"She's up there." He pointed apologetically up the hill. "I tried to bring her down, but there was no way. Going downhill seems to be really tough for her. I quit trying to lead her when she almost rolled end over end on top of me."

"Can you fill this with water for me?" I passed him my stainless steel bucket.

"Does it have to be hot?"

I shook my head. "As long as it's clean."

I draped my stethoscope around my neck and grabbed a ther-mometer while Joe filled the bucket from the garden hose. I stuffed the bottle of calcium in the back pocket of my coveralls. "I think we might need this."

"What's that for?"

"It's calcium….I think she may be dealing with milk fever."

"I don't think so," Joe said. "I thought of that, too, and felt her udder. It was nice and soft."

"Not mastitis—I was thinking more of a condition we see in horses called eclampsia. Milk fever's the slang term we use for the same condition in cows—only cows go down and can't get up again. It's a result of a difference in sensitivity to low levels of serum calcium. In the cow it prevents muscle fibrils from contracting; in the horse it causes nerve impulses to keep firing."

I kept my eyes focused on the narrow path the horses had trod-den into the rocky terrain as I followed Joe up the mountain. At times, I had to step from boulder to boulder because there wasn't room enough for my big feet between them. Joe had cleared several benches of the land recently, and although there was evidence of blades of grass growing here and there, horse tails, ferns, and fire-weed still seemed to predominate.

"There they are," Joe puffed between gulps of air. "Tinker's still up…I was half expecting her to be lying in a heap the way she was acting when I left."

Even from a distance I could see that the mare had an unusual stance. Attentively watching our approach, she stood with her head pointed towards the downhill slope. Her front legs were crossed; her hind legs spread wide apart.

"Look at the way she's standing," Joe groused.

"I am."

I stopped ten feet in front of her and sat on a waist-high boulder to watch her. Joe was right…although the horse was bright, she swayed back and forth as if she'd had a few drinks too many. Her back was arched. Her front feet straddled a rock several feet in diameter and her hind feet appeared lodged behind a couple of boulders. It was as if she was trapped by circumstances and the unfortunate placement of immoveable obstacles. As we watched, the foal jockeyed for position to suckle her mother, almost squatting to get low enough to get mom's teat in her mouth.

"The foal sure looks like she's doing well."

"I know," Joe responded. "She's been doin' great till now…" He gave the mare a mournful look. "But what's going to become of her with her mom in this shape?"

As if in response to Joe's spate of negativity, the mare stumbled forward, with legs flailing madly. The foal flipped sideways, rolled end over end over the rocky terrain, then scrambled to her feet apparently unharmed. Joe rushed to his mare's head and grabbed her halter as she staggered uncontrollably down the hill, stumbling through the weeds well off the side of the trail.

"Easy, girl…easy."

By the time I was in a position to help steady the mare, she was in that awkward stance with her front legs crossed and her hind legs splayed. Turning her head, she looked frantically in the direction of her foal.

"Why's she standing like this?" Joe asked again.

I ran my hand over the horse's neck, over her tight, trembling muscles. As if in frustration, she bowed her head, grasped a mouthful of weeds, and munched furiously.

"She still wants to eat," Joe noted.

"Seems to."

The last thing I had done before leaving the office was to have a quick read from my Blood and Henderson text about eclampsia. Their comment about how animals would attempt to eat and drink, yet be unable to swallow, was very much in mind as I watched the fronds of the bracken fern slowly disappear.

"Let's see if she wants a drink." I retrieved the bucket of water from where Joe had set it down and held it in front of her muzzle. The mare gulped the water until she sucked at the little that remained in the bottom corner.

"She was sure thirsty," Joe observed.

"She sure was…it may have been longer than you thought since she was able to get down for a drink."

"I'm sure they were down to the corral day before yesterday."

I lowered the bucket and watched the horse grab another frond of the bracken fern and begin munching. I clapped my hands together in front of her face and watched her eyes.

"What you looking for?" Joe inquired.

"Watching her third eyelid," I mused, extending my hand and tapping gently at the medial canthus of the eye. "If this were tetanus, she'd be prolapsing her nictitating membrane—that's the pink thing in the corner of the eye."

My mind was in a spin as I continued my examination. I inserted my thermometer in the horse's rectum, then slipped the tips of my stethoscope into my ears. The text had mentioned that with eclampsia, the pulse was usually elevated and respirations rapid, almost violent. Now that she had settled down, Tinker's breathing appeared pretty normal to me.

I slid the stethoscope head to a point behind the foreleg and held my breath. There it was—thump thump. I moved the stethoscope head and listened again, waiting for another. I stared at my watch and listened on. Thirteen beats in thirty seconds—the heart rate for a normal horse was around forty per minute.

Joe was watching my face intently. "Something wrong?"

"Her heart rate's incredibly slow."

"What does that mean?"

"That I haven't seen my first case of eclampsia in a mare," I responded almost glumly. As if to confirm the fact, the mare hunched and defecated. "They usually can't pee or take a dump either," I muttered.

I poked through the feces to retrieve my thermometer. Luckily enough, it was still intact and read 37.8 degrees Celsius.

Joe looked hopeful. "Is it normal?"

I nodded in affirmation. "She read the book."

I palpated the mare's udder and squirted a few jets of milk onto the palm of my hand. All seemed normal. I ran my hands along her back, then focused on her head; I felt under her jaw and down her neck. "I'm looking for signs of a tick," I explained. "It's later than you'd expect one, but in our area, you can never rule out the possibility of paralysis from a *Dermacentor andersoni* tick."

After checking her entire underbelly and her groin, I plunked on a rock twenty feet from the horse to watch her. "Just let her be for a bit, Joe."

The moment Joe released her head, Tinker turned and whinnied to her foal. She looked in our direction when her foal trotted up to her, then staggered to the edge of the small shelf of land and started munching at the weeds that surrounded its perimeter. Aside from being uncoordinated, the mare was bright and obviously caring about what was going on around her; there was no questioning the concern for the well-being of her baby.

"Have you got any ideas?" Joe asked apprehensively.

"Are you feeding her at all?"

"I've thrown out a few flakes of hay down at the corral, but for the most part Tinker and the foal have been sticking to themselves up here on the pasture."

"Let's take a walk," I suggested.

We followed the winding trail up the mountain. In the steep areas, little of the surface had been disturbed, and although there were tufts of grass around the base of boulders and trees, most of the hill was covered by native vegetation—predominantly bracken fern and fireweed.

"See this, Joe." I pointed to a dried-off stalk that protruded from the ground.

He nodded. "That was a fern, wasn't it?"

"Sure looks like it." I pulled the stem from the ground to reveal its black pointed root. "We used to have wars with these and throw them at each other like spears when we were kids. They were everywhere in the bush out in Casino near Trail where I grew up."

"We gather them as fiddleheads in the spring," Joe offered.

"I've never tried them. Are they good?"

"You bet."

"They're toxic to horses and cattle, you know."

"Are you serious? Tinker eats them—do you think that could be what's wrong with her? There are more of them mowed off over there." He pointed to the undergrowth beneath a nearby clump of trees. "My other horses hardly bother to come up here, but she hangs around this area with her foal, and I know for a fact she eats them all the time."

"I think it's looking likely...I've ruled out most everything else I can think of."

"Is there a treatment?"

"With horses there is...consuming bracken is thought to cause a thiamine deficiency with them. In cattle it causes some sort of clotting problem and it's almost always diagnosed on post-mortem."

Time was going to tell whether or not I was right about Tinker. I treated her with an IV injection of thiamine and left Joe with injections of B-vitamin complex. He had carried feed and water up to the horse, and as I was leaving was constructing a bit of a corral to keep her from stumbling farther down the hill.

When I got back to the office around four, I plucked the Blood and Henderson text from the shelf in the darkroom and started reading. I smiled as I closed the book and set it aside—I was more convinced than ever that I was right.

"Jack Rodgers called!" Doris hollered from the surgery. "He says he'll have the rest of the drywall up in the clinic today and will start taping tomorrow." She suddenly poked her head around the corner. "Brenda Freeman came in for another tube of ophthalmic ointment today. Rosco's holding his eye open all the time now, and she's sure he's able to see with it...And the Margarets and I went over the colour chart you picked up. We can't decide between the lemon chiffon and the goldenrod yellow. We're sick of living in a dungeon. We want something bright and cheery."

She presented the colour fan to me and pointed to the two they had selected. I took a quick look at them.

"Either one would work for me," I offered gallantly.

"You're a big help," she groused. "I was hoping you'd say lemon chiffon, because the two Margarets want the goldenrod yellow."

She went back to the front counter to check the appointment book. "Mr. and Mrs. Reid are bringing in Poco—things aren't sounding good. Martha said she and Jim have made up their minds to put the old guy to sleep...she asked me to talk to you before they got here so you don't get Jim's hopes up about something else you could try. Poco kept them awake all night with his coughing, and Martha says he won't eat a thing. Even Jim is certain his time has come."

I had finished discussing a lab report on the phone with John Partington when Doris called out. "I think they're here!" She'd been watching out the front window for the Reids, because with all Jim's paraphernalia to ensure his supply of oxygen, it was usually necessary for one of us to help them maneuver through the door.

"Do you think they're ready for me to give them a hand?" I asked.

"I don't know," Doris said, peering around the hibiscus plant for a better view. "They look like they're squabbling about something... maybe Jim has changed his mind."

I went to the surgery and pulled back the curtain. There was no question about it—Jim and Martha were still in the car, and from their agitated gesticulations, they were in the middle of a heated debate.

"I think we better wait here until we see the car door open. They're obviously in disagreement over something. Give me a holler when you think they're ready."

I went to the back room and drew up six millilitres of Euthanyl while Doris continued her watch. I could imagine how hard this was going to be for Jim. I think the old guy had really believed that he'd pass over before his buddy. I could almost see those fancy urns sitting side by side on Martha's coffee table.

"What's up, Doris?"

"They're still in the car, arguing."

"Maybe I better go out and see what's happening…I promised Bernie Meekes I'd stop and check out a cow he's having trouble with. If I don't get out there soon, he'll already be started milking."

Jim opened the passenger door of the old Chevy the moment he saw me. He was gaunt; his skin had a terrible pallor.

"Goddamned things," he cursed, adjusting the tubes in his nose. Glaring in Martha's direction, he shifted Poco to the seat beside him and began the difficult procedure of extracting himself from the car. I held the door open while one after the other, he lifted his legs to the curb. I stooped down to see what Martha was up to, as she was usually the one to assist Jim. She was staring down the street, giving not the slightest indication that she was going to help him.

Poco emitted a harsh, hacking cough; his sides flailed as he struggled for air. Jim stared at me with blank, expressionless eyes. He moved his lips and muttered something incomprehensible.

I leaned closer to the man. "I'm sorry, Jim, I didn't get what you were saying."

"Damned old age," he rasped in a voice barely above a whisper.

I nodded and waited for him to gain some momentum. Grasping the door of the car, he pulled himself from the seat. I steadied his arm as he tottered precariously first in one direction, then the other. He nodded at me, then motioned to the trolley in the back seat.

"I'll need that damned thing."

I wrestled the apparatus out and set it down on the street. Jim passed the clear plastic hose around the upright of the car and repositioned the tubes in his nostrils. He stood resolutely staring at my office door as if it were a goalpost, or a finish line in a race.

"Can you pass me Poco?" he asked.

"I'll carry him," I replied.

Jim shook his head with determination. "You can push that thing...seeing's it doesn't seem like Martha's coming." He glanced in his wife's direction, then gave the oxygen tank a look of disgust.

As I stooped to pick up the old dog, Martha lifted him to her breast and hugged him tightly. Her eyes brimmed with tears as she calmly said, "I'll bring him out."

She stepped onto the street. I closed both doors and waited to see what would take place between the Reids. Martha calmly walked up to Jim and placed Poco in his waiting arms.

"You ask!" she said with determination. Wiping tears from her eyes, she grabbed the handle of the oxygen trolley and followed Jim as he shuffled towards the clinic door.

I ran ahead to grab the stool from the surgery. By the time I got to the exam room where I anticipated doing the euthanasia, Jim had collapsed on the bench in the waiting room. I positioned the stool at the head of the exam table and waited while Doris talked to the Reids. As I returned, Martha burst into tears. Giving Poco one last pat, she kissed him and ran from the building.

Doris was leaning towards Jim with a look of bewilderment. "Dave? Can you come here?"

Tears flowed down Jim's cheeks as he tried to speak. He sat for ten seconds just sucking in air as if preparing for a tremendous exertion. His face was ashen, his lips a hideous blue. Although he was making an obvious attempt to breathe in the oxygen-enriched air through his nose, some whistled through his tightly pursed lips with a strange hissing sound.

Doris sat next to Jim and I knelt on the floor at his feet.

"I couldn't understand what you wanted, Jim," Doris said.

The man opened his mouth as if to speak, then closed his eyes and continued his erratic breathing. I looked at Doris. She shrugged her shoulders and shook her head.

"Did you have a special request, Jim?" I finally asked.

"I…we…Martha wanted to know…" he began. Before he could continue, Poco wheezed and gagged as if he were going to vomit. Extending his head, he wretched up white froth, then continued breathing with his mouth open and his head reaching towards the ceiling. Jim closed his eyes and continued his own battle for air. It was several minutes before he was able to continue.

"We were wondering…if…" He stopped and struggled with tears. "Could you collect some seed from Poco?"

"Seed?"

"Jizz!" Jim blurted with passion. "Martha wants to know if you could freeze it till she can find a bitch she likes…she doesn't want to be alone."

I was at a loss to respond. I had collected semen from several males and inseminated bitches when the pair was just too stupid to figure out the mating procedure, but that necessitated getting the male's penis erect and collecting a sample into a tube.

I shook my head. "Poco's in no shape to give us a semen sample."

Jim gasped. "You'd have to jerk him off?"

I nodded.

"I told Martha that, but she thought there might be some way of getting it after he was gone."

I shook my head again.

"Then I guess that's it," Jim said resolutely. "Just wish you could do me first."

"Do you want to be with him, Jim?" I asked, without acknowledging his last comment.

The man nodded. "Can we do him here?" he whispered.

I glanced at Doris; she nodded.

I went to the exam table for my syringe. Wetting a swab with alcohol, I returned to the waiting room. Doris had already positioned herself at Poco's elbow. I stroked the vein on the dog's foreleg and looked up at Jim. When he nodded, I threaded the needle into the vessel and began the injection. By the time the syringe was empty, Poco lay still.

Chapter 11

Wizardry

I kept firm tension on the strand of suture material until the knot disappeared into the subcutaneous fat. Tunnelling a final stitch beneath the skin, I poked the needle through and cut off the excess thread. Frank, the rosy-cheeked observer across the surgery table, stripped off his cap and mask and tossed them in the laundry hamper.

"I love the way that subcuticular suture pattern hides every-thing," he said.

I patted a tiny drop of blood from the site my needle had exited and smiled. I loved it, too. As I stripped the drapes from the cat's tummy, it was hard to see that I had even made an incision. If I could have replaced the hair I'd shaved away, no one would guess that Bailey's uterus and ovaries had just been extracted.

Margaret removed the ties from the cat's legs, then disconnected the endotracheal tube from the anesthetic machine. "You'd better quit admiring your work and get out to Riehls. I promised Bernie I'd get you there by ten. He has a dairyman's meeting this afternoon and doesn't want to be late."

She tugged at her mask until it rested under her chin. Although she still hated wearing the gauze barrier over her mouth and nose, she had developed into an iron lady in the surgery. She watched the patients as if each breath the animal took was her own, and never seemed to fluster when four-letter words echoed from the walls.

As Margaret and Frank supervised Bailey's recovery, I made a quick run to the truck. Sorting through my drug box, I replaced the bottle of penicillin I'd left at the Dortmans the night before.

As it turned out, this had been a good week for a student to observe the practice. Jim had taken a few days off to be with his wife, Mary. She was already several days over her due date, and both she and Jim were anxious to get the delivery over with. I always found having students in the practice refreshing and never refused a request. Marcie had been an observer in my practice when I first met her. There was something about the enthusiasm of students that reminded me of why I wanted to become a veterinarian.

Frank had called a few days before arriving in town to ask if he could ride along with me. A big-city boy who had finished his second year at the Western College of Veterinary Medicine in Saskatoon, he was anxious to see what life as a rural vet was really like. Over the last few days he'd been exposed to a bit of everything: routine spays, office appointments, and herd health sessions on dairy farms. The cake was iced last night at the Dortman farm with a wee-hour Caesarian performed in a remote shed by the light of a lantern and a flashlight whose beam seemed to come and go of its own volition.

By the time I had the truck sorted out and my coveralls on, Bailey had settled into a dejected ball of fluff in the farthest corner of the recovery kennel. Her head tucked into her flank, she growled softly with each breath. I opened the kennel, stroked her a few times, then rolled back her lip to check her perfusion. I found what I was hoping for—nice pink gums. She meowed plaintively and opened her eyes to mere slits. I ruffled her ears before closing the kennel door.

Margaret was washing the instruments in the sink as we headed out. "Dave, Jack brought in a list of materials he wants you to order for the new clinic, and he has the quotes for the cupboards in the exam rooms and surgery!" she called. "And Bernie needs a dozen herd health sheets and some oxytocin."

Bernie Riehl stood waiting at the door of the steel Quonset building where the farm records were kept. As soon as I introduced my ride-along to the tall, dark dairyman, he shook Frank's hand warmly. Plucking a small red notebook from his coverall pocket, he scribbled "Frank" across the top of the page. He grabbed a sheet from the counter and handed it to me.

"I got the results of my feed analysis back from first cut...what do you think?" He watched my face as I surveyed the figures.

"Looks like you got it up in pretty good shape, Bernie. The protein's twelve and a half per cent, but the calcium/phosphorus ratio is way out of whack. We might have to bump up the brewer's mash and get more phosphorus into the milking herd if we want to be seeing heats."

I passed the sheet to Frank. "Remember in your animal science nutrition course how they always harped about keeping a two-to-one ratio between calcium and phosphorus? Some of our clay soils here in Lister are loaded with calcium, and ratios of ten or twelve to one are not uncommon."

Bernie screwed up his face. "They hate the taste of that last mineral we tried...they even left some of the brewer's mash behind when I tried to mix it in."

We followed him to the corral where he had his milking cows confined. He unlatched a chain and opened a ten-foot metal gate far enough for us to enter. Frank followed nervously as we made our way through the tightly packed herd. Cradling a three-ring binder on his arm, Bernie fumbled through the hardboard herd health sheets until he selected one that was clipped with a wooden clothes peg.

"Number 53 calved on the fifth of March and we still haven't seen a heat on her." He tapped a big black cow on the rump and followed her into a stall. I slipped my arm into a plastic sleeve, then squirted it with soap. As I pushed through the cow's anal sphincter and forward into her rectum, Bernie held her tail to one side and scratched vigorously at the base of her spine.

Frank focused on my hand as it expelled handfuls of manure

to the concrete floor of the paddock. He fidgeted, turned uncomfortably towards the cow licking at the sleeve of his coveralls, and tapped her on the nose. I smiled as the big black and white cow persisted, stretching her long tongue in a tortuous arch in search of Frank's golden locks, the ones that curled over his collar.

As I continued to evacuate the cow's rectum, I grasped the ligament that suspended her uterus and tipped the organ into the pelvis where it could be examined easily. Both horns were firm and well-toned. As I manipulated the organ, a stream of shimmering mucus spilled over and stretched to the ground. It hung there tenuously for thirty seconds, then broke free to settle in a clear puddle on the manure-covered concrete floor.

"She's in heat today, Bernie."

I followed the broad ligament to the right ovary, a fluctuant structure the size of a plump, ripe cherry. Slipping across to the left side, my index finger explored the crater created by her ovulation. This was where the corpus luteum would develop to maintain a pregnancy if she was properly inseminated. "She has a follicle on the right ovary and a new corpus luteum on the…"

I was unceremoniously jostled by a cow as Frank jumped backwards and startled the animals behind him. His mouth gaping open, he peered into the rafters of the barn. I glanced up in time to see the disappearing figure of Bernie's thirteen-year-old son. Leaping from one open rafter to the next, he ran the length of the barn faster than I could have done it on the ground. I chuckled as Frank looked at me in disbelief. Bernie smiled meekly.

"That's Bernie's son, Doug…as you can see, he's part monkey."

Bernie continued writing as if nothing were out of the ordinary. "Should I breed her tonight?"

I nodded.

After making a notation in the herd health book, Bernie removed his trusty red booklet and wrote down the cow's number. Frank was still gazing in bewilderment into the rafters of the shed as I followed Bernie in search of the next cow.

We were almost back to the golf course on our way to the office when Doris came on the radiophone. "I just got a call from Carol Gilmour. She says her cow cut its teat and needs it sewn up."

I pulled into the golf course access, checked for traffic, and backed onto the highway. The Gilmours lived in Canyon and we had to retrace our path towards the sheer cliffs of the Skimmerhorn Range. My student sat passively staring out the window as we drove through the rolling hills of Lister past fields of lush green alfalfa. We were almost to Canyon when Frank spoke up.

"You sure live in a beautiful part of the world."

I nodded at him and smiled. "I sure do."

"I'm sorry I almost got you trampled today." He gave me a sheepish grin. "I guess I have to learn to move a little slower around livestock. It was weird...I was checking things out to get a feeling for their set-up when I looked up and saw that boy squatting there watching us. When he knew I saw him, he took off and startled me...Did you see the way that kid ran those rafters? If he'd fallen he'd have gone splat on the concrete—that has to be twenty feet up and those trusses must be three or four feet apart!"

I chuckled. This wasn't the first time I had witnessed Doug's performance. "Yeah, he's quite a kid...he loves living on the edge. The first time I saw him do that was a couple months ago. We were joking around after we finished working with the cows. When I swatted him with a shit-filled glove turned inside out, he gave me a crack on the butt with a stock whip. Poor Bernie...when I took after Doug, he thought I was going to wring the kid's neck. But Doug got over the gate, up the wall, and was gone like a shot—just like today."

We had turned up 48th Street and were climbing the last hill before Canyon Park when Doris called again. "Dave...I got another call from Carol Gilmour. She said not to go to their old place in Canyon...she's out in Lister now. She and John bought the Art Sommerfeld place."

I felt an immediate jolt through my body and pulled over to the side of the road.

Doris's voice crackled over the radio again. "Dave? Did you get that?"

I picked up the receiver and mechanically depressed the button on the mike. "Yeah, Doris, I copy."

"What's the matter?" Frank asked with concern. "You look like you've seen a ghost."

I held my face in my hands and leaned forward on the steering wheel. "You're not going to believe this." I took a deep breath. "Have you ever heard people talking about the feeling of déjà vu… when you're sure you've been somewhere before?"

Frank nodded. His face betrayed his bewilderment. I avoided his gaze and focused on the escarpments of Thompson Mountain.

"I know this sounds crazy…but when I spent some time at an ashram over two years ago, I had this dream."

"What dream…and what's an ashram?"

"An ashram's a yogic retreat, a place where you try and figure out why you think the way you do, and attempt to understand yourself better."

The look on Frank's face brought me up short. "Sorry," he said after a long silence. "Somehow, I have a hard time picturing you contemplating your navel."

I stepped on the gas and pulled onto the roadway.

"Aren't you going to tell me the dream?" Frank pleaded. "I didn't mean to insult you."

I drove to the top of the hill and pulled into the drive that had been the Gilmours. A prominently displayed Veitch Realty *For Sale* sign had a bold *Sold* across it.

"Do you see that building over there? John Gilmour built it recently so they'd have a place to milk their cows. He's applied for the building program that the milk board started to encourage new dairies." I put the truck in park and faced Frank. "When I was at the ashram, I was driving a Volkswagen sedan—I just bought this truck a month ago. I know it sounds silly but I never thought about what colour it was when I bought it…it was a plain-Jane vehicle that the Ford dealer brought in for me."

I hesitated a moment longer as an involuntary shiver ran up my spine. "In my dream, I was driving a yellow truck exactly like this one when I got a call on the radio from Doris that Carol Gilmour had a cow with a cut teat...I got here, and when I was about to this very drive, Doris came back on the phone to tell me that Carol called her again. She said that she and John had moved to Lister— that they'd bought Art Sommerfeld's place."

I looked over at the young man next to me, willing him to believe me. "You have to realize that back then I never had a radio in my car and when I got one put in here, I never gave it a second thought."

"So, that's the whole thing?"

"No, there's more...I drove to Lister and turned down Sommerfeld hill. When I got to their place, Carol waved at me from the other side of a barbed-wire fence. She wasn't happy. The moment I got out of the car, she started grumbling. She said, 'That darn John...just when I got to the point where I had a nice place to milk my cow with a milking machine and all...look what he does. He up and moves us. See where I have to milk my cow now.' She pointed to a tiny log building that used to serve as a shelter for the Sommerfeld horse. I straddled the fence and walked with her to the log building. The whole time, she's complaining about how hard it is to go back to a set-up like this when everything was fixed up so nice at the other place.

"When we got to the shelter, we looked through a little door that had a plank nailed across it. Inside was a big black and white Holstein cow that almost filled the entire space, and a newborn calf with marking almost exactly like hers...only the calf was red and white. Carol pointed to the cow's udder and her right hind teat. Without even going into the stall, I could tell there was nothing I could do. It had been cut off flush with the udder, and milk dripped steadily from the crater onto the straw."

I backed onto the roadway and started retracing our track towards Lister. As we turned onto the upper road above the valley, Frank smiled tentatively. "How much farther is it?"

I didn't answer him, just kept driving until I turned off

Canyon-Lister Road and headed down Sommerfeld hill. The moment we made the turn, I could see Carol standing along the road on the opposite side of a drooping wire fence.

"Is that her?" Frank asked impatiently. "Is that the woman?"

Frank opened the passenger door before the vehicle came to a stop. I got out and headed towards Carol.

"Thanks for getting here so quickly," she said. "This has turned out to be the damnedest morning. We got everything else moved over here on the weekend—the last thing we had to do was bring the cow. Wouldn't you know it, I'd gotten to the point where I had everything set up nicely over at the other place. John made me a nice stall with gutters, and we had the milking machine all set to go." She jerked her head towards the little log barn that stood in the middle of the pasture. "Look where I'll have to milk her now."

Frank nodded at me, smiled crookedly, and vaulted the top wire on the fence. Before I could even respond to Carol or introduce him, he was off at a run towards the barn.

Carol scowled in his direction, then turned to follow him. She grumbled as she walked, "I don't know how John expects me to manage with this set-up."

I swung my leg over the fence and hurried to catch up with her. As I approached the barn, I saw Frank craning his neck and squatting for a different view.

"Where's her calf?" he blurted as Carol approached.

"She isn't due for several more weeks," she responded.

"Well, at least you got the tit right!" said Frank. "It's the right hind."

Carol gave me an inquisitive look as I crawled under the rail and entered the pen. "It happened somehow when we were moving her. John thinks that she pinched it with her dewclaw."

"Easy, girl," I said as I patted the expectant mother's right back leg and slid my hand towards her udder. A semi-circular cut began at the top of the teat and ran its length to the tip on the inside. The moment I touched it, she flailed at me and circled to avoid me.

"It's okay, Gertie," Carol crooned in a sympathetic tone. "Settle down, girl." She grabbed the cow's halter and tied her lead shank to a big brass ring in the corner. "She's been a pretty easy cow to milk, but she wasn't very happy about riding over here in the back of the pickup…she's still pretty worked up."

I knelt beside her for a good look at the wound. "The cut's not into the teat canal, so I think we can sew it without much trouble. I'll get my kit and see if we can do it with just a local."

While I got things ready, Carol went to the house for a bucket of warm water. When she returned, Frank was still giving me a hard time about the dream and bantering about the low percentage of cattle that carried the red factor in the Holstein breed.

"I'm sure that they told us in animal science classes that it's less than five per cent," he asserted. "If that's what it is, it could only show up in two and a half per cent of births."

"Do you know how to apply a tail jack?" I asked, trying to change the subject.

"Sort of," he said hesitantly. "They showed us how it worked a couple times in medical exercises class."

"Push Gertie's tail straight ahead over her back. Remember that it will only keep her from kicking me if you maintain the pressure straight ahead."

I watched as he tentatively grasped her tail and lifted it over her back. Flopping the tail back and forth several feet from the base, he limply pushed it forward.

"You need to have more control of it," I counselled. "Slide your hands down further where you can keep a steady pressure."

"But she's all poopy down there," he whined.

"Poop washes off, bruises don't."

I began scrubbing her wound, keeping a watchful eye on my wary assistant. Squirting surgical soap into the cut, I scraped chunks of straw and pieces of dirt from the raw surface. As I began injecting lidocaine, the cow danced up and down, continually taking pokes at me with her right hind foot.

I glared at Frank as he tried to distance himself from her menacing blows. It was a resounding thump to my left shin that convinced me it was time to consider a new approach. With tears pooling in my eyes, I fumbled through my kit for a bottle of Rompun, a new drug that had been on the market for only a few months. I had used it on several occasions on fractious bulls, with good results.

"I'm going to sedate her, Carol. As you can imagine, this is a very sensitive area to freeze."

I drove a needle into Gertie's right thigh and injected a millilitre of the clear liquid. Taking a step back, I pulled up my pant leg for a look at my shin. It was throbbing like the dickens and a bit of hide had been displaced.

"Are you all right?" Carol asked.

"Yeah, nothing that a week or two won't fix."

Within five minutes, Gertie decided it was time to lie down for a snooze. With her head tucked into her flank, she slobbered away, groaning with each breath. I injected a line of lidocaine adjacent to the wound, then began trimming up the margins.

"What's this red factor you guys were talking about?" Carol asked as I began suturing. I nodded in Frank's direction and shrugged.

"Before I came over here, I told Frank about a dream I had a couple years ago. It really doesn't make a bit of sense, but when I was at the ashram recording my dreams, I dreamt that I was out doing rounds when I got called to your place—that you had a cow with a cut teat. I was almost to your driveway in Canyon when Doris called me and told me you had called back to tell me that you'd moved to Art Sommerfeld's place in Lister."

Carol screwed up her face. "How could you have known we were going to buy Art Sommerfeld's place two years ago...we never even thought about it until last month. And how could you remember a dream that you had two years ago? I can't remember the ones I had last night."

I cringed and wished I had kept my mouth shut. Things like this had a habit of getting around; the last thing I needed was to be branded by the farmers as some sort of weirdo. I sighed and looked up from suturing.

"I don't understand it any better than you do, Carol…but I still have that dream written down at home and remember it like it happened last night. I spent almost two days trying to interpret it as part of my assignment…analyzing what you and John meant as characters; what Art Sommerfeld meant to me; what a little red and white Holstein calf meant. It wasn't something I'd soon forget."

"Red and white calf?" The pitch of Carol's voice went up several octaves and her eyebrows lifted.

"Yes, that's what Frank's been razzing me about."

"So, what haven't you told me?" Carol asked insistently.

Frank smiled at me and shrugged.

"That you would greet us at a barbed-wire fence that we would have to climb over…and that from the moment we got here, you'd be ranting about how that darned John had moved you away from a finished barn with a gutter and a milking machine to a dinky log shack that had a plank nailed across the door."

Carol flushed and I detected a hint of anger. I stopped talking and focused on my suturing. After a long pause, she began again.

"What's this about a red and white calf?"

I placed the final two sutures at the top of the wound, then stood up and threw my instruments in the bucket of water.

"When we got to the barn in the dream, I just stood at the door because there was nothing I could do. The Holstein cow had stepped on her right hind teat and cut it right off at the bag. Lying in the corner of the hut was a little red and white Holstein calf."

"Well, at least she didn't lose her whole teat," Carol quipped.

I gave Gertie an injection of penicillin before retreating to the car with my instruments. I handed Carol the remainder of the bottle of penicillin and the syringe. "Give her thirty millilitres a day for the next three days starting tomorrow."

Carol nodded. Frank had retreated sheepishly to the truck. He hadn't spoken again since Carol began her interrogation.

"I better not tell John about this," she said. "He's Catholic, you know…and probably wouldn't have you back on the place if he found out that you were some sort of wizard."

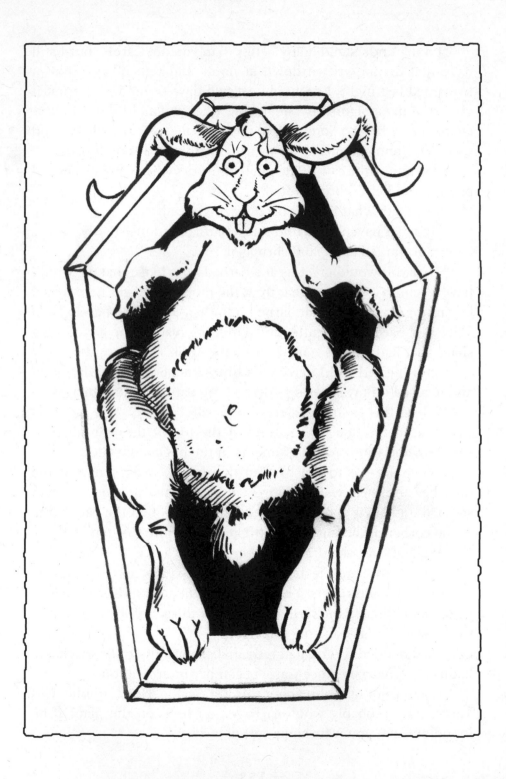

Chapter 12

Open Casket for Elvis

Dan Hurford was waiting at the office door when I arrived on Monday morning. Doris had called before I left home to let me know she was driving out to West Creston to pick up Margaret Berg and might be a few minutes late. Margaret's car was having some work done on it this morning at the Last Chance Garage on Nicks Island Road, and she had no other way of getting to the clinic.

"You running the show on your own today, Dave?" Dan joked as I came around the corner.

"I hope not...the girls should be here any minute."

"You heard that Jim's a daddy?" he asked.

"No, I didn't...tell me more."

"Mary delivered last night—a little girl."

"Oh, really...everything went well?"

"Yeah, great."

"When did you see Jim?" I asked.

"He and I walked into Nun Lake on Friday to try our luck at fishing."

"Fishing? Nun Lake?"

"Yeah. Don't you remember how we've been talking about trying our luck there."

"Yeah..." I nodded. "Yeah, I do."

Dan had been one of my biggest supporters since I started my practice in the valley, and I considered him one of my best friends.

He and his family ran Tsolum Farms, the second largest dairy in the area.

Dan and I had taken a weekend off the first year I was here to sneak off to Boundary Lake near the U.S. border for a few days of fishing and camping—that was before he got married and started a family of his own. We had passed the sign to Nun Lake on the way to Boundary and made a pact to walk in and check it out at some future date. There wasn't a month went by without our talking about that trip. In our busy lives it had developed into one of those never-never things that we'd someday have time to do.

"How was it?" I asked half-heartedly, a bit sorry for myself that my new assistant was reaping the benefits I was hoping for.

"Oh, great!" Dan replied enthusiastically. "We ate all the fish we could get down on Friday night, then the same on Saturday. We walked out Sunday afternoon and got home before Mary went into labour."

"How did you get away from the farm for that long?"

"Just decided it was time to start doing some of the things I've been putting off," he answered resolutely. "It worked out really well…Trish had Mary out to the house in case she had any trouble, and Jim and I got to wind down a bit."

I took a deep breath, then asked, "Can I get you something?"

"Yeah, I need a gallon of Ketol, a couple boxes of Biotef, four bottles of penicillin, a 250-mil bottle of Tasvax, and some herd health sheets."

I quickly threw everything in a box and handed it over.

"You wouldn't have a couple of ice packs would you, Dave? I won't be heading home for a bit yet."

"Sure thing…"

"I'm going over to Jim's to give him a hand fixing up a few things. I'm helping him with some plumbing for their new washer and dryer."

Doris and Margaret arrived as Dan was leaving.

"Isn't it exciting," Margaret gushed to him. "Jim and Mary have a little girl. Her name's Cynthia."

"You knew about it, too?" I asked.

"Yes," she said hesitantly. "Doris told me last night...Jim called her the minute it happened."

I looked at Doris. "I seem to be the last one to know what's going on around here."

She was about to say something when the phone rang. She picked it up and handed it to me. "Dave, it's Joe Jacks again."

"Good morning, Joe. Are things still okay out your way?"

"As right as rain, Dave...as right as rain. Like I told you last week, Tinker's never looked back. I gave her those shots and fed her in that makeshift corral I threw up, then brought her down here to the house. She followed right along like there'd never been a thing wrong with her. Not a stumble, not a missed step. I've been feeding all of them hay down here...I'm scared to let her go back up the mountain."

"I would be, too, Joe."

After making an appointment to vaccinate Joe's mares and foals, I hung up the phone.

Doris came out of the darkroom still doing up the snaps on her smock. "Well, shall we premed the spay?"

"I guess..." I said dejectedly.

I had amputated the uterus of the six-month-old golden cocker, Tippy, and was just beginning my closure.

"What's wrong?" Doris asked.

"Nothing," I answered glumly.

"Don't give me that. I know you well enough to tell when something's eating at you."

I aggressively tied the first knot, then took a bite through the muscle layer again.

"Was it something that Dan said?" Doris guessed.

I continued suturing and was halfway along the two-inch incision with my closure when I answered. "Why can't someone I hire get friends of their own? Hell, for that matter, why can't they get lovers of their own?"

I looked up at Doris, instantly regretting my outburst. She stared at me through her horn-rimmed glasses for a full minute. Adjusting her mask, she finally replied, "It's natural that Jim would attract similar friends as you when he does the same job as you do."

"Natural? Was it natural for Cory to show up for work on his first day with the girl of my dreams in tow? Was it natural that Dan and I planned a bloody fishing trip to Nun Lake for five years... then Jim shows up, and five weeks later they've already gone and done it?"

"You're being unreasonable. You introduced them. They have lots in common...Dan and Trish are married with a little one, and Jim and Mary were a couple expecting a baby...now they have one. Mary and Trish hit it off really well...so, yes, it's natural."

"I gave Jim a week off to spend with his wife when she was ready to deliver, not to take the fishing trip I've been planning for five years."

Doris sighed and watched in silence as I continued suturing.

Tippy was awake and sitting up in her kennel when I left her and headed for the front office to see my first appointment.

"Hello, Alex," I said with as much enthusiasm as I could muster.

"Hi, Dave."

"Come on into the exam room." I struggled to add a bit of a swagger to my step.

"Late night last night?" he inquired.

"It's that obvious, is it?"

Alex smiled and said no more. He was a slim man in his mid-fifties. He and his wife, Alice, had a bed and breakfast facility on Kootenay Lake and also ran a kennel. He was clutching their miniature poodle close to his chest.

"Teddy's not been doing well the last few days. We noticed him shaking his head a couple days ago and started putting this in his ears." He pulled a depleted tube of Panolog from his pocket and set it on the exam table. "Alice said she had only enough left to do half a treatment yesterday. When he threw up this morning and wasn't interested in his breakfast, she got kind of worried."

The dog was a trembling mass. Although he had been recently groomed, and I could still detect the scent of perfume, it was over-powered by the offensive odour of decay. Teddy's eyes were half closed and he looked dejected. Slime matted the grey hair on the side of his face and his right front leg.

"Did he vomit on the way in?"

Alex nodded. "There was some mucousy-looking stuff in his carrying kennel...I doubt that he had much in his tummy to throw up, though. He's right off his food."

Even in his owner's arms I could see that Teddy's head tilted dramatically to the right.

"Can he walk?"

"I think so," Alex replied. "But to be honest, I haven't been dealing with him. Alice kennelled him and put him in the car just before I left...I only took him out of his crate to bring him in here." He put the dog on the floor at his feet. The poodle stood uncertainly in a wide stance. Alex backed off a few steps and called, "Come here, Teddy...come on, boy."

The dog hesitated, took a few uncertain steps, then flopped onto his right side.

"Alice never mentioned he was having trouble walking," Alex said defensively.

"Just pop him up here, Alex."

Teddy sat uncertainly where he was placed with his head moving ever so slightly in a rhythmic motion. I stooped for a closer look. His eyes were in continual motion, rotating slowly to the right side, then flicking rapidly back to the left.

I lubed a thermometer and stuck it in the poodle's rectum. While it was cooking, I let my mind wander. Dan was right—the time to do the things we had been dreaming about was now. It really irked me that he had taken the trip to Nun Lake with Jim and not me, but when would I have had time to go? I would have felt guilty about not working on the house or not helping Jack at the new clinic. Heck, we should be relocating up the street in a few weeks—how were we supposed to get enough time for the move? I'd have to shut the clinic for at least a day.

I sighed…all I wanted to do now was go home, pull the covers over my head, and sleep the rest of my life away.

"What do you think's the matter with him, Dave?" Alex asked tentatively.

I withdrew the thermometer and studied it before answering. It read 40.1 Celsius. I leaned forward to smell the dog's ears; the stench was overwhelming. A watery, serous fluid drained from his right ear. His left was inflamed as well.

"I suspect most of what we're seeing is the result of a middle ear infection." I held Teddy's head firmly in my hands. "See what's happening with his eyes?"

Alex bent forward for a closer look.

"Watch how his eyes rotate slowly towards the right, then flick rapidly back to the left."

Alex puckered his lips, then nodded.

"That's called nystagmus—to him, the whole world's turning towards the right and he follows it with his eyes. When they rotate as far as they can go in that direction, he quickly snaps them back to catch up when it comes out the other side."

"Does that mean it's his right ear that's affected?"

"That's the worst one…but from what I can see, both are a mess. The symptoms suggest that only the right side has the labyrinth involved."

"Would that explain the vomiting?"

"What would happen if someone stuck you in a barber chair and spun you round and round in circles?"

"I'd probably lose my balance and throw up."

"That's exactly what Teddy's doing."

I grabbed my otoscope and fished a tip from the cold sterilization vat. Locking it on, I sank to my knees beside the table and pulled Teddy towards me. The left ear looked raw and painful, and the lateral ear canal was filled with yellowish, watery debris. The right ear was brimming with the same material.

"Well, we better get him started on antibiotics to see if we can get things straightened out."

"Do you think he'll be all right?"

"I suspect he will...so long as we choose the right antibiotic and he has no permanent damage to the vestibular apparatus. Most times when I treat cases like his, the head tilt and nystagmus have sorted themselves out within three or four days. It'll take a lot longer than that to get those ears back to normal, though. I'll send you home with some topical medication as well...and we'll use an anti-inflammatory to try and get the labyrinth to return to normal more quickly."

While Doris was getting the medications ready, I swabbed Teddy's ears and headed to the lab. After streaking a blood agar plate and throwing it into the incubator, I sank into the swivel chair, laid my head back, and focused on my breathing. I couldn't let a little thing like a missed fishing trip derail me.

A few minutes later, Doris came around the corner. "Mrs. McAlister is out front and wants to talk with you."

"The Elvis and Costello McAlister?"

Doris nodded. "Elvis isn't doing well."

"Oh darn..."

The McAlisters were a tight-knit family with four girls between the ages of four and ten. Janet, the mother, was a slim, youthful woman who didn't look old enough to have parented any one of the children, never mind all of them. I had yet to meet the husband, John, who worked at Huscroft Sawmill, as he was most often at work when something was up with their critters. The only reason I knew his name was that Janet was most insistent Doris make the record cards out in his name.

Until recently, the McAlisters had been proud caretakers of a guinea pig named Costello and a rabbit named Elvis. A few days after Jim arrived on the scene, Janet and the girls had brought Costello in to be put to sleep. For a guinea pig, he had lived to a ripe old age. Amanda, the oldest of the McAlister girls, told me tearfully on his day of passing that he was just a week short of his eighth birthday.

At the time, Janet had been concerned about how much Elvis would miss Costello, because the two of them were best buddies and constant companions. Elvis himself was an ancient bunny—Janet was sure that the girls had the rabbit at least two years before his guinea pig companion arrived on the scene.

I felt like an undertaker creeping into his parlour for the first meeting with a bereaving family member. There was no way this was going to be easy for Janet.

She was sitting alone on the bench in the waiting room with her hands folded in her lap and a parcel wrapped in a brown paper bag beside her. In her grief she looked even paler and slighter in build than she actually was.

"Hello, Janet." I took a seat next to her on the end of the same bench.

"Good morning, Dr. Perrin. Sorry to come with such a sad request."

"Elvis is not doing well?" I prompted.

Tears welled in the woman's eyes as she lowered her head and shook it slightly from side to side.

"He's not been right since we had Costello put down...we've been tempting him with his favourite foods, but he's just not interested in eating anymore. The girls have spent the last two weeks running around the yard looking for the youngest and tastiest dandelion leaves—they were always his favourite food, you know. I don't think he's eaten a bit of hay or pellets since Costello left him. When I got him out of his cage this morning there was a heap of vegetables and treats that he hadn't touched. The girls have tried broccoli, lettuce, apple slices...Amanda even read about rabbits liking willow bark as a tonic when they're sick. John went out and cut him some."

"So you think his time has come?"

Janet nodded. "He's old and he misses Costello so much...they were always together. They ate together, they slept together...spent hours grooming one another."

I sighed deeply. "Do you have him with you?"

"Yes…" she said hesitantly. "I have him out in the car…"

I bowed my head as Janet was overwhelmed with tears. She looked at me earnestly and struggled to go on. "We have a special request. It's about his presentation."

"His presentation?"

"Yes," she responded, unwrapping the parcel. "John has made another coffin for Elvis…just bigger than the one he made for Costello."

The woman opened the lid of the beautifully crafted box. I remembered thinking what a shame it would be to bury Costello in the other one, when it would have made such a great jewellery box for the girls.

"We would like to have him wrapped in his blanket," she went on. "The girls have spent hours cuddling him in it over the years. They didn't give Costello his, and Julie is worried that he may be missing it."

I nodded.

"And please, please, please, close his eyes when you're done with him. Faith and Julie were certain that Costello would never be able to sleep in heaven because you left his eyes open after you gave him his needle."

"I'm sorry, I wouldn't have thought of that."

Mrs. McAlister stood and headed for the door. A few minutes later, she returned with a cat-carrying box. Extending it to me, she asked, "Can you finish by noon?" With tear-filled eyes, she continued, "We've got the service planned for one o'clock. The girls' grandfather ministers a church in Invermere and will be coming to say a few words at his burial."

I looked at my watch and nodded. It was only eleven-thirty, so that gave us plenty of time to prepare him.

She had her hand on the doorknob to leave when she turned and said, "You will remember the eyes, Dr. Perrin. The girls want an open casket."

The moment the door closed behind her, Margaret and Doris emerged from the surgery.

"That's the darndest thing I've ever heard of, Dave," Margaret pronounced. "Can you imagine? A funeral for a *rabbit*? I just put six of them in the deep-freeze last weekend, and I certainly didn't say a prayer over any of 'em."

"Think about it as a service for the children's loss, Margaret. I can remember burying my pets. It's not easy accepting the end of anything—never mind a pet—when you're a kid. Kids think good things should go on forever."

"Look at all the work that man put into making this coffin," Margaret said, running her hand over the freshly varnished surface of the lid.

"That's what I mean," I said. "He obviously values his kids' feelings."

She followed me to the exam room, shaking her head in amazement. I placed the carrying case on the table and opened the folding cardboard lid.

"Oh, the poor thing," Margaret crooned.

"It is his time," I muttered, lifting the emaciated creature from the case.

In the surgery I drew up some euthanasia solution while Margaret stroked the bony old bunny. Putting a 25-gauge needle on my syringe, I returned to the exam room, grabbed a gauze, and soaked it with alcohol.

"Hold off at the base of his ear, Margaret."

As she cramped her finger below the ear, I scrubbed along the margin with the swab until I could make out the dark blue tract of the ear vein. Threading the tiny needle into the vessel, I nodded at Margaret and began injecting. Elvis took a deep breath, quivered slightly, and lay still.

I sighed, then went out into the waiting room for the coffin. No matter how many times I played God to end an animal's life, it never got any easier. If there was a job in my profession I liked less, I couldn't think of what it was.

I carefully wrapped Elvis in the blue cotton blanket and placed him in his final resting place with only his head and long floppy ears protruding. The last thing I did was close his eyes.

The moment I took my hand away, his eyes popped open again. "Damn..." I tried again...same response.

"In the movies the doctor just reaches up and gently closes them," Margaret said innocently.

"Well, this isn't a movie, Margaret!"

"What's wrong?" Doris asked as she left her station at the front counter.

"I can't get his bloody eyes to stay closed."

I glanced at my watch. It was quarter to twelve—I had fifteen minutes to remedy the situation.

"Doris...bring me a package of fine Dexon."

I had a needle driver ready by the time Doris returned, and quickly placed a suture through the margins of his eyelid. The problem was, on either side of the suture, the lids struggled to stay open, revealing snippets of Elvis's pink eye beneath. I would have had to place at least three sutures to keep it properly closed.

"That's no good," I said in disgust.

"Why not?" Margaret asked. "It's almost closed."

"If the girls see those, they'll be sure that Elvis'll never be able to open his eyes in heaven. To them, that may be even worse than his never sleeping."

"You could glue pennies to his eyes," Margaret suggested. "Isn't that what the Irishmen always do?"

"That's it, Margaret...you're a genius!"

"I am?" She shot a questioning look at Doris.

"You are! Doris, take some money from the till and rush down to the hardware store for some crazy glue. I tried that stuff at home to fix Mom's broken glasses and almost ended up with my fingers glued together."

I checked my watch again. It was ten to twelve.

Five minutes later, Mrs. McAlister and her four daughters showed up to collect their treasured pet. I had moved Elvis and the coffin to the surgery room and left the door that exited onto the street unlocked.

Margaret went to the waiting room to explain that the doctor was just finishing up a procedure on another animal and that he would bring Elvis out to them shortly. I removed the suture I had placed, blotted the puncture wounds flat, and waited impatiently for Doris's return.

She was huffing and puffing when she finally threw the door open and passed me the tiny bottle of glue.

It took only a matter of minutes to have Elvis resting in peace. After tucking a bit more blanket under his head as a pillow, I closed the coffin lid and marched out to the waiting room.

Mrs. McAlister quickly got up from her seat and took a step towards me away from the girls. Leaning close to me, she whispered, "You remembered his eyes?"

I nodded as I passed her the coffin.

"Yes, I remembered his eyes."

Chapter 13

Big Problems in Small Spaces

The aging Hereford cow snorted and tossed her head in warning as I took a step closer. The granulating pink masses in her right eye were large enough to distort both lids.

"There's no way, Bob...it has to go. It's involving the lacrimal duct as well as the eye. If you tried to ship her now, she'd never pass inspection."

Bob nodded and motioned to the six-hundred-pound heifer calf that stood behind her.

"Damn shame—just look at her calf. Should have my arse kicked for letting it get ahead of me like this. I noticed a little pink bleb on the edge of her eye when we kicked them out to pasture earlier this spring."

"That would have been the time to catch it...we could have frozen the tumour then."

"Never heard of such a thing," Bob said, shaking his head. "But when Willie and I were out on pasture the other day, we saw another one with some pink growing on the white of her eye."

"Maybe you better get her in, too. This old girl's too far gone, but the other one may be a candidate. Cryotherapy's sort of new to vet medicine. We brought a clinician up from the Pullman vet college for a continuing education session, and he went on and on about all the success he'd been having with it. He claims he's gotten rid of tumours twice the size of your hand by just freezing them

again and again. This guy has actually manufactured a bunch of metal probes for the purpose. You stick one of them into a canister of liquid nitrogen until it's the same temperature as the nitrogen... then you put it on top of the tumour and freeze it into a lump. Squamous-cell carcinomas like this one are apparently more susceptible to freezing than most."

Bob looked skeptical. "Why wouldn't it kill everything when you stick something that cold on it?"

"Apparently healthy cells are more resistant than cancer cells. You kill some of them by freezing an area, but the normal tissue regenerates quickly."

"Do you have the tools to do that?"

"I bought some probes from the guy when I was at his seminar, and I've been dying to try them out."

"We better see about getting that other cow in for you to check out, then...Willie and I can get her in some time next week." Bob gave the cow in front of him a look of disdain. "How do you think she'll manage with just one eye?"

"About as well as she manages now." I examined the weeping mass that was once her eye. "I'd bet she can't see a thing out of that one now."

Bob nodded and said reluctantly, "I suppose you want her in the head gate?"

"Yeah...there's no doubt about what has to happen."

Bob stepped between the cow and her calf and gave the mother a slap on her rump with the flat of his hand. The critter took a few steps down the alleyway, then put on the brakes and started lumbering backwards.

"No, you don't, old girl..." He quickly slid a metal bar behind her to halt her retreat. "This old bat's always a pain when you have to work her. She's been down this chute enough times to know the ropes."

"You get the head gate ready, and I'll see if I can get her up there."

It took ten minutes of poking and prodding to get the wily old cow into the squeeze and close the end gate behind her. Even then she refused to stick her nose between the pieces of the metal V that would trap her head. It was only after I pried her forward with a metal bar that we were able to catch her. Bob stood back and wiped his brow when the gate finally clenched on either side of her neck.

"I swear she gets smarter and ornerier every time," he groused. "She's horrible to handle here, but I'd hate to be without her out on pasture. It's amazing…if I convince this old girl to do something, the rest of the herd follows her like she's the Pied Piper."

I climbed over the rail of the corral and made my way to the front. Bob peered in disgust at the affected eye. The inside corner and lower lid were distorted by mounds of scabby, discoloured tissue. Several pinkish plaques grew from the margins of the sclera towards the centre of the cornea. The animal squinted constantly, and the tears flowing from her eye coalesced into a wet fan on her lower jaw.

"Do you think removing it will cure her?" Bob asked, swatting at the flies that circled her face.

"It's hard to know for sure. Most cancers involving cows' eyes are malignant. When cells from a squamous-cell carcinoma metastasize, they're likely to travel either by the lacrimal duct or the lymphatic system. With lymphatic system spread, we see a swelling under the jaw or behind the ear where the downstream lymph nodes enlarge. Once that happens, or bone gets involved, it's pretty much game over."

I reached under the jaw to feel the nodes; the moment I touched her, the old cow tossed her head and struggled to be free of her shackles.

"Watch out!" Bob warned as she suddenly twirled her head in an attempt to trap my hand against the metal upright.

"Feels normal enough at the moment." I stepped back to be clear of her flailing head.

"Well, I obviously can't ship her like this," Bob said matter-of-factly.

"She'd be condemned at slaughter for sure," I agreed. "Either we remove the eye today, or you let her finish raising the calf, do her in, and put her in a hole. The way the eye's looking right now, it's got to be pretty uncomfortable."

Bob shook his head decisively. "Can't leave her like this...she's been a great old cow. We've got two of her heifers out on pasture, and I'm planning on keeping this one, too."

"Keep in mind that research suggests this condition may be heritable."

Bob grimaced at the word "heritable."

"The thinking is that the cancer results from exposure to ultraviolet radiation. Skin with no pigment absorbs more UV radiation than skin with pigment, so you should always try and select for brown skin around the eyes of both bulls and heifers. It makes sense, because it's a big problem for the industry—most tumours leading to condemned carcasses at processing plants are from cancer eyes."

Bob sighed deeply. "What happened to the good old days when people just wanted nice-looking critters...I tell you, farming's getting more complicated every year." Again, he shook his head in disgust. "Let's get her done."

"We'll need her snubbed up with a halter, so I can work on her."

Bob lengthened the loops of a rope halter shank and threw it over the cow's stub horns. "Watch out!" he hollered as I flipped the loop under her jaw and pulled the halter tight. The cow stretched her neck and bellowed in frustration when I wrapped the rope around one of the pipes of the head gate and began to cinch it tight.

"I don't think she likes what you have in mind any better than I do," Bob said ruefully.

"We'll need an extension cord for my clippers," I said, hauling in another couple of inches of slack.

The ancient chute rattled and creaked as the cow struggled to free herself. With her head secured, I gently prodded the margins of the crusty lesions, trying to determine if there was any involvement of the bone. The margins of the orbit felt clean and sharp.

By the time Bob had the extension cord stretched out to the

chute, I had lugged my surgery box from the car. The old girl had still not become resigned to her fate—the moment the vibrating blades of my clippers touched her skin, she bellowed in defiance and rattled the chute with renewed vigour.

"Easy there, old girl," I crooned, cutting a swath of hair above her upper lid. "You'll be okay."

Bob watched warily as I swathed a wide halo around the cow's eye.

"Can you pour the water for me as I scrub her up?"

"You're not going to just start cutting, are you?"

"Not till I've frozen her."

"Oh, good." Bob sounded relieved.

I slathered the clipped area between her right eye and ear with surgical soap, then nodded at him to pour some water from a gallon jug that I had brought along. After several more scrubs, I plucked a three-millilitre syringe from my coverall pocket and filled it with lidocaine.

"Is that the shot to freeze her?" Bob asked.

I nodded. "It's the first one."

I palpated the margin of the bony ridge beneath the cow's eye and slipped the fine needle under the skin where it met the bones of her skull.

"She didn't mind that," Bob said optimistically as he watched me inject the contents of the syringe.

I scrubbed the area one more time while waiting for the local anesthesia to take effect.

"Oh…that's a bigger one," he said when I grabbed a 14-gauge, one-inch needle and snapped the protective plastic sheath off with my teeth.

He grimaced when I placed it in the same location as the last injection and drove it through the skin. The old cow never moved as I directed the needle as deep as the hub. Leaving it there, I went back to my surgery box and opened a package that Margaret had labelled "Long Needle." Bob's eyes bugged as I unfolded the cotton wrap and removed the six-inch, 18-gauge needle.

When I held it up and bent it into a gentle C-shaped curve, he turned his head. I threaded the point of the long needle through the hub of the bigger one and advanced the tip until it ground against the underlying bone of the cow's skull. Applying a syringe, I aspirated to make sure I wasn't in a vessel. When nothing came back, I drew up twenty millilitres of lidocaine in another syringe and slowly injected it. The cow blinked her eye, struggled briefly against the halter, then stood stoically as I pulled the needle back and redirected it to block the nerve to freeze her eyelids.

"Need some more water?" Bob asked.

I nodded and handed him the pail. He looked relieved to be getting away as he headed to the house with his Border collie, Pepsi, close at his heels.

I had everything I'd need laid out where it was easily accessible before he returned with the water. After scrubbing up, I dried myself, slipped on my gloves, and locked a blade into my scalpel handle. I incised the skin a centimetre below the lower eyelid and carefully examined the weeping tissue on either side of the wound, making sure it looked healthy. As my blade left behind a trail of blood above the cow's upper eyelid, Bob turned his head again.

I followed the margin of the upper lid, gently curving my incision to meet the lower one near the corner of the eye. With scissors, I dissected bluntly to the tough white connective tissue that lined the eye socket. Pushing downward, I opened my scissors, tearing away connective tissue to the level of the muscles that circled the eyeball. I repeated the procedure again and again, until all that remained was to sever the muscles and cut through the optic nerve. Soon, the eye was staring up at me from the ground at my feet.

As I focused on the glistening hole where the cow's eye had been, searching for anything that could indicate remnant islands of cancer cells, Bob hollered, "Pepsi, no!" Before either one of us could react, the dog was gone with the eye in her mouth.

Bob was right—this was a gross procedure that even I found disgusting. As I packed the eye cavity with gauze and began suturing the wound, I mused about my choice of starting practice here in Creston. Maybe I should have gone to Calgary or Vancouver, where I could have specialized in vaccinating kittens and trimming the sharp points from puppies' nails.

"You better clean up your act, Doc." Jim was standing at the kennel room door as I stripped off my dirty coveralls. "And don't see any patients till you have a peek in the mirror."

I headed around the corner to the darkroom where my smocks were hanging.

"Are you sure you don't want me to look after your first appointment?" he hollered after me. "I've got time."

"No…it won't take me long to get ready." Glancing in the mirror, I discovered a speckled trail of blood beginning at the bridge of my nose, crossing my cheek, and ending inside my right ear. I quickly washed up and was ready to throw on my smock when Doris piped up.

"Better check the high-water mark." She was giving me the once-over from behind.

I lifted first my left, then my right arm. Sure enough, there it was—a montage of blood and hair up the back of my triceps, extending down into my armpit.

"You know, Doris, there are days I wish I'd taken a job in a small animal practice where the job was clean and the critters were manageable."

Doris chuckled. "Keep scrubbing…you missed a spot."

When I finally passed her inspection and headed to the waiting room, it became clear why Jim had offered to help me out. We had all noticed over the past few weeks his penchant for good-looking women—especially blond good-looking women.

Lynn Schiavon was both blond and beautiful. In fact, the thirty-ish bombshell was probably responsible for more cricks in more necks than almost any other woman in the area; it was a riot to watch all the grey heads turn as she journeyed down Canyon Street when Creston's male retirees were out in force.

The Schiavons lived on the shore of Kootenay Lake in the community of Gray Creek, and Lynn's husband, Gerry, was the principal of the Crawford Bay School. Lynn had a zest for life and an absolute passion for two very disparate critters—ladybugs and St. Bernards. The cute little cottage she and Gerry shared with their two children was decorated from top to bottom with red and black knick-knacks in the shape and colour of ladybugs—ladybug ornaments, ladybug pictures, ladybug cushions. She owned two huge St. Bernard dogs, and one of them, of course, was called Ladybug.

In the waiting room, Lynn was sitting with her hand resting pensively on a cardboard cat box. She was wearing a bright red blouse with black shorts. Her ears were adorned with ladybug earrings.

"Hey, Lynn…how're you doing today?"

"I'm doing fine, but poor old Archie's seen better days."

"What's his problem?"

"He's been scrapping again," she said with a sigh. "He's at it all the time, and I'm constantly cleaning up little booboos…but this one's way beyond me. It looks to me that half the skin on his neck's gone."

"Oh no…"

"He must have been in the fight a couple of days ago. I never saw him yesterday, and when he came out to pick at his food this morning, I knew there was something wrong. He's pretty much an outside cat now because he's so antisocial. He really likes me, but wants nothing to do with Gerry and the kids."

Lynn indicated the box beside her and frowned. "Gerry didn't even want me to bring him in. He thinks we should get someone to do away with him, then find a kitten that the kids can actually play with." She frowned and raised her eyebrows. "There's no way I can do that."

She sat staring at the box beside her. "In a way, keeping him's not fair to the rest of the family—this cat is truly a holy terror. Gerry won't even try to hold him for me anymore, and Archie actually stalks the kids—as if he's hunting them. They're terrified of him…

he'll hide behind the couch or the corner of the house, then jump out and claw at their legs. He's even tried that with Gerry."

"He sounds like quite the cat," I muttered with a noticeable lack of enthusiasm.

"I can only imagine what he's going to be like today after riding to town in this box…you better be careful."

Lynn stood and cautiously lifted the carry kennel. I was beginning to think I had been a bit hasty in my desire to be a small animal vet—at the moment, a wily old cow didn't sound so threatening.

In the exam room, Lynn set the kennel on the tabletop. She had a worried expression. "Shouldn't we be in a totally closed room in case he gets away?"

"You don't think you'll be able to handle him?"

"I don't feel comfortable with the idea right now—the two-hour ride to town has gotten him worked up."

I went to the surgery and returned with the restraint bag that we routinely used to confine fractious cats. Opening the zipper, I placed it face up on the table.

"You better get a bigger one, Dave. You'll never squish him in there."

"Let me take a quick peek at him," I offered, unfolding the latch on the cardboard case and prying it open a bare inch.

"Watch out!" Lynn warned as a grey paw flashed through the crack. "Oh gods!" She struggled to keep the lid on Pandora's box. "I warned you," she said, watching the blood drip from the end of my index finger.

I hurried to the front, wishing I had allowed Jim to handle Archie. Doris looked at the blood oozing from my finger as if she saw it every day, and passed me a paper towel. "You must be slowing down in your old age," she quipped.

Wrapping the paper towel around my finger, I peered at the appointment book, trying to figure out one of the notations on this afternoon's page. "Doris, what's this? I'm going to need to book time to do something with this crazy cat, but I see I have a three-o'clock appointment."

Doris checked the book, smiled at me, then shrugged her shoulders. "Coccasomething? Trim nails," she guessed hesitantly.

"Coccasomething? Could it mean cockapoo?"

"I don't know. You better ask Margaret...that's her writing."

I opened the sliding door to the surgery and hollered to Margaret, who stood watching a cat on the anesthetic machine. "What in the world does coccasomething mean?"

Margaret shot me a worried look; she could tell by the tone of my voice that I wasn't thrilled. "A lady called in and wanted a nail trim for her bird," she said tentatively.

"Her bird?"

She nodded, then stooped to check the colour of her patient's gums.

I stared glumly at the word "coccasomething" on the appointment page. "Did she say cockatiel or cockatoo?"

"Dave, you know I haven't got a clue about birds. All I can tell you is that a lady called saying she was worried that her bird's nails were too long. She said she was scared to cut them herself because she didn't want to make them bleed. "

I closed the sliding doors and continued to glare at the coccasomething notation. If there was anything I hated in practice, it was uncertainty. I preferred working on things I knew I could handle. Cockatiels fell somewhere behind budgies, canaries, gerbils, and rats in my comfort zone. Cockatoos...

I opened the door to the surgery again. "Jim, maybe you can handle this bird call while I'm suturing up Archie."

"Sorry, Doc." Jim looked up from his surgery with a smile. "I'm already booked to vaccinate a couple horses out in West Creston."

The moment the door swung open just before three o'clock, I suspected I was in trouble. All I could see beyond the huge domed cage were arms embracing its sides and stubby legs trundling beneath it.

Only after the shrouded enclosure was settled on the bench did I get a look at the woman who had carried it in. A short, stout redhead in her early forties stepped forward and extended her hand.

"I'm Maggie Schroeder, and this," she said, turning and whipping a cotton sheet from a bronzed wire cage, "is Snowball."

The woman looked disparagingly at my bandaged finger. "A difficult patient?"

"An occupational hazard," I responded.

"Are you familiar with parrots, Dr. Perrin?" Mrs. Schroeder quickly changed the subject. "My sister says it's very easy to make them bleed to death if you cut their nails too short."

I stood transfixed as the big white bird extended its neck, opened its grey beak, and glared at me with dark, almost black, beady eyes.

"Snowball's a white cockatoo," the woman continued blandly. "I'm told that they originate from the Indonesian islands."

All I could focus on was the long curved beak. Only a couple of weeks ago, I had splinted the wing of a budgie that had crash-landed against a kitchen window. By the time he left the office swaddled with judiciously applied adhesive tape, my fingers were riddled with tiny bleeding bite wounds. As I stared at this menacing bird, all I could picture was that pruning-shear-like structure chomping on one finger after the other.

Margaret and Doris stood as if pinned to the floor. It had taken both of them to help me overpower the budgie, and neither of them seemed anxious to be assisting me with Snowball.

The bird kept his beady eyes focused on me as he advanced a few steps closer along his perch. Cocking his head to the side, he extended a large fan-shaped crest of feathers on top of his head. He continued to stare straight at me, letting out a screech that sent my heart racing and induced me to take a hesitant step to the rear. Both Doris and Margaret disappeared from sight.

"I think Snowball finds your size intimidating," Mrs. Schroeder noted out of hand.

"I know the feeling," I mumbled, still unable to take my eyes off his enormous grey beak.

"My sister's birds can actually talk, but all Snowball ever does is screech. He was the sweetest thing when we brought him home," she said dreamily. "My sister raises these birds in Calgary, and when she offered to give one to my teenage daughter, I caved in." Her nostalgic tone suddenly took on an edge. "That was before I got sucked into paying five hundred bucks for this gilded cage, and," she said after a moment's hesitation, "before the bird grew up."

She paused for a moment, then said, "You know, when he was young, he was as much fun as a puppy, and I thought I had made a great choice. My daughter played with him for hours and hours, and her friends were drawn to the pair of them like pieces of metal to a magnet."

"I can see teenage girls really being attracted to a young bird like that," I said. "It'd be quite a novelty."

"He used to sit on their fingers and kiss them and cuddle with them…then he had that incident…"

"Incident?"

"Yes…" Mrs. Schroeder became pensive. "He bit one of Angela's friends on the tip of the nose. We were still living in Red Deer then. Angie called me in tears when I was at work. I had to rush the poor girl to the hospital…there was blood everywhere. The doctor had to graft skin from the back of her ear onto her nose—poor thing still has a scar right across here." She ran her finger over the tip of her nose.

Snowball stepped off his perch to cling to the metal bars of his cage.

"His nails really don't look bad," I offered with the slight hope that my opinion might sway Mrs. Schroeder's decision in the matter. The truth was the nails could be curling fully around a perch a second time before I'd voluntarily suggest intervention.

"To be honest, I wouldn't have bothered…" the woman admitted, "but my sister's coming to visit." She rolled her eyes and shook her head slowly. "My sister's an even bigger pain in the arse than this bird, and I'm not up to listening to her going on and on about how I'm not looking after him properly."

I laughed out loud. Although I wanted nothing to do with her pet, I was developing an appreciation for this client.

"I don't have a lot to do with Snowball," she went on. "Now that Angela's off to college, he doesn't get anywhere near the attention he deserves." She sighed deeply. "To be honest, I always thought birds belonged outside in the wild."

"I agree, and I've been told that they need a lot of human interaction to keep them sociable."

Mrs. Schroeder frowned and nodded her head. "That's what my sister keeps telling me. She spends three or four hours a day working with hers, but I work full-time and have a lot of things I'd rather be doing."

"Are you able to handle him enough to get him out of his cage?"

"Hell, no!" she said emphatically. "As a matter of fact, I get all stuffed up from his dander the moment I'm in the same room with him." She demonstrated by taking a few quick breaths through partially blocked sinuses. "I can work up the courage to stick my hand in his cage to feed and water him, but nothing more than that. Last year when I still had my place in Red Deer, I felt sorry for him and let him loose. Boy, was that a big mistake—he wrecked all my plants, destroyed half my picture frames, and shredded my wicker baskets. When I tried to make him stop picking at my favourite basket, he chased me across the room, screaming and flapping his wings like a maniac."

"How did you get him back in?" I asked in awe.

"I trapped him in Angela's room where his cage was and left his food and water inside it. I kept opening the door a crack and peeking in. Finally, he got hungry enough to get back in his cage, and I locked him in. He's been in there ever since."

"What do you plan on doing with him?"

"I'd love to get rid of him, but Angela keeps telling me she wants him back when she has her own place. My sister says the damned things can live for up to one hundred and twenty years, so I hope she keeps her word. I don't plan on living that long, and I sure as heck don't want to spend the next eighty years with him."

I stared into Snowball's menacing black eyes, willing myself the courage to do something with him.

"We better take him into a confined room, just in case he gets away on us," I said, hefting the bulky cage and moving it to the surgery. "How does your daughter get him out when she handles him?"

"She doesn't," Mrs. Schroeder said, following me around the corner. "She tried to stroke him under his chin when she was home last week and get him to sit on her finger...he used to really like that when he was a youngster. But this time he nailed her good."

"Are you going to come in and give me a hand?" I asked, trying to sound assertive.

My client smiled reassuringly and returned to the waiting room. "I'll leave him in your capable hands while I go do some shopping...I really don't want to get in your way."

I heard the door open, then Mrs. Schroeder advising Margaret, "Just warn the good doctor to be careful...Snowball can crunch hazelnuts with a single bite."

With her words ringing in my ears, I plucked a pair of nail trimmers and a container of cauterizing sticks from the cabinet drawer. Contemplating my patient for several long minutes, I tried to conceive a plan of action. The cage was criss-crossed with perches, and I could see no way of avoiding contact with them in order to extract him easily.

"Margaret...you better come give me a hand!"

My courageous assistant slunk around the corner as if she were being summoned through the doors of a gas chamber. "Dave, I'm scared spitless of that thing."

"That makes two of us...but you know who made the appointment. It seems only fair that you get to help me."

I opened the sliding door of the cage and stuck my hand into parrot territory. Watching me warily, the bird sidestepped his way farther along his perch.

"Are you going to just grab him and pull him out?" Margaret asked.

"I don't know what I'm going to do."

"Why don't you put these on?" Doris suggested from the safety of the front room. She produced the welding gloves that I used on occasion when dealing with an unruly cat.

Pulling the right one on, I trespassed into Snowball's cage again. I hated trying to do anything with these bulky things—it was a bit like trying to work with boxing gloves on.

"Don't worry, boy," I said, working my hand through the maze of perches. "We're not going to hurt you."

I was poised to make a desperate lunge for the bird when he grabbed hold of a cage bar with his beak and hopped nimbly to the next perch. He turned to face me, extended the crest feathers on the top of his head, and emitted a horrendous screech. I jumped back so quickly that I tripped over Margaret in my retreat. Grabbing hold of the wall to regain my balance, I looked sheepishly in my assistant's direction and pulled off the glove. Beads of sweat were magically popping out across the woman's brow.

"Dave, I swear if he does that again, I'm going to wet myself. How do you expect me to help you with this creature? Look at that beak…"

"Believe me, I can see it."

"Maybe we should just tell the lady we can't do it," Margaret suggested. I could see her glance pleadingly towards Doris, who was now peeking between the panels of the folding doors.

Margaret's words seared my delicate ego like acid. I'd love to have sent the damned thing home, too, but I hated to admit to Mrs. Schroeder that I wasn't man enough to handle her pet. Placing the domed cage on the floor, I resolutely knelt beside it.

"When the going gets tough, Margaret…" I said with determination. "You go over there and hold his attention, and I'll grab him while he's looking at you."

She hesitantly shuffled her way around to the far side of the cage, making certain to give the structure a very wide berth.

"Okay, get his attention."

The bird stared straight at me as I extended my arm upwards towards his perch.

"For God's sake, Margaret," I chastised as she ineffectually waved her hand back and forth in front of him. "He can't jump through the bars to bite you. You need to hold his attention…get closer!"

"But, Dave…" she whined.

I lunged for the bird and closed my hands over his wings before he could flap them and hurt himself. I had him halfway to the door before he took aim on the end of my finger.

"Aaaaaaaah!" I cried in agony as his beak clenched over my pinkie finger. "Aaaaaah!"

Before I could react, the determined bird twirled his head one hundred eighty degrees and crunched down on my thumb. "Son of a bitch!" I bellowed, trying to get hold of his head with my other hand.

"Let him go, Dave!" Margaret screamed.

I was trying to work my other hand through the cage door when Snowball let go of my thumb and took possession of my bandaged appendage. Releasing my grasp on the demonic bird, I yanked my finger free.

"Oh, Dave…" Margaret muttered.

Blood ran freely from all three fingers as I danced around the surgery waving them in the air. Snowball settled himself on his perch still holding my Band-Aid in his beak. No longer a pristine white, his wing feathers, cheek feathers, breast feathers, and crest were now a crimson red. As I ran for a paper towel to stop the flow of blood, he grabbed the Band-Aid with one of his claws, anchored it to the perch with his foot, and systematically shredded it to tiny pieces with his beak.

"Get me the vet directory, Doris," I growled in the front office.

She dug through the bottom drawer of the file cabinet and produced the spiral-bound book.

"Find me Dave Huff's number," I ordered curtly.

"Huff Animal Hospital?" Doris asked hesitantly after a flurry of flipping pages.

I nodded and she dialled the number in Tsawwassen.

I had sat next to Dave Huff in several sessions at the last B.C.

Veterinary Medicine Association convention, and he had mentioned that he was working with more and more exotic animals and birds in his own practice. Surely, if there wasn't some sort of a trick to handling these patients, he'd have long since been working without fingers.

While the receptionist went in search of Dr. Huff, I plucked off the blood-soaked paper towel and tentatively examined my wounds. My pinkie had a nasty gash below the first knuckle that continued to ooze. With my index finger it appeared that Snowball had just deepened the wounds left by Archie's claws. My thumb…

"Hello, Dave, how are things up in the wilds of the Kootenays?"

"They've gotten a heck of a lot wilder since a big city client dragged in a cockatoo."

"A cockatoo, eh? What's his problem?"

"His biggest need right now is a bath to get my blood off him. His owner brought him in requesting a nail trim, and so far the only nails that have been trimmed have been mine."

I looked mournfully at the split that ran the length of my thumbnail and gingerly poked at a nail bed that was still seeping blood.

I held the telephone away from my ear as Dr. Huff roared with laughter. "Did you use a towel?"

"A towel?"

"Yes, you need to get a towel or blanket over him, then gently compress him. That way you can get your assistant to hold him on his back so you can work on his nails. Once you get his head covered and control his wings, he'll be easy to handle."

"Oh, I sure hope so."

"It's much easier and less stressful on the bird if the owner will get him out of the cage for you."

"I can well imagine, but my owner's even more terrified of him than I am."

"You know, there are more of these birds that people want to find a home for than you can shake a stick at. A lot of people would be better off getting a lovebird or canary, rather than a cockatoo. If parrots don't get enough attention, they can be hard to handle."

"So I've noticed."

By the time I had the courage to tackle the bird again, my fingers had almost stopped bleeding. Snowball watched suspiciously from his upper perch as I carefully removed several of the lower ones. My hand was trembling when I grabbed a hand towel and advanced towards him. Somehow he sensed something was different, because he immediately climbed onto the bars of the cage and started screeching.

"Oh my goodness, Dave!" Margaret blurted. "Who could live with one of these things in the house?"

Snowball somersaulted to avoid me and dropped to the bottom of his cage. The moment he lighted, I pounced with my hand outstretched. The towel flopped over his head and my fingers closed over his wings to firmly capture his body. Within seconds, he was upside down in Margaret's trembling hands.

Doris came in to observe as I systematically snipped one nail after the other. Within minutes, the procedure was complete and Snowball was back in his cage preening himself.

I was feeling somewhat elated as I covered his cage with his sheet and carried him to the table in the examination room. "Margaret, reassure Mrs. Schroeder that all the blood on Snowball is mine and not his."

I turned around to see Doris standing behind me with her hands on her hips. "Well, are you ready for Archie?"

Chapter 14

Canada Day Celebrations

"Doris, where's the spare ophthalmoscope? This one wasn't plugged in last night, and the battery's dead!"

I was trying to get finished with Patches, the big calico cat that I had just spayed. The Schultzes had recently inherited her from a neighbour who moved away. Although she'd been an inside cat in her previous home, she seemed to be adjusting to life in the barn with several other feline companions. When Mrs. Schultz dropped her off last night for the spay, she requested I check her ears, too, as she'd noticed her scratching at them.

"I'm supposed to be at Tsolum Farms at ten," I grumbled. "How am I going to get finished here, when I don't have any equipment to work with?"

"Check in that box by the kennel room door—the one with the drapes piled in it."

I rummaged through the box, picking up one linen-wrapped bundle after the other.

"It's not here!" I hollered.

"Ye gods," Doris groaned. "Margaret probably took it over to the new clinic in the last load."

I sighed. Practice was hard enough at the best of times, but it was next to impossible when half my equipment was disappearing.

"Come watch Patches for me, while I have a look under the microscope."

I swirled a cotton swab around in the sleeping cat's ear, then stood watching Doris for signs that she had heard me.

After throwing several piles of files into a box she'd labelled D to F, she slowly got up from her chair in the office and drifted into the surgery.

"I'm getting too old for this," she pronounced.

"Aren't we all," I responded, heading to the lab. "Thank God they haven't run off with the microscope yet." I knelt down in front of it. "When did Margaret take my chair?"

"A few minutes ago…she loaded it up with boxes and wheeled it down the street."

"It's a good thing we're only moving half a block," I said, rolling the cotton swab back and forth across the surface of a glass slide. "Aren't you going to miss this place just a little?"

"What are you mumbling about?" she hollered back at me.

"Aren't you going to miss this place?"

"Are you kidding…I can't wait to see the last of it!"

I positioned the slide on the microscope at low power and perused from one end to the other. It was on the third trip across that I saw it—the familiar globular creature with six legs paddling back and forth, dragging itself aimlessly across the glistening surface of the glass slide.

Patches's ears weren't the typical wax-laden ears that we usually found in adult cats infected with ear mites. She must have picked them up from the other cats after arriving in her new home.

"Can you imagine working in a place that isn't dark and dingy all the time?" Doris called back. "Where you can actually clean the floors right to the corners!"

"She has ear mites, Doris!" I got up off my knees and walked back to the surgery. "We better dose her ears now and send the Schultzes home with enough medication to treat the rest of the cats—they probably all have them."

"The Shultzes will be happy to hear that," Doris said flippantly. "Can I wake her up now?"

"Yeah, I'm done with her."

As Doris went about working ointment into Patches's ears and waking her up from anesthesia, I went to the kennel room and grabbed a pair of coveralls. I looked around me, at all the bulky things in the room; these would definitely be the most difficult items to transport to the new location.

Although I'd miss this rickety building, I was looking forward to an end of the turmoil associated with moving. We had been in a state of total chaos for the last three days, with the girls packing things up and lugging them over to the new facility.

The big impetus for the move was Doris's desire to host the open house on Saturday with everything set up and ready for business. I proposed quietly making the changeover, but she insisted that she wanted to celebrate the event, and she wanted to celebrate it this Saturday, in conjunction with the Canada Day celebrations. Seeing as Saturday was tomorrow, we had a lot to get done in a very short period of time. When Doris Currie made up her mind to do something, I knew it was best to either help accomplish her task, or get out of the way.

I was happy enough with the new layout. It could have been bigger, but we now had a cozy waiting room with an actual desk for Marg Rogers to sit at while she groused about the finances. There were two brightly lit exam rooms, a properly enclosed surgery suite, and a well ventilated kennel room. There was no question that new clients would get a better first impression walking into that office as opposed to this one. It was also a step up from the facilities of our two competing practices.

When it came down to it, the physical space wouldn't make much difference to the type of care we offered—we had done some great work in this old building. Although I had learned a lot over the last five years, it was still attitude that made more difference than anything else to the outcome of the patients that came through our doors. It was all about wanting to have the best for both our patients and clients. The colour of the paint on the walls would have little to do with any of what really mattered in a veterinary practice.

I was in a pensive mood as I drove west across the flatlands towards the mountains in the distance. Summer was such a beautiful time of year, and with all the rain we'd had over the past month, the valley had become a showcase for the colour green—the light greens of the new barley and oat fields, the deep greens of the now knee-high alfalfa, the yellow-greens of the cottonwoods lining the banks of the Kootenay River, the blue-greens of the trees facing the mountains in the distance.

I crossed the bridge over the Kootenay River and slowed to watch a boat navigate its placid waters. Would I ever get to row these channels as I had been visualizing for the past few years? I hadn't been in a shell since I was on the UBC rowing crew in 1969, but that didn't stop me from knowing that the long straight stretches of slow-moving water this river offered lent themselves to rowing. I could picture my slender shell cutting through the calm. I could almost see the blades of my oars flashing.

I turned onto Nicks Island Road and parallelled the river for a few kilometres. Crossing a little bridge where the irrigation ditches drained into the Kootenay River, I stopped to watch a deer and her fawn graze on the far bank. In my first years here, I had spent hours paddling my canoe down the long ribbon of water. That stretch was populated with almost every species of bird seen in western Canada. It was hard to believe that I hadn't wet my canoe in over three years.

I felt uneasy as I got close to Tsolum Farms. Maybe I was reading too much into things, but it seemed as if my relationship with the Hurfords and Dan in particular had changed since Jim had come on board. Last week, Jim had asked if I'd mind letting him take over the herd health sessions on the Hurford farm. He had been less than satisfied when I told him I'd like to continue doing them myself. Now, I was wondering if the suggestion had come from Dan himself.

He was waiting for me at the milk house door. "Well, you almost made it on time." I glanced at my watch…I was fifteen minutes late. He smiled and led the way through the milk house to the parlour where we processed the cattle. As he started down the three steps into the pit, he set the dials on the feeders to run a bit of grain into each.

"How are things going for you these days?" he asked. "Now that you have Jim around to share the workload, you must really be making headway on your house."

"I don't know…" I pulled on my palpation sleeve and followed him into the pit. "It seems like I still never get anything done. Father put up the forms for a new pour weeks ago, and I haven't gotten around to doing it. What with trying to get the new clinic ready for Doris's grand opening, the house is on the back burner…I was at the clinic painting until two last night."

"Are you going to finish on time?" Dan asked, opening the gate to the parlour and allowing cows to work their way through the herringbone structure. "You'll be in deep shit with Doris if you don't get it done by tomorrow."

"I can see that Jim's keeping you posted."

Dan laughed as I grabbed hold of one of the galvanized support pipes and hoisted myself out of the pit to the level of the cows. Working my way between them, I tapped an old girl on the forehead to back her up. When she was clear, Dan opened the back gate. I swung in behind the last cow, pulled her over with her tail, and proceeded to evacuate her rectum.

"She's a thirty-day check," Dan said. "She calved normally and has been milking well. Dad made a note that he thought she was in heat three days ago."

I worked my hand back and forth, sending jets of manure through the grates on the parlour floor. When she was cleaned out, I pushed forward to my armpit, grasped her utero-ovarian ligament, and followed it to the right horn of the uterus. Curling my fingers, I retracted the organ and turned it upside down in the pelvis where I could examine it completely to make certain that the animal had cleaned up after calving and was ready to rebreed.

"The uterus has contracted down nicely…the right ovary is three centimetres with a new corpus luteum on the anterior pole.

The left is two and three-quarters. She's cycling and has just gone through a heat."

Dan made notations in his big blue binder. I withdrew my arm, pushed the last cow back into her stall, and squeezed by her.

"That one's a preg check," Dan advised.

I began evacuating manure from the new cow.

"She was bred fifty-three days ago." Dan frowned. "I sort of wondered about her last week—she was playing around with 289 when she was in heat. I ran the pair of them in and checked this cow, too, but she didn't have slime and wasn't really toned up, so I left her."

I retracted her uterus and manipulated the horns—the left was fluid-filled. I gently pinched the wall and felt the characteristic fleeting of fetal membranes.

"Just as well you did…she's pregnant."

We finished checking the cows and were leaving the barn at noon when Dan's father, Herb, pulled up in his new John Deere tractor towing a dust-covered green swather. Throwing open the door to the cab, he wearily stepped down from the machine.

"All done with the cows?" he asked.

I nodded and pulled off my manure-spattered coveralls. "For another couple weeks." I threw the coveralls into the back of my truck.

"Did you discuss the minerals?" Herb asked Dan.

Dan shook his head. "No, but Jim thought it was a good idea."

I waited for Dan to fill me in.

"Why don't you come in for lunch, and we can talk about it over a bite to eat," Herb said, heading to the house. "I'm sure Ev can scrape up enough to feed another mouth."

"Sounds good to me," I said, looking out of the corner of my eye in Dan's direction. He smiled and pointed to the house.

"I better clean up a little better in the barn first." In the milk house I turned on the tap in the big double sink, squirted on soap, and scrubbed away. After I was happy with what I could see, I lifted my arms, checking my pits for the characteristic veterinary high-water mark.

"It's good there, but I noticed earlier you had a couple gobs on your forehead." Dan was standing behind me in the doorway.

I stooped over, cupped water in my hands, and scrubbed at my face, then dried vigorously, rubbing especially well over my forehead.

"So, what you got going over the weekend?" I asked. Although I knew Dan wasn't big on celebrating such things as Canada Day, it meant there'd be more than usual going on in our little town.

"If it stays nice, and we get the silage up early enough, we'll take in the fireworks. Jim and Mary asked Trish, me, and the Turners to come in for supper before we head up to the Rec Centre…You've met Bob Turner, my new milker. He and I are going to put Jim through a milking just for the experience."

"That'll be good for him," I agreed. "Bob's married, too?" I assumed he would have to be, to fit in with the other couples.

"Yeah," Dan answered. "Trish and Bob's wife, Alyssa, get along pretty good, and we three couples have been kind of getting together once in a while." He turned on his heel. "I don't know about you, but I'm hungry." I followed him across the yard to his parents' house.

As we settled at the table, Ev's mom, Grannie, as everyone in the family affectionately called her, bowed her head and asked the blessing. As she said grace, I stared past Herb's bowed head at the familiar picture on the wall directly across from me. I thought of the countless times I had sat at this table staring at the haunting painting of an old prairie farmer with his head bowed over his bowl of soup. I wondered if I'd see it as much in the future.

I had finished my bowl of beef vegetable soup and was making a second ham sandwich when I got around to asking Herb what he wanted to know about the mineral.

Herb looked at Dan and then at me. "You know how we've been putting that mix you guys concocted onto the belt when we feed the cows?"

I nodded. They had a large conveyer belt which brought feed into the barn from an adjacent silo and deposited it evenly into a central feed trough. Walter Goertzen, the nutritionist at the local B.C. Agriculture office, and I had designed a high-copper, high-selenium mineral mix to meet the requirements of local livestock. We had calculated the amount of mineral that someone had to dump onto the belt in order for it to deliver an average amount to each cow.

"Well, we were talking to the Unifeed salesman about simplifying things and cutting back on how much we have to pour on. He suggested that they just add their own mineral to the pelleted grain they bring us...That way we won't have to stand up there when we're feeding, dumping so much of the darned stuff on the belt."

I paused while I pondered the idea and poured myself a glass of milk. "How are you going to make sure that each cow gets the amount of mineral she needs on a daily basis?"

Dan interjected, "When they go to the challenger feeder, they'll get the amount of grain that we set for their necklace, and we know we'll still have to add some to the belt."

A challenger feeder was a metal station set up for a cow to enter to get a feed of grain. The necklace or transponder she wore around her neck was programmed to dispense enough grain to support her level of production. On a farm the size of this one, a half dozen feeders were spread around in the loafing area to reduce congestion and avoid long line-ups for entry.

"We calculated your mineral consumption on roughly two ounces per thousand pounds of body weight per day," I recounted. "That means we want them to get that same amount every day—like if you were taking a multi-vitamin tablet with each meal."

Dan nodded.

"If you add it to the grain, then the cow that's just freshened or the cow that's close to drying up is getting hardly anything, and the one that's putting out a hundred pounds of milk a day and getting lots of grain to support that production could end up with two or three times as much as she should have."

"We thought of that—that's why we decided to cut your mineral in half," Dan answered.

I shrugged. "Well, if the feed company thinks they can work it out, it may be all right. You know how hard it is to see heat cycles when the cows are low on minerals. Besides, selenium and copper can be extremely toxic when they're fed to excess. And you'll really have to pay attention to the dry cows…they won't be getting much grain except when you're steaming them up."

Dan smiled. "We won't change a thing from what we do now on the dry side—and of course we'll still have some free-choice mineral at a lick box."

Dan and Herb looked at one another and nodded confidently.

"We already have the first load coming," Herb said.

Doris was still roaring around stuffing things into boxes when I returned to the office. "I hope you've eaten, because your first appointment is already in the back."

"I thought you were cutting back on appointments so we could all focus on the move."

"That was the plan, but you know what this place is like. The phone hasn't stopped ringing and everyone swears their situation is urgent."

I checked the book and cringed. "Not Archie Schiavon! Doris…"

My girl Friday gave me a look of consolation. By the time we had discharged the cat last time, he had terrorized everyone in the clinic.

"What's up with that miserable old bugger now?"

"Lynn said that the spot on his neck, where you sewed him up last time, broke open again."

"That's impossible…I left those stitches in over three weeks before taking them out and that was a week ago."

Doris shrugged.

"And what's this about a pig?"

"Mrs. Robertson out in Arrow Creek has a problem with her

pot-bellied pig. She said he hasn't eaten in two days, and she's really worried about him."

"Is that the Mrs. Robertson with Alex and Frederica...the lady who lost her husband right after she moved here from Calgary?"

"That's the same one."

I remembered the woman well. She and her husband, Bernard, had brought their two dogs in shortly after they bought property in Arrow Creek. They had been so happy to get back to their rural roots and out of the big city; both of them had originated from a small town in Manitoba. The day after they presented their dogs for their annual vaccination, Bernard had a massive heart attack out in the garden and died on the spot. I was sad to hear that their enjoyment had been so short-lived, but I hadn't been surprised—both he and his wife were grossly overweight.

"What's Jim doing?"

"He's out tending a colicky horse in Erickson. He and Margaret picked up the dolly from Creston Hardware and moved the fridge over just before the call came in."

I wandered into the back room to throw my dirty coveralls in the laundry basket, and to check on my first patient. I stopped short. I should have stayed at Herb's. The washer and dryer were in the middle of the room, all the shelves for my coveralls had been dismantled, and the laundry basket was nowhere in sight. The only things in their original position were the banks of kennels. I chucked my coveralls in the corner and opened the door of the bottom cage. Gently conveying the still-closed carrying case to the surgery, I set it on the table.

"Poor Lynn was fit to be tied," Doris chimed from the front office. "Her husband hates that cat and wants it done away with, but you know what she's like."

"I do."

"She did say, though, that if it was going to cost as much as last time, you better call her so she can think about it."

I cautiously opened the top of the box and peered in. The big grey cat cowered in the corner, glaring at me with malicious green eyes.

"Thank God Lynn put that Elizabethan collar back on."

"She said he was scratching at it, and she wanted to protect the wound from getting any worse."

"Wound, hell…with that on, I can get hold of him without getting bitten."

I grabbed the big brute by his scruff with one hand, stuck the other under his butt, and hefted him onto the table. When he swatted at me, his claws slid ineffectually over my forearm; I was so glad I had trimmed his nails again before taking out his stitches.

I laughed. "Poor guy is totally humiliated. With this hat on and his claws blunted, he's not anywhere near as tough as he thinks he is."

Doris reluctantly got up from the floor where she had been cleaning out the ancient cupboards and stuffing packages of ear and eye ointments into a cardboard box.

"What do you want me to do?" she asked.

"You can hang onto him while I have a better look."

Doris leaned over the table, sandwiching the cat between her elbow and her upper thorax. As if understanding that his defences were grossly diminished, Archie sat quietly while I gently lifted the plastic collar and examined the wound.

"It's the darndest thing." I was looking at a red granular circle about twice the size of a quarter, and on either side was an elliptical line where the sutures had held it together. "It's as if the cat isn't producing collagen," I muttered. "The subcutaneous tissue didn't bind together at all. The only thing holding it was the skin itself."

Archie cooperated surprisingly well, and Doris and I were able to mask him down without much struggle. Within five minutes, he was asleep and intubated. After debriding the entire wound surface and inserting a drain, I stitched the underlying tissues together for the second time in a month and closed the skin with non-absorbable sutures.

By two-thirty I was in coveralls again and on my way to Arrow

Creek with Lug on the seat beside me. As I drove east on Highway 3 through Erickson, I was recognizing the familiar warning signs of an upcoming downer—every second thought found me worrying about what I had done to lose the Hurfords' trust. Feelings of inadequacy plagued me, and waves of emotions rushed through my body. I was eight years old again, standing alone at the edge of the schoolyard—I was big, I was dumb, and no one wanted to play with me. I was feeling sorry for myself again!

Why couldn't I deal with this issue once and for all, and be done with it? Being a veterinarian on the Hurford farm was one thing, being a friend of the family was another. I had to somehow detach one from the other, to let go of the emotional attachment I had to all my clients. How else could I survive in business? How else could another vet, like Jim, ever feel successful in my practice?

I thought back to the day I came rushing in from the Wienses to find Sorina Maletta leaving the office with a big smile on her face. My initial reaction was one of relief, but the truth was I'd been mortified to discover that Jim had been able to please her. I'd have been much happier to see her sitting there with a scowl on her face because she wanted to see only me and was tired of waiting. And that was not a healthy state of mind for anyone, especially me.

And I certainly knew how Cory felt when he arrived at Verna's place to find Jim and me already there. If things had been reversed, and Cory had arrived there first, I'd have sulked over the situation for weeks. Man, it seemed like life was working overtime to highlight my weaknesses and insecurities.

As I climbed onto the upper bench of the Arrow Creek community, I slowed and pulled up the drive to park in front of a nicely appointed modular home. Mrs. Robertson had obviously busied herself with landscaping her yard. When she and her husband arrived, this plot of ground had been little more than a poorly maintained pasture. Now, an array of flowers abounded in elevated wooden beds that surrounded the house.

A spate of barking erupted from the house as the dogs recognized the presence of a foreigner. Lug snapped to attention immediately, but I pushed him back on the floor and opened the door.

"Down you get!" I snarled as he grumbled under his breath.

A sliding door on the edge of the patio opened and both a long-haired Scotch collie and a shaggy Airedale burst forth.

"Alex! Frederica! Settle down!" a woman yelled.

Both dogs approached, still barking, but with tails wagging. I held my hand on top of Lug's head as I got out of the vehicle and pushed the door closed. "That's enough, you two…" I cautioned, extending my hand.

Mrs. Robertson was standing at the edge of her balcony looking down on me. "Don't worry, they're a pair of pantywaists."

"Your place is beautiful," I said. "I'm amazed what you've done with it."

"Thank you," she responded with a broad smile. "The flowers still give me lots of pleasure." Her smile faded. "I've sort of let the rest of the grounds go now that Bernard isn't around to help. He so loved his garden, you know…the whole time we were in the city, he dreamed about being able to go out to pick his own peas and pull his own carrots from the ground."

"I know what you mean. I love browsing in my mother's garden that way."

"Gardening's not been the same since I got Rosalie, either," she said sadly. "That's why I had all my flower beds built up like that… Right from a piglet, Rosie loved to root. The first year I had her, there wasn't a flower left in my beds…I planted a little vegetable plot last year, but she had it dug up long before I could use anything. Maybe next year I'll hire someone to build me a fence to keep her out." The woman suddenly looked sombre. "I'm really worried about her. I'd never have thought I could get so attached to a pig, but she's a real character, and such good company."

I checked my pockets for my thermometer and stethoscope before heading to the house. Alex stuffed his furry face into my hand for a sniff, then lifted his leg on the front tire of my truck.

"What seems to be the problem with Rosie?" I asked.

Mrs. Robertson watched me scale the three steps to the deck before turning her massive body and hobbling through the sliding door into the living room. She waited until I passed through, then closed the glass panel in the dogs' faces to keep them outside.

"She's just not been herself the last two days," she huffed between breaths. "She barely picked at supper last night and wouldn't eat a thing this morning."

"Has she done anything that would contribute to her acting strangely? Run around more than normal, gotten into compost, coffee grounds, or wild mushrooms?"

She shook her head, pointed to the big black mound stretched out on a cushion in the middle of the living room carpet, and sank into a big felt recliner. "She's never out of my sight, and we've hardly been out of the house this week except to tend to the flowers. This sudden change in temperature has gotten both of us down." Mrs. Robertson removed a hanky from her sleeve and patted her brow. "We're not designed for the heat."

"What's her stool been like? Has she had diarrhea or been constipated?"

"She certainly hasn't had diarrhea…I don't think she's moved from her cushion since this time yesterday…and she'd never mess in the house."

I knelt next to my lethargic patient and rested my hand on her black, bristly side—she felt overly warm. I turned my head away from my client, and spat on my hand. Rotating a thermometer in the spittle, I grabbed hold of Rosie's tail and gently inserted the glass cylinder. She grunted and raised her upturned snout from the pillow to get a better look at me.

"That's the most activity I've seen from her all day," Mrs. Robertson said woefully.

I ran my hand over the rotund pig's bristly side as the thermometer was cooking, and spent more time investigating the sow's upper thigh and brisket.

"What are you checking for?"

"She's got thickenings of the skin in a number of places. See here..." I traced a rhomboid lesion with the tips of my fingers. "It looks darker in colour, too, and has a purple hue."

Mrs. Robertson struggled to lean her heavy body forward. "Yes, now that you point it out, I can see it...that's certainly not her normal colour."

I withdrew the thermometer and rotated it in the light to read it. "No wonder she's not up dancing a jig...41.7."

I slipped the tips of the stethoscope into my ears and slid the head of the instrument along Rosie's side. There was a definite increase in lung sounds; her heart rate was elevated.

"What do you think's wrong with her?" my client asked apprehensively.

"I suspect she has erysipelas...the high temperature and the diamond-shape skin lesions are characteristic of the disease."

"How could she get such a thing? She's never around other pigs."

"Erysipelas tends to be a soil-borne organism that becomes endemic where pigs are raised. Hogs are the main animals affected, but it can infect birds and be transmitted by them as well." I hesitated a moment, then added, "It can produce disease in humans, too."

"Is there a treatment?" Mrs. Robertson's voice was trembling.

"The organism that causes it is very susceptible to penicillin. Most animals respond quite quickly, but occasionally we can see a chronic form of the disease, where there's involvement of the joints and the valves of the heart."

I shifted position and palpated the pig's limbs, flexing them and pressing on the joints. Rosie gave a shrill squeal when I flexed her elbow, and with a concerted effort, she struggled to her feet. Standing on the very tips of her toes, she took a stiff step forward and shifted from one leg to the other, as if bearing weight on any of them was painful to her.

"Oh, Rosie...I don't want to lose you, too." Tears pooled in the woman's eyes as she watched her pet standing like a statue with every muscle in her body trembling.

"I'll get the medication ready."

I went back to the truck and drew up twelve millilitres of penicillin in a syringe. When I returned, the pig had hardly moved.

"Do you think you could hold her, Mrs. Robertson?"

If this were a commercial animal, I'd have worked either a rope or a chain into her mouth so it looped her upper jaw. The pig would have predictably pulled back against the tether and squealed until it was released. In the meantime, I'd have been able to administer the injection.

"How do you want me to hold her?" the woman asked tentatively. She levered her weight onto the arm of the chair, then launched herself to her feet.

"I'm going to have to give her a shot in either the neck or the butt, so you'll have to keep her steady enough for me to pop the needle in and inject the medicine."

"Well, I'll try," she said resolutely.

Bending over at the waist, Mrs. Robertson positioned one stout leg on one side of Rosalie's neck, and one on the other. I was poised to drive the needle into the animal's well-rounded ham when she suddenly backed up, and her owner stumbled awkwardly towards me. I braced myself as the large woman crashed into me, grabbed hold of my arm for support, and hoisted herself erect.

"That didn't go well," she said with a hint of frivolity.

I chuckled, thankful that I hadn't administered the injection in the wrong well-rounded ham. We stood by the sliding glass doors and watched as Rosie tottered shakily around the living room.

"What do you suggest now?" her owner asked.

"Well, if this were a piggery, we'd run her down a chute or trap her with a plywood moving board until we could give her the shot…How about if we pull the sofa out from the wall on this end, and see if we can get her to go into the V. Maybe you can hold her in there long enough for me to give her the injection."

While Mrs. Robertson scratched Rosalie's back, I pulled the patent leather sofa away from the wall.

"Okay, I think we're ready."

The moment I walked in front of the pig, the animal turned and shuffled to the farthest corner of the living room.

"Just stand a little bit out from the sofa," I suggested.

As the pig made her way along the wall, my client followed in after her. I had my syringe at the ready, but could see nothing except the woman's corpulent posterior as she bent forward holding her pet in place. I tried to stretch around the side, but couldn't begin to reach my target. Kneeling behind my hefty assistant, I peered into the space between her huge legs at the pig's derrière. I kept telling myself that I could get the job done, but lacked the courage to proceed.

"Can you get her?" Mrs. Robertson gasped.

"Just a second."

Taking my shoes off, I stood on the seat of the sofa and hung over the back with my butt in the air. Mrs. Robertson and I were head to head when I plunged the needle into Rosie's neck and injected the penicillin.

"That's it!" I exclaimed. "You can let her go."

I went to the car to count out the pills for Rosalie's continued treatment. When I returned with the medication, the pig was once again stretched out on her pillow. She lifted her head slightly and followed me with her eyes as I walked into the room. My client had returned to her refuge in the recliner and tipped it forward to grasp the medication.

"Give her one pill with her food twice a day."

"Thank you so much, Dr. Perrin...I hope this gets everything back to normal around here."

"So do I, Mrs. Robertson...so do I."

As I headed for the door, she leaned back and lifted her over-sized legs.

"Dr. Perrin, please let Alex and Frederica in on your way out."

After the day I'd had I wanted to head home to the farm and collapse in a heap, but if I did that, Doris would never forgive me. She was determined that things would be ready for her big do tomorrow.

Now that half the town was invited, I could admit we'd look pretty slack not presenting our new facility at its best.

It had been so long since I had spent any time working on the house that I was feeling guilty about letting things slide. This was my weekend off and right at the moment mixing concrete and placing stones sounded far more attractive than moving kennels and hefting washing machines and dryers.

When I got back to the clinic, I was delighted to see that Margaret and Jim had been busy in my absence. Jim had gotten back shortly after I had left, and the two of them had already moved the washing machine to its new spot; Jim was busy with its installation. While he was connecting hoses and levelling it, Margaret and I wheeled the dolly back down the street and strapped up the dryer.

It was after midnight by the time we got the kennels wheeled over and the record cabinet in place. Although we had called a time out for Chinese food at the Club Café, everyone was exhausted. Doris and Margaret were to meet again at six in the morning. They were determined to have spotless floors and everything situated when the first client stepped through the doors.

As tired as I was, my mind was trying to play catch-up, and it took me forever to get to sleep. Because Jim was on call this weekend, and the open house wasn't slated to start until eleven, I decided to sleep in as long as possible.

At quarter after five the next morning the telephone rang. I pushed Lug off the bed so I could get out from under the sheets, and stumbled towards the phone.

"Hello," I croaked.

"Dave, it's John Gilmour."

"Good morning, John. Is there a problem?"

"I want you out here to look at this damned cow."

"How about I stop by at ten on my way to the office?"

I had run into John when leaving the Depot Restaurant a few days ago. When I asked about the cow, he said she had healed up beautifully. At the time, I had watched his face for some sign he had found out what had taken place on my last trip out there. If he knew, he gave me no indication. He had asked at the time if I could come out soon and remove the stitches because Gert was due any day, and he didn't want them bothering her during milking.

There was a moment of silence on the phone before John spoke. When he did, his tone left no room for question. "I want you to look at her *now*!"

"Okay, I'll be out there in a few minutes."

John was waiting patiently by the barbed-wire fence when I pulled up. I got out and pushed Lug back into the truck when he tried to follow. John never uttered a word, but started to the barn the moment I stepped over the fence. He stopped in front of the door and peered into the pen. I maneuvered past him to get a view of the cow.

I couldn't believe my eyes. Gert was busy licking away at her calf in the corner of the stall. Her baby was the spitting image of her, except it was red and white.

"My God, I don't believe it."

John gave me a steely stare. Turning back to Gert, he pointed to her right hind teat and said, "No, look at that!"

I felt the blood drain from my face when I saw the udder. Was this my dream or a nightmare? Gert had somehow stepped on her right hind teat and torn it right off. Not a stitch remained. Milk dripped steadily from the crater onto the straw at her feet.

Chapter 15

A Hitch in the Gitalong

"It's Eleanor Blair, Dave." Doris held her hand over the mouthpiece of the phone. "It sounds like she needs you out there again."

I had finished neutering Goliath, a three-year-old St. Bernard, and Margaret and I were about to move him to the recovery kennel.

"Have her hold for a moment, Doris."

Looking to Margaret, I wrapped my arms around the dog's massive torso. "Just manage his head while I lift him down." I hefted the bulky creature and took a shaky step backwards. While Margaret cradled the dog's head, I struggled to my knees and began sliding the animal's back end into the kennel.

"I'm glad I'm not paying his grub bill," Margaret grunted as we positioned him on a blanket and pushed him the rest of the way in. She stood beside the kennel watching our patient as I rushed to the phone.

"Hi, Eleanor...how are things?"

"It's Wee Jordie again..."

"He's locked up?"

There was a long pause, and I could picture my friend taking a prolonged drag on her cigarette.

"Yes," she finally went on in her hoarse voice. "I haven't been able to get him to move since yesterday, and I've been carrying hay and water to him." She hesitated again. "I hate seeing him like this. Can you make it out here sometime today to work your magic? I don't know how you do it, but you always seem to be able to get him moving."

Upward fixation of the patella can be a perplexing problem for horse owners. The equine stifle differs from those of most other species in that it has three patellar tendons instead of one. That difference, when the mechanism works as it's supposed to, allows the horse to sleep standing up. When a horse happens to be excessively post-legged with less than normal flexion in its hocks and stifles, it can develop a tendency for the stifle to lock in extension.

This was the case with Wee Jordie. Most other cases I'd seen had been far less obvious and more difficult to diagnose; they exhibited more of a 'hitch in the animal's gitalong'—a slight hesitation in the way it brought its hind leg forward. Jordie was different. When he locked up, he was planted for extended periods.

He had presented in this paralyzed state a half dozen times over the past few years. Each time, I had resolved the situation in the same crude manner—a hard whack across his hindquarters with a freshly picked switch. As cruel as this sounds, it was the only way I had been able to get him to contract his quadriceps muscles rapidly enough to release the patellar locking mechanism. The trick to successful resolution of one of these events was getting Eleanor out of my hair long enough to perform the task. She was such a pacifist that I was sure she'd allow him to stand like a bronzed statue for weeks rather than allow me to hit him.

I was on my way out the door to Eleanor's when Lynn Schiavon pulled up in front of the clinic. I waved at her and opened the truck door for Lug to hop in. I had just stuck the key in the ignition when she came running over.

"This is it!" she cried. "You have to put him down."

"What's the matter, Lynn?" She was distraught, and by the look of her eyes, she had cried most of the way to town.

"It's broken open again…there must be something terribly wrong with him."

"Again? That's impossible." I had left Archie's sutures for almost a month before digging through the regrown hair to pluck them out. I had been absolutely convinced that the wound had healed.

"I'm going to just leave him with you," she blurted tearfully. "I can't deal with burying him now."

I got out of the truck and followed Lynn to her car. Damn… why was this cat tormenting me? Just the thought of euthanizing him now after all this effort seemed such a travesty. Lynn handed me the travelling carrier, looked at the box, and burst into tears.

"Take him." She climbed into her car, backed out of the parking lot, and drove away.

It was after two in the afternoon by the time I crossed the meridian of the highway and pulled up in front of Eleanor's gate. All the way out to Canyon, I worried about what to do with Archie. Rather than carry out Lynn's wishes, I had stuffed him into a kennel with the notion that I'd decide his fate on my return.

It wasn't as if I had grown fond of the cat—Archie was one of the most obnoxious patients I had ever dealt with. And Gerry was right. The kids would be much happier with a kitten that they could actually play with. But that wasn't the point. Putting him down now would be admitting defeat…surely, I could find some way of gluing that wound together.

I opened the truck door and squeezed out, being careful to keep Lug inside. I struggled for several minutes to get through Eleanor's front gate. The top hinges had rusted away, and it was necessary to hold the gate up, then wrestle with a chain that hooked on a nail of the opposite gate. The moment it let go, the top of the log structure dropped precipitously in the direction of the truck. I grabbed hold of it to keep it from falling flat on the ground, stepped through the crack, and tugged it upright again. After securing it in position with the chain, I went in search of Eleanor.

The first thing I always checked when approaching the old clapboard house that my friend called home was the front door. The entry to the dilapidated building had long since been distorted by the sinking of the underlying support beams. As a result, the door no longer latched but was secured with a butter knife in the jamb when Nell was inside, or a couple of wraps of twine around a nail when she was outside. The twine was wrapped around the nail, so my client had to be somewhere outside. Walking past the rickety veranda, I headed to the broken-down shed where Eleanor housed her stallion.

"Hello, Eleanor! Are you around?"

"Over here!" she hollered in her raspy voice.

I made my way to an old lean-to farther back in the yard where my friend was doling out hay to her ancient steeds. O'Brian, the old gelding, was nothing more than a rack of bones. I thought he was on death's door several years ago when I treated him for an impacted caecum, but somehow Eleanor kept willing him to live on. She constantly referred to him as the horse that couldn't be ridden; according to her, she had saved him from being put down after he'd killed a rider at some small-town rodeo. It was a point of pride for her to affirm that no one had ever gone the distance when riding him.

Honey, the dun quarter horse mare, had been Eleanor's personal mount. Although she had missed riding in the Blossom Festival parade this year, she and Honey had been adding flavour to the May event for decades. Even up to a few years ago, they had been an impressive sight—Honey groomed and decked out with side-saddle, and Eleanor all gussied-up in her English riding habit.

"I don't know what to do with him anymore, Dave."

Eleanor sounded tired. I hadn't seen her in weeks, and I was surprised how gaunt and pale she looked; she was becoming as decrepit as her equine companions. I often wondered how the poor woman kept body and soul together. Other than a few heels of bread that she stashed in a metal box out of reach of the cats, I couldn't recall seeing any human sustenance in the house. Her main concerns were keeping hay in front of her horses and food in the bowls of her feline dependents. I had never seen anything resembling a fruit or vegetable in her room; she had no refrigerator and no means of keeping things fresh. Two items were absolute staples for Eleanor—Red Rose tea and Player's Light cigarettes.

"He's been standing like a statue all day," she said. "I've lifted his hay and water up on top of an old washtub so he can reach it, but he can't keep going like this."

"Have you given him a hot bran mash yet today?"

Eleanor squinted as the cigarette in her mouth smouldered, and the smoke encircled her face. She shook her head. "No, but I was considering it."

We walked side by side to the paddock where Wee Jordie was penned. The horse was standing in a most unnatural stance with both hind legs extended well back beyond the axis of the hips. When he turned his head to check us out, his right rear fetlock knuckled and he struggled to drag his toe forward.

Several years back, when Eleanor first noticed a minor lameness, I could only pick up the occasional catch on his right hind leg. At that time, the other leg never bothered him at all.

"I still think we should geld him, Nell, so you can get him out of this little corral and let him run with Honey and O'Brian. He needs more exercise."

Eleanor glowered at me but said nothing in reply. Pulling a slightly crumpled packet of Player's Light from her pocket, she flipped it open and grabbed another cancer stick. Lighting it from the stub of her dying butt, she closed her eyes and took a deep drag.

"I think, Dr. Perrin," she said in a deadpan fashion, "it's time for you to brush up on your anatomy...his patellas are a long way from his testicles."

I sighed. We had had this argument many times before. In my mind, not gelding this horse was a major contributing factor to his lameness. By law, a stallion was not allowed to run at large. Because Eleanor didn't have the wherewithal to build a proper enclosure, he was confined to this twenty-by-twenty space where he couldn't begin to get the exercise he needed to stay healthy.

"The conformation that leads to this condition is definitely heritable, Eleanor. Why would you want to breed Jordie and put his offspring through the same thing?"

"It's only gotten really bad in the last year," she said defensively.

"And that's when I started mentioning the physiotherapy. Remember we talked about taking him up on the hill at the back of your place and walking him up and down the incline to help stretch out the ligaments?"

Eleanor focused on the tip of her cigarette, giving no indication that she had even heard my question.

"You mentioned the possibility of surgery," she finally said.

I nodded. "There is a surgical correction, but I've never done it…"

She gave me a knowing look and a sarcastic smile. "Why would you let that stop you? When you first got here, you had hardly touched a scalpel, and how many different surgeries have you done since then?"

Eleanor knew my deficiencies more than most people. I had frequently confided in her about how apprehensive I got when tackling new procedures with my textbook open on the surgery table next to me.

"There are downsides to the procedure…" I justified. "If we sever the medial ligament, the unequal pressures applied by the other two ligaments could make him more susceptible to patellar fracture…besides that, he'll never be able to sleep standing up."

"I can't sleep standing up, either," she said. "And I seem to be able to make do."

Eleanor took another deep drag on her cigarette and stared at her horse thoughtfully. She watched as I cautiously checked the split-cedar corral rails in preparation for scaling them. This enclosure was a long way from what I considered necessary to enclose a stallion—if Jordie were halfway sound and chose to challenge the fence, it wouldn't begin to hold him. The top slab seemed firm enough; the middle two were bound with only plastic twine. I carefully stepped onto the bottom rail, tested it a few times, then swung my long leg over the top one.

I dropped to the ground next to the slight black stallion and dragged the rusting galvanized tub that Eleanor was using as a feeder towards the fence. A reference I had read suggested mechanical manipulation of the patella in the hope of releasing it. I pressed downward on the bony structure as hard as I could without effect—like every other time, the medial ligament felt so taut that it may as well have been part of the bone. Working my way to his front shoulder I tapped him repeatedly in an attempt to make him take a step backwards.

"I've read that getting a locked horse to back up is the most effective way to relieve the problem," I explained to Eleanor, who attentively watched the goings-on from her post outside the rails.

In an attempt to startle the horse, I gave him a sharp slap on his chest with the flat of my hand. He tossed his head, and although his left fetlock knuckled, the upper portions of his legs remained planted as if splinted in place.

Eleanor's eyes smouldered as she butted her half-smoked cigarette on the side of a fence post and turned towards the house. "I'll make up the mash," she said abruptly.

She must have been really annoyed to extinguish a cigarette before she had sucked all the smoke out of it. Her sulky look told me she wasn't happy with my treatment of her horse. In the six years I had been around her, I had yet to see the woman lift her hand against a single critter.

I watched until she was out of sight, then climbed the fence and broke off a branch from a clump of willows. Standing to one side, I brought the switch down with a sharp crack across Wee Jordie's rump. The horse crow-hopped, lunged forward, and walked away from me, dragging the toe of his right hind leg. I followed to keep him moving. Although he was now able to move the legs enough to walk, the patella would catch on every second or third step and cause the toe of the right hind foot to drag. Not being able to plant his foot effectively led him to stumble erratically. By the time we had completed several trips around the paddock, the dragging of his toe became less pronounced and his movements more fluid.

I threw the willow over the fence onto the neighbour's property and sidled up to Jordie, intent on ruffling the hair on his hindquarters and removing the incriminating line of dust that so perfectly outlined the force of impact from the switch. Every time I approached the determined animal, he accelerated his pace to stay beyond my reach. With each pass around the corral, his toe dragged less and less, and his movement became freer.

I moved to the corner of the corral and looked in vain for some sort of rope or twine to catch the horse. Eleanor had been in the house for some time now, and any moment she'd be returning with the hot bran mash. I knew she'd instantly pick up on the clearly defined switch mark. I had felt my friend's wrath on several other occasions when she disagreed with my handling of her animals, and the last thing I wanted today was conflict.

I had a touch of panic when she emerged from the house, but I waited until she was halfway back before hollering to her. "Can you bring the halter and lead shank?"

She stopped and watched as Jordie and I made yet another round about the paddock. With a big smile, she set the mash on the ground and returned to the house. In desperation, I moved the washtub and balanced a broken rail from the tub to the top rail of the fence. Waving my arms, I chased Jordie between it and the fence to trap him in the corner. He quivered as I patted my hand along the line of impact. I was still rubbing his back end when Eleanor arrived.

"You worked your magic once again, Dr. Perrin," she said enthusiastically. "Is that your secret? I've never tried massaging up there before…I've always focused my efforts on his stifles and hocks." She shook her head in admiration. "I guess that's the difference between a layman and a professional."

She passed me the halter and lead shank, then wrinkled her brow and asked, "Why didn't you ever suggest massaging his hips before?"

Lug got excited as I drove through Canyon on my way to Lister. When I kept going onto 28th Street instead of turning onto Canyon-Lister Road towards home, he whined and continued to stare out my side window in the direction of home.

"Sorry, boy, but we're not done yet."

By the time we reached Lister Road and turned west onto 24th, he had flopped onto the seat and plunked his chin on his feet. It was almost four when I turned off Highway 21 and onto the gravelled road to the Creston dump. I made my way past the general dumping location and pulled up next to a red white-faced cow that was lying on her back with her feet in the air.

Gene Vogel from Wynndel had recently purchased three cows at the Pincher Creek auction sale in Alberta to help keep down the grass on his twenty-acre holding. He had returned from a few days camping on Kootenay Lake to find one of his newly acquired assets lying dead by the water trough. He called this morning wanting me to look at her; he wanted to rule out that she had died from something that could be contagious to his other two animals. I made arrangements for him to leave the critter at the dump where she could be properly buried after I was finished performing a post-mortem.

Even though the heat was stifling inside the pickup, I wound up my windows and closed the side flaps. Lug would have to bear a few minutes of discomfort. The windshield was already covered with hundreds of flies, and I didn't want to let any more of them in than I could help.

As I was opening the back of the canopy to get my knife and gloves, a John Deere loader rumbled past in a cloud of dust. The side panel was open, and the balding operator smiled and gave me a big wave. Harold had been managing the landfill since it had been moved here from the far corner of Lister. He was a real character with a gritty personality, and I had gotten to know him well over the past few years. Harold knew everything that went on at this facility, and rarely missed an article of value that was being discarded by one of his patrons. This was his playground, and I was sure he made more money from peddling items he recovered from the trash than he did driving the loader. I often wondered if his sense of smell had been completely eroded, because on days like today the stench was almost overwhelming.

Lug peered out the window watching me as I pulled on shoulder-length plastic palpation sleeves and covered them with rubber gloves. I sharpened my post-mortem knife with a steel, grabbed my axe, and stuffed a few empty sleeves in my pocket before approaching the cow.

She was moderately bloated, but that wasn't surprising after being several hours in the sun. I ran my hand over the body looking for the crackling that could indicate gas being produced by organisms under the skin. There was none, but the ribs seemed more prominent than I would have anticipated—this hadn't been a fat cow before her death.

I waved my hand around her face to temporarily clear the area of flies, and opened her mouth. Although the mucosa was already covered with fly eggs, there were no lesions on her lips, gums, or tongue. I moved to her back end. Her tailhead was clean—she didn't have diarrhea. I lifted her tail and inspected the rectum... there were a few hard chunks of fecal material that were reminiscent of horse turds. The poor girl hadn't been eating well for several days before her demise.

I grabbed the left front leg, plunged the knife into her axilla, and carved at the skin while lifting upwards. Before long, the cow's leg was pointing to the pit that lay at her back, and her entire rib cage was exposed. I ran my hand over the pre-scapular lymph nodes to check for enlargement, then examined the subcutaneous tissues for evidence of pre-mortem bruising. There was nothing abnormal.

I shifted to the cow's back end, grabbed her left hind leg, and lifted it onto my shoulder. Driving the knife into her groin, I cut through the skin and muscle, all the while lifting the leg higher and higher. When my knife reached the level of the hip joint, I severed the joint capsule and the ligament holding the head of the femur in the socket. With a final heave, I cut the remaining musculature so that the hind leg was also pointing upward parallel to the front one. I slashed through the muscle looking for abnormalities in colour and texture, but other than there being a relative absence of fat, there was nothing to note.

I cut down the cow's midline, then severed the muscles along the last rib, lifting the musculature from the cow's side to expose her abdominal contents. I cut through the gristly material at the costochondral junction where the ribs tied into the sternum, separated each rib one at a time, and heaved upward to break it as close to the spine as possible.

I had most of the animal's chest exposed when the loader pulled up beside me. I peered through a cloud of dust as Harold hopped down from the idling machine. He was used to seeing me carve open carcasses in order to determine a cause of death and had a keen interest in what I found.

"Hey there, Doc...how's it going?"

"Pretty good...can't think of a place I'd rather be right now!" I hollered in order to be heard over the rumbling of the loader engine. I waved my hand at some particularly annoying flies that insisted on landing on my face.

"What ya findin' with this one?"

"Getting down to the nitty-gritty now," I grunted, heaving up on one of the last ribs. It broke with a resounding crack and further exposed the contents of the chest cavity.

"You vets are just like dogs on a gut wagon." He laughed. "Even the bears we see out here tear apart a body with more finesse than you guys."

I smiled as he moved in closer and stood looking over my shoulder. I plunged my knife into the hugely bloated rumen, and backed up as gas whistled through the gaping hole.

"You're sure a glutton for punishment," Harold said, raising his arm to his nose. "Don't you think it's ripe enough around here as it is?" He waved to the bottom of the pit where legs of other animals protruded from a scant covering of dirt.

"Didn't think that after all this time you even had a sense of smell."

He chuckled as I worked my hand between the second chamber of the cow's stomach and body wall, and peeled away its attachment.

"She doesn't have much grub in her, does she?"

"She doesn't." Harold was right—now that the pent-up gas had been released, the organ was virtually devoid of content. The rumen of a healthy, full-grown cow like this one should have contained close to forty gallons of water and ingested food.

I continued rolling the rumen forward until it was free of the body except for its attachment to the reticulum and omasum, the cow's second and third stomachs. It was when I gave an additional tug to separate the reticulum from the diaphragm that the diagnosis became obvious. A gallon of fetid-looking material gushed from beneath the organ.

"That doesn't look good," Harold stated in a deadpan fashion.

"No, it doesn't."

"What is it?"

"Pus…this cow died from hardware."

"Hardware?" He looked confused. "What do you mean, hardware?"

"It's a slang term for traumatic reticulo-peritonitis."

Harold rolled his eyes. "I can see why you call it hardware…but what does it mean?"

"It means this cow inadvertently swallowed a piece of metal that punctured the wall of the pouch called the reticulum. When stomach contents leaked through, it caused an infection between that part of the stomach and the body wall."

I reefed on the reticulum to further separate the organ from the body cavity, then ran my hand to a cylindrical tract running forward through the diaphragm. I sliced it open and showed my enthusiastic student a dark, inflamed circle where a foreign body had exited.

"It just looks like a hole," Harold said.

"Unless I miss my guess, we'll find something lodged in her heart."

"The heart…isn't that a long way for anything to travel?"

"Not in the cow. When I do surgery for removing a wire or nail, it's the neatest thing…you cut a hole in her stomach and reach down to search for it. When you get down here," I said, indicating the honeycombed structures of the reticular endothelium, "you can feel the heart beating right under your fingertips."

Harold shook his head in awe as he watched me continue my dissection. I cut off the trachea just before it entered the chest, then gave a few good tugs to free it to the level of the diaphragm. Cutting the diaphragm from the body wall, I lifted the lungs and heart from the cow.

"Is that normal?" Harold asked, staring at the massive globular structure where the heart should have been.

"No," I replied. I sliced through the thick sack that was the pericardium, and backed up as half a gallon of rank-smelling fluid poured to the ground.

I ran my hand along the inside of the pericardium to the area that was closest to the reticulum. A thick mass of scar tissue adhered the pericardium to the heart. When I cut into it, my knife grated on something metallic. Turning my blade parallel to the foreign object, I pared away until I spotted a pointy end. I gave it a tug, and when it didn't pull free, cut along it, well into the muscle of the heart.

"Voila!" I pulled forth a three-inch wire and held it up for Harold to examine.

"Who'd believe it?" he asked in amazement. "Why in the world would a cow swallow something like that?"

"This was once a piece of barbed wire...by the look of these sharp ends, whoever put up this cow's feed must have swathed too close to the fence, then pounded it into a bale. Cows are amazingly unselective about what they eat—she probably wolfed it down with a big mouthful of hay."

"Could you have saved this cow by doin' surgery?"

"Early on, when it was still in the reticulum," I surmised. "I'd have thrown a magnet into her first, though."

"A magnet?"

"Yeah," I said. "If we had gotten a magnet into the reticulum early enough, it would have had a good chance of grabbing hold of the wire and pulling it back into the stomach where it wouldn't have caused any trouble."

"How in the world would you get it in there?" Harold asked.

"They're made so we can pop them in with a balling gun. Once you get it over the big lump on a cow's tongue it's a done deal. The movement of the cow's stomach will keep it there where all the other garbage she eats is likely to collect."

"That's what I like about this job. There's not a day goes by that I don't learn something new." Harold snorted. "Well, we'll catch you later."

With that, he climbed onto his loader and dropped onto the seat. I carefully tucked the piece of wire into one of my rubber gloves to show Mr. Vogel and tossed the remaining gloves into the pit. I was about to hop in the truck when Harold hollered down from his machine.

"Be careful when you're backin' up, Doc!"

I looked behind my truck. "What do you mean?"

"You vets are about as wild at drivin' as you are at hackin' up critters…it got that pretty little thing you had working for you a couple months back into trouble. She came out here to cut up an old sow for someone, and when she went to leave, she backed right up on top of the pig pieces. She was pretty humble when she come over t' the shack askin' me for help."

Harold revved the loader and roared off. I chuckled at the thought of Trudy being high-centred on the corpse of a pig. I'd have to give her a rough time about it, when I saw her at the next convention.

It was after five-thirty when I got back to the office. Jim and Margaret had already left, but Doris was still sitting at her desk justifying the cash for the day.

"How'd it go?" she asked.

"About as good as it gets when you spend your afternoon at the dump."

"Did you get things straightened out for Eleanor?"

"Sort of…Jordie's walking again."

"That's good." Doris closed the big black day book, and leaned back in her chair. "I'd love to go home and put my feet up, but we have to bowl a makeup game tonight. I…" The telephone cut her off.

"Ye gods, what now?" she groaned and picked up the receiver. "Creston Veterin…"

I closed my eyes and waited for the other shoe to drop as she stopped halfway through her standard spiel. When someone was in that much of a hurry to spill out what they had to say, they were most likely in a state of panic.

The tension built as Doris answered, "Yes, Agnes, yes…one moment."

She covered the phone with her hand and gave me a forlorn look. "It's Agnes Spy," she finally said.

"Oh no." My heart sank at her words.

If there was one client I could magically remove from both my records and accounts receivable list, it would be Agnes Spy. I'm sure almost every business has a client like her—a person who is so annoying that everyone in the office dredges up an immediate excuse in order to avoid dealing with her.

I hadn't heard a peep out of Agnes since her confrontation with the SPCA, and had sort of hoped I'd heard the last of her. She'd been furious with me when I refused to come to her defence after a neighbour complained that she wasn't looking after her animals properly. She'd come to me certain that I'd pen a letter telling the inspector she was a great caretaker. It was hard to say no to her, but they were right—she had far more animals than she could possibly take care of. I knew if I were a critter I'd want to live as far away from the woman's place as I possibly could.

Doris sat with her hand over the phone for well over a minute while I fumed. I looked at my watch. Why couldn't the bloody woman have called during office hours when Jim was able to deal with her? Finally, I held out my hand and took the receiver from Doris with as much trepidation as if she had handed me a live hand grenade.

"Hello."

"Oh, Dr. Perrin, it's awful…just awful!" Mrs. Spy's coil spring was wound to the max once again.

"What is it, Agnes?"

"The coyotes got one of my triplets!" she shrieked. "Oh, why, why, why does it always happen to me?" She broke down and sobbed noisily on the other end of the phone.

"Is it one of your goats, Agnes?" I carried on, hoping to settle her down.

"Yes, it's Jessica!" she sniffled. "One of Heidi's babies."

"Is it still alive?"

"Yes…James tied a piece of twine around the top of her leg to stop the bleeding."

That made sense…James, Agnes's teenage son, was the only Spy with a lick of common sense. On several occasions I had wondered if he had been adopted into that crazy family.

"There was blood all over, Dr. Perrin…those damned coyotes. If it hadn't been for my dogs running them off, it would have been the end of her."

"Can you bring Jessica in, Agnes?"

"No…" Mrs. Spy's wailing increased in intensity. "The transmission on my Chevy packed it in, and my husband is away with the truck. Can you please come out and fix her up, Dr. Perrin? Crystal and I are here to help with whatever you need."

My chest tightened and I stopped breathing for a moment before I could reply. There was absolutely no way I could handle dealing with Agnes's daughter, Crystal—that demon-woman was something else. The first time I met her, I took her to be a child of eleven or twelve. Closer examination revealed that although she was tiny, barely four feet in height, she was, in fact, in her mid-twenties. In her formative years, she had been stricken with a skeletal deformity that left her stunted with hunched shoulders and stooped spine.

It was when she opened her mouth that I realized Crystal was not the sweet, innocent creature she first appeared to be, and it was immediately obvious that the agility of her tongue had in no way been impaired by her physical problems. The way she attacked me from the moment we met made me certain that she was resentful of my height. She had taken an instant dislike to me, and within minutes of our first encounter I couldn't wait to put distance between us.

"Just a second, Agnes..." I covered the phone and looked to Doris. "Is there any way you can stay late tonight? They have a goat kid that's been chewed up by a coyote."

"The girls will kill me if I miss this game," Doris whined.

"And I may kill myself if I have to work with those two. Agnes says Crystal's there. There's no way I can spend a couple of hours out at their place."

Doris closed her eyes and shook her head. She knew how I felt about Agnes, and she shared my opinion of Crystal.

"Please, please, please," I begged.

"Okay, but you better get a move on...I have to be out of here and at the bowling alley by eight."

I quickly threw on coveralls. Lug was on my heels as I reached the exit, but I pushed him back and gently closed the door in his face—there was a good likelihood that I'd be bringing the kid back with me in the front seat, and I didn't need him there to complicate the matter. I jogged to the truck, tore out of the parking lot, and headed towards Erickson.

By the time I turned off the highway and drove up the dirt side road that led to the Spys, I was already uptight. There was something about dealing with the women in this family that stripped me of my confidence and left me wanting to run and hide. Although there were similarities between Agnes and Eleanor in the way they collected critters, there was a big difference in how I viewed them. When I dealt with Eleanor, I always left wishing I could help her out more. When I was done with Agnes, I left scheming for a way to never see her again...and then there was Crystal.

The Spys lived in an older home at the bottom of a wide gully beneath a cluster of newer homes that had been built on the ridges above them. From the number of calls I got from the owners of those homes, and the SPCA, I knew there was constant conflict between the Spys and their neighbours. It was obvious many of the new folks were unhappy that the view from their living room windows was of Agnes's property. The fact that the Spys' fences were not maintained also meant a constant flow of animals marauding through adjacent lawns and gardens.

I stopped at a sagging four-strand barbed-wire gate, got out of the truck, and removed the wire loop that held the barrier upright. Dragging the three-posted structure to the side of the road, I drove through. I hadn't gone more than fifty feet up the driveway before my vehicle was surrounded by a pack of barking dogs. Although a few of the bigger animals had the sense to run to the side, a half dozen shaggy mutts of poodle ancestry milled just a few feet from the front of the truck. I took a deep breath, leaned forward as close to the windshield as possible to avoid hitting them, and slowed to a crawl.

Near the house I could see the Spys congregated in a circle in their backyard next to an aging Ford pickup. Although the grass in their lawn had never seen a mechanical mower, it had been cropped within a few millimetres of the earth by constant attention from the horses and goats. The moment I stepped out of the truck, I was almost overwhelmed by the dogs. The smaller ones continued yapping, stopping only for periods brief enough for them to quickly dart in and sniff at my legs and shoes.

"That's enough!" screeched Mrs. Spy. Launching herself to her feet, she raked dangling strands of greying hair from her face and stomped towards me. Stopping halfway between us, she planted her feet, tensed her body, and screamed at her dogs, "Enough! Enough! Enough!"

As she carried on, a bigger dog that had evidence of Airedale and German shepherd ancestry, pushed forward and rooted my hand for attention. The curly, coarse hair on his jowls and chest were crusted with dried blood. I glanced from him to Agnes.

"He was the one who took on the coyotes," she declared.

When I gave her a look of incredulity, she dramatically thrust an arm to her face to wipe at her eyes. "I just can't take any more of this!" she wailed. "It's as if God's picking on me…why, why, why are these things always happening to me?"

Without heeding the woman's rhetorical question, I continued past her towards the rest of the family. Her husband, Lyle, who I thought was off somewhere with the truck, was stretched out on the hard-packed ground with his eyes closed, seemingly oblivious to the goings on. James and Crystal were holding my patient.

"So, what's happened to her?"

"Duh…" Crystal said sarcastically. "Can't you see?"

She removed a blood-stained blanket from the front half of the tiny, grey pygmy goat to reveal a limb that dangled precariously from the upper foreleg by shards of skin and muscle.

I spoke to Agnes, who was still sniffling. "That's definitely going to mean an amputation."

She closed her eyes and stamped her feet like a spoiled child who had been refused a candy bar. I closed my eyes, wishing I could be anywhere else in the universe but the backyard at the Spy enclave.

"Will she be able to survive with only three legs?" asked James, with real concern in his voice.

"She'll do fine so long as she hasn't lost too much blood," I assured him. Silence reigned for almost a minute.

"Will you do it here?" his mother finally asked.

I shook my head. "Doris is waiting for me at the office."

"It'll be cheaper if he does it here with my help, Mom," Crystal crabbed.

"Believe me, Agnes, it won't," I replied quietly. "Doris has everything ready to go at the clinic. She's already stayed late in anticipation of my coming back, and with her help, the job will go much quicker."

I knelt on the hard-packed ground to examine the poor creature. Crystal glowered as I ran my hands over the kid's body checking for other injuries.

"It looks like he just got hold of one leg and held on," I observed.

"They were all around her," Crystal insisted indignantly.

"Then only one did any damage," I replied.

The kid gave a frightened blat and struggled briefly when I rolled up her lip to examine its mucous membranes.

"She's a bit shocky," I mused. "But I think she'll be up for the surgery."

I wrapped the blanket around the young goat again, then lifted her into my arms. Crystal glared at me as I carried the trembling creature to the truck.

Agnes followed me and opened the passenger door. "I'm sure I must be one of your best clients, Dr. Perrin," she said as I settled the kid on the floor of the truck.

"You'd be surprised, Agnes," I said without a hint of emotion. "You'd really be surprised."

Chapter 16

Temperature Rising

"I tell you, Doc, that ejaculator's a piece of junk!"

Jim furrowed his brow and took a sip of his coffee. "What do I tell the poor guy about his bull? The animal's testicles measured up, and he looked physically sound, but I couldn't get a sample. It's possible the critter's shooting blanks, but I think it's more likely that archaic machine of yours just couldn't get him to ejaculate."

I sighed. I had to agree with him. The device had seen better days—it was old when I bought it second-hand two years ago.

Because it was a matter of economic survival for ranchers to be certain that the bulls they ran with their cows were fertile, evaluating a bull's ability to produce sufficient volumes of quality semen was part of our job. After a bull was examined rectally to ensure that his organs were normal and healthy, a good massage of his accessory organs usually got him primed for action. That's when we slipped a big rubber probe with impregnated metal electrodes over the base of his penis inside his rectum. By slowly turning a knob on a boxed panel, electrical impulses were sent via a long cord through the probe. On turning the knob further, the intensity of the impulse increased. Waves of impulses in ever-longer bursts usually caused the bull to extend his penis and produce a sample of semen.

Although collecting semen from bulls was as much an art as it was a science, having a good machine simplified the task. I was

convinced there was something wrong with the dial on my apparatus, because I could turn it and get no visible response from the bull, then turn it again the same amount and give him a jolt that would almost bring him to his knees. I had been on the lookout for a new machine for months, and although Marg wasn't convinced I could afford it, I was determined to get one before I needed to do the bull evaluations later this winter.

Doris had been on the phone for several minutes while Jim and I were having a coffee in the waiting room. I heard her wind up her conversation.

"Okay, okay, yes…we'll get someone out there as soon as possible." She hung up the phone and turned to us. "Which one of you wants to go to Lister to check out a horse with diarrhea?"

Jim took a sip of his coffee and winked at me. "You look like you need a shitty start to your day, Doc."

Doris raised her eyebrows and shook her head in disapproval.

"I thought we were doing Bob Rogers' cow this morning," I said.

"I have you both down at eleven for that," Doris replied. "Unless… only one of you wants to go to Bob's."

"No," I insisted, "we're both looking forward to trying out those new probes on a cow."

We had both had a chance to use the smallest cryotherapy probe to remove warts and small tumours on dogs, but still hadn't used them on a horse or cow. According to the professor from Pullman, Washington, whom I had bought the probes from, it was the answer to early cancer eye lesions in cows and annoying tumour-like lesions called sarcoids on horses. There was something about all the hocus-pocus of using the stuff that brought out the kid in me every time I poured the boiling liquid nitrogen into the four-litre thermal canister. It certainly got the client's attention when I slipped the metal instruments into the steaming cauldron and waited while they bubbled away to a final violent frothy release of heat when they reached the same temperature as the surrounding liquid.

"I'll go do the horse, if you want to stay and do the spay and neuter."

Jim nodded his consent. Setting my coffee cup aside, I headed to the kennel room and grabbed a pair of coveralls.

"What's the story on this critter, Doris?"

"It belongs to Ruth Boehmer. She said it was off a bit yesterday, but today it's got a watery diarrhea and is really depressed. She says he's drinking but won't even look at his hay."

"That doesn't sound good."

"I don't remember your having another call for a horse with diarrhea," Doris mused.

I grabbed a container of activated charcoal from the shelf in the pharmacy and headed to the truck with Lug on my heels. He waited impatiently at the door as I checked through the back to make sure I had oral electrolytes and Stat, a kaolin-pectin-based product I used frequently for cattle with loose stools.

I pulled out of the parking lot and turned in the direction of Lister, glancing at the notations Doris had made on the paper she'd given me. Lyons Road—that wasn't far from my place—somewhere out near the Blackmore compound and the old Creston dump.

I began wondering how close to the old dump they lived; maybe the animal had gotten into something toxic there. Doris was right. Acute, watery diarrhea was not common in horses. Salmonella was certainly a possibility, but I hadn't seen a case in a horse since I'd been here. It was a condition that was often associated with some sort of major stress. The only diarrhea I had treated in horses had been a pair of ponies that broke into a grain bin where a backyard farmer had stored the wheat for his chickens. Those two had been a real challenge; the owner didn't call me until they were both foundered and standing like statues because of severe pain in their feet.

Lug did his usual performance as I approached my farm. When I drove past our yard, he barked to let me know I had missed the turn.

"Not yet, old boy…you haven't put in a day's work yet."

I headed east where Canyon-Lister Road butted into Huscroft

Road, straight towards the sheer cliffs of the Skimmerhorn. This mountain amazed me—its demeanour changed on a continual basis depending on the position of the sun, the cloud coverage, and the time of year.

I could see the Boehmer house as soon as I turned onto Lyons Road. It was a modest one-storey structure surrounded by an acre or two of closely clipped pasture. Halfway down the road to the house, a young woman was standing next to a horse under a narrow, tin-roofed lean-to. I pulled up next to them and shut off the ignition. I glanced at the woman, an attractive, well-rounded blond, as I stuffed my stethoscope in my pocket. She was dressed in blue jeans; her grey flannel work shirt had the sleeves rolled up past her elbows. The tan she sported accentuated heavy freckling on her arms and face. I focused on her for a moment, wondering where I had seen her.

Before I could decide, I was distracted by the appearance of the horse. The slightly built animal was standing with its head only inches from the ground; its water-drenched tail hung heavy with encrusted fecal particles.

"Hello," I said, getting out of the truck. "I'm Dave Perrin."

"Ruth Boehmer," the woman replied. She looked towards her horse and shook her head slowly. "This is Coconut."

"How long has he been like this?"

"The diarrhea must have started sometime during the night, but yesterday when I went riding he wasn't himself. He was real doggy. When I got back home, he passed manure that was loose— sort of cow-pie texture."

"Is there any way he could have gotten into something? Could he have eaten too much grain?"

She shook her head, then added timidly, "Mom's really careful with the grain."

I slid on a palpation sleeve and lifted the horse's soggy tail. The moment I stuck in the thermometer, he hunched and strained without bothering to lift his tail. Watery, tea-coloured stool with tiny flecks of partially digested hay ran down his tail and onto the ground. The horse flinched as his guts emitted a sustained grumble.

"You haven't changed his feed or introduced anything different in the last few days?"

Again, the quiet blond shook her head. "No...Mom has baled up our hay from the same place for the last few years, and we've never had trouble before."

"And it's not mouldy?"

She produced a flake of hay from a manger at the head of the lean-to and extended it for me to look at. It was green and timely baled—good horse hay—an alfalfa, brome, timothy mix.

I removed the thermometer and rotated it in the sunlight to view the mercury. "It's forty-point-two."

"What should it be?" she asked.

"The same as humans."

Before I could continue, she said, "Thirty-seven, eight," and added, "I'm a nurse," when I looked surprised at her rapid response.

"Oh..."

I pinched the skin on the side of the horse's neck, then moved to his eyelid. Each area I tented stayed exactly as I left it.

"I was sure he was dehydrated," she observed.

I nodded. "The colon and caecum are proportionally much larger in the horse than they are in most other species—that's where they break down the fibre that most simple-stomached animals like pigs and humans can't digest. So, when an adult horse gets diarrhea, it's often an explosive event where they lose large amounts of fluid rapidly."

"Mom thought maybe he had worms."

"It's not impossible...but the temperature suggests we have something else going on."

I lifted Coconut's head and felt along the angle of his jaw for his pulse—his heart rate was rapid, his pulse thready. I took out my stethoscope and listened to his chest. His heart was beating at over sixty-five per minute; it should have been under forty. Tinkling sounds emanated from the entire left side, and on the right, one gushing rumble followed on another as fluid was being dumped from the caecum to the colon. I plunked along his right side, checking for evidence of a gas pocket that could result from a twisted bowel. My client watched intently.

"You've got a pretty sick animal here. He's secreting tremendous amounts of fluids into the bowel...unless we can slow down the process and replace as much of it as possible, he's going to crash."

"What do you think's causing it?" she asked softly.

"I'm not sure, to be honest. The increased temperature would suggest that it's infectious—salmonella and *Clostridium perfringens* would be most likely—but when I was at the last veterinary convention at the Coast there was talk of a new disease called Potomac horse fever that can present exactly like this." I hesitated a moment. "Until we find out otherwise, we better treat it as if it's salmonella...I'm sure I don't need to tell you that it affects humans as well. I'd be super careful about cleaning up after handling him, and keep other people away from him as much as possible."

Ruth nodded.

"Are you going to be able to keep checking him throughout the day?"

She nodded again, then said quietly, "I'm just starting four days off...Amy Helme and I were planning a ride up the mountain this afternoon, but I guess that's not going to happen now."

"I'll pump some fluids and electrolytes into him and do what I can to stabilize him, but unless he rallies, we'll have to start fluids intravenously."

Ruth sighed and shrugged. "I guess we'll do what we have to."

I produced my bucket. "I'll need this full."

While she was filling it from a garden hose near the side of the lean-to, I dug out the equipment I'd need from the back of my truck. She returned with the bucket full to the brim. I dumped out a bit of the water, added a few glugs of Stat, a bottle of electrolytes, and a handful of activated charcoal. Coconut stood complacently as I grasped his nose and applied the chain of the twitch around his upper lip.

"Can you hold this," I instructed, presenting Ruth with the

wooden handle of the apparatus. "My patients aren't as cooperative as yours, and this'll keep his attention while I pass the tube."

She hesitantly took the handle. With a hint of sarcasm, she replied, "Mine aren't always as cooperative as you might think."

Coconut stared dejectedly ahead as I inserted the tube and started advancing it down his nose. When I reached his throat I rotated it and started moving it back and forth. He swallowed; I pushed the tube forward. Puffing on it to dilate the esophagus, I advanced it until I was rewarded with a gush of warm, sweet-smelling air.

I displaced Ruth's hand on the twitch. "I'll need you to pump in the water while I hold everything in place...just cram the tube onto the spout of the stomach pump, and start stroking the handle up and down." She did as she was instructed, and the slurry was soon flowing down the tube. "Keep stirring it from time to time... that darned charcoal sticks to everything, and we want it coating the inside of his gut rather than the inside of my bucket."

Ruth was puffing by the time the bucket was empty and the pump began slurping air. I was appalled at how inefficient the stomach pumps used in veterinary practice were, and how hard one had to work to displace a few gallons of water.

"I hate to tell you this, but I'd like to give him more...if you think you can manage it, let's give him another one."

Ruth compliantly filled the bucket and returned to her appointed task. By the time the last of the water disappeared down the clear plastic tube, her arm was trembling and beads of sweat had formed on her brow. She looked relieved when I withdrew the tube and removed the twitch from her horse's nose.

I gave Coconut an injection of Demerol in the hopes that the narcotic would slow the contractions of his bowels and cut back on the loss of water. I debated what to do about antibiotics; there was still a lot of argument in the veterinary literature about the merit of using antibiotics for salmonella. I decided to wait until I saw the results of the blood work. Driving a needle into the horse's jugular, I collected a sample.

I was feeling uncomfortable when I was ready to leave; my gut was telling me that this horse needed more than I had provided, and I had trouble with the logic of not using antibiotics for a potentially infectious condition.

"Let's see what this does," I said hesitantly. "Call my office this afternoon to bring me up to date and let me know how he's doing. If he continues to dehydrate, we'll have to go with intravenous fluids."

Jim and I arrived at the Rogers' farm a few minutes after eleven to find Bob waiting next to the chute. A Hereford cow was standing quietly with her head trapped in the head gate.

"I'm all ready for you!" Bob hollered as we got out of the truck and walked through the hay shed to join him. "I'm glad you didn't come in your eggbeater today. Every time you go by here in that krautmobile of yours, that old cow you took the eye outta goes on the prod."

He motioned to the corral fifty feet to the north where the one-eyed cow and her calf stood watching intently. "The moment your car gets off the bridge and turns the corner in this direction, she tosses her head and starts tearing around the corral. One of you must have been heading down to Herb's the other day in the Volkswagen…When you went by, I thought she was going to take out a couple of rails and head for the hills."

"I guess she's determined to keep her other eye," I joked.

"Do you want me to go bring the nitrogen?" Jim asked.

"Why don't we check her out first? Make sure she's a good candidate."

"I hope it hasn't gone too far," Bob said apprehensively. "I don't want to go through removing another one. This girl's only a third calver."

When we approached the head gate, the cow looked at us with both eyes open. She didn't appear to be in any discomfort. I knelt a few feet in front of her for a closer inspection. She was a classic example of selecting cows with pigment around their eyes. The skin around the right eye was pigmented and perfectly healthy. The skin surrounding the left eye was totally white—its upper lid had two crusty, wart-like lesions. The bottom lid had an ulcerative area about three millimetres in diameter. On the surface of the eye, just a centimetre from the corner of her eye, was an elevated pink bleb.

"What do you think?" Bob asked.

"Seems like a good candidate to me," Jim answered. "Don't you think so, Doc?"

I nodded and got to my feet. "Looks like a go."

"I'll get the canister filled," he said, heading to the truck.

I took a bottle of topical anesthetic from my pocket and unscrewed the lid. Grabbing the cow by the nose, I worked my hand under her chin to steady her, then instilled three or four drops into her eyes.

"That'll keep her from feeling anything when we freeze it," I told Bob.

"I still can't picture what you plan to do."

"Come, have a gander at the equipment...it's really pretty simple stuff."

Bob and I arrived at the truck as Jim was manipulating the bulky artificial insemination tank from the front seat. Insulated tanks like this one, filled with liquid nitrogen, were usually used to store straws or ampules of frozen semen for extended periods of time. When a farmer needed to breed a cow he would choose a sample from the bull of choice, thaw it, and insert it into her uterus with a plastic straw. We used the tank just as a storage vat for the liquid nitrogen.

"Do you want to pour, or shall I do the honours?" Jim asked.

I grabbed the four-litre Plexiglas thermos and situated it on the ground in front of the tank. Jim removed the lid from the bigger vessel and began pouring the steaming liquid.

"That's scary-looking stuff," Bob said as it boiled away in the container.

"And these are the instruments." I showed him the machined stainless steel and copper heads that screwed onto a soft plastic handle. "You select the size of head you need according to the size of the tumour…the idea is to be able to freeze the whole thing solid with one application."

I screwed the handle onto the head with the smallest diameter tip, and plopped it into the nitrogen. As the liquid boiled around the outside of the stainless steel probe, we made the trek back to the cow. Jim put a halter on her and cranked her head hard towards her good eye. The cow struggled and rattled the chute as I scrubbed her lids with alcohol and injected a small amount of local anesthetic at the base of the tumours. She stood quietly as I snipped the curly warts off.

I removed the instrument from the container and applied it to the bleeding surface on the upper lid. The instant it made contact, the blood and underlying tissue froze into a solid lump. I left it there for a good thirty seconds before removing it, then applied it to the other site.

"There's not much to that," Bob said as he watched over my shoulder. "It doesn't seem to bother her at all."

I moved the probe to the raw lesion on the bottom lid and applied it until the tissue was frozen solid for several millimetres on either side of the instrument. I dropped the probe back into the canister.

"So that's it?" Bob asked.

"Not quite," I replied. "We're going to freeze each site three times. If you think of the stories you've heard of people freezing their toes: thaw them slowly and carefully, and they might survive; freeze them and thaw them several times, they become gangrenous. Same thing goes here, and we want all the tumour cells dead."

"What about the one on the surface of her eye?"

"That'll be a bit tougher to get at…I think Jim and I'll have to gang up on her and control the lids for that one."

The other two applications on the lesions went without a hitch, and the probe was soon back in the canister. I put another couple of drops of the topical anesthetic in her eye and turned to Jim. "Do you want to do the one on the eye…I'll hold the lids."

I pressed my hip against the cow's neck for better control and pried open her eyelids. She struggled against me to close her eyes, and the moment Jim brought the probe towards her eyeball to freeze the lesion, she prolapsed her third eyelid to cover it completely.

"This isn't going to work, Doc," Jim said with conviction. "I think we'll have to pop it."

"Pop it?" Bob and I both blurted at the same time.

"Proptose it," he clarified.

Bob was mystified. I raised my eyebrows and shook my head in bewilderment. "Never heard of it."

"They didn't teach us how to do it in college either, but the guys I worked for last summer were really good at it."

As Bob looked on in horror, Jim grabbed a pair of surgery scissors from the cold sterilization tray. Opening the scissors fully, he pressed the handles steadily against the lids, depressing them further and further. The cow began to struggle, and I was about to intervene when the eye suddenly popped free of the socket.

"I'll be damned," I muttered, staring in amazement at a globe that now stuck out several inches from the skull.

"Just keep pressure on the handles, Doc, while I get it frozen," Jim instructed.

With the eye fully exposed, it was a simple task for him to apply the probe directly to the surface of the globe without interference. In less than ten minutes, the eye was back where it belonged, and our job was done.

"That was pretty impressive," I complimented Jim as we were driving back across the flats towards Creston. "Getting that eye out where we could work on it made all the difference in the world. I would have been hard pressed to get a good freeze on it otherwise."

"It is a pretty neat trick," Jim agreed. "But every once in a while they just won't let it pop. Doc Travis, the guy I worked for last year, had a couple he had to inject first. Once he froze their intraocular muscles, it worked even easier than this one."

I was feeling good right now about my decision to hire an assistant. It was amazing how many new techniques one could pick up working with different veterinarians. It was also a benefit that came from hiring someone who originated from a totally different background from mine. Despite his ongoing flirtations with some of the female clients, Jim was proving to be a valuable addition to the practice.

We drove in silence until I crossed the Kootenay River bridge.

"What do you know about Potomac horse fever?" I asked.

"Not a lot, other than it wiped out a whole mess of horses in DC last year. As far as I know, no one has discovered what causes it yet."

"They said at the B.C. convention this year that although they were sure it's infectious, no one has figured out how it's transmitted."

"They had a horse come in to the college from south Texas after we got back to school last year. The powers that be had us all running around with gloves on thinking it was salmonella, but the white count wasn't right. They were never able to grow anything so they were wondering about Potomac."

"What happened to the horse?"

"It shit through the eye of a needle for three days, then got so badly foundered, the owner had them put it down."

His words about founder hit me like a hammer—I hadn't considered the possibility of laminitis with Coconut. Any time a horse was exposed to a major stress or toxin as he had been, it was at risk of getting an allergic reaction that caused swelling in the laminae of the feet. The condition could often be severe enough to cause permanent lameness and render the horse useless for riding. I'd have to start him on antihistamine first thing when I got back out there.

"You worried about that horse you saw this morning?"

"Yeah…he was pretty dehydrated, and the manure was still running out of him like water. I hate it when we need to give fluids IV to large animals. You can't get enough into them when you fiddle with a litre of the prepared fluids at a time, and there's no way of knowing that the solutions are sterile when you dump a jug of Ionalyte and five gallons of tap water into a carboy."

"Yeah, I know what you mean. You'd think that one of the drug companies would start making saline in ten-litre pouches…Are you going back out there?"

"The owner was supposed to call and let me know how she was making out, but my guess is, yes. I didn't give the horse antibiotics either…half the references recommend using them for salmonella, and the other half say no. They're big on tetracycline for Potomac horse fever, though."

"You don't think Potomac horse fever could be way up here, do you?"

"Who knows, especially when no one is even sure what causes it. I collected some manure to send to the lab, but I can't say that I'm holding my breath for an answer. Most stool samples of diarrhea I've sent in the past never got a definitive diagnosis. I just want to make sure I cover all the bases."

Doris and Lug met us at the door when we entered the clinic. "This dog has been driving me nuts," Doris grumped. "He hates it when you run off and leave him."

"I know." I settled on the waiting room bench to scratch Lug's ears. "But there was no room for him today."

"You better head out for lunch if you plan on eating…you both have a crazy afternoon ahead of you."

"Have the Boehmers called about their horse?"

"I just got off the phone with Ruth…she says the diarrhea has slowed a bit, but the horse still isn't looking good."

I sighed and headed to the lab, resigned to going without lunch. "Did you get his blood count done?"

"Yes, and the smears should be dry and ready for you to read."

I plunked myself in the chair in my spanking new laboratory and slid one of the glass slides that Doris had prepared onto the microscope. The moment I sat down, Lug rooted his nose beneath my fingertips.

"Not now, pal…I've got work to do."

After giving him a cursory pat, I opened the lab book and

checked the notations Doris had made. The blood's packed cell volume was elevated—48 compared to a normal of 40—but that wasn't a surprise. I knew the horse was dehydrated. The white cell count was slightly over 11,000 per microlitre. That wasn't really elevated when I considered the degree of dehydration, but it wasn't what I'd have anticipated with salmonella; usually that organism wiped out most of the white cells.

I scanned the edge of the field on low power to get a feeling for the relative number of cells present. The blue-staining white cells had a normal distribution throughout the red cells. I put a drop of immersion oil on the smear and went to the high-powered lens. I was halfway through the count when I stopped to dig out my hematology notes.

After rummaging through the badly earmarked pages, I found my notes. Just as I remembered—an acute fulminating attack with this organism usually caused a general depression in all leukocytes and a severe depletion of neutrophils.

That wasn't what I was seeing. Neutrophils were present in relatively normal numbers, and there were more monocytes than normal.

I finished my count and sat back in my chair. Both neutrophils and monocytes were cells involved with chewing up damaged cellular debris and bacteria. Usually, when they were elevated, it indicated the body was responding to a bacterial invasion.

I removed the cover slip from the test tube that Doris had set up to look for parasite eggs and dropped it onto a clean slide. After placing it on the microscope and scanning the whole field, I saw only a single *Strongylus vulgaris* egg; although this type of blood worm was a frequent cause of colic, I didn't consider finding one egg significant, even with the dilution of a watery stool.

There was nothing here to clinch or rule out a diagnosis, but salmonellosis seemed less likely than it had this morning. I'd just have to treat the animal symptomatically and hope for the best. It was time to get tetracycline on board.

It was mid-afternoon when I lugged the five-gallon carboy full of electrolyte from the truck. While I hefted it, Ruth secured it to a rafter in the lean-to with a piece of baler twine.

We had already administered more Stat and activated charcoal with the electrolytes, and I had given Coconut his first injection of antihistamine. He wasn't looking good—in fact, the animal was so dejected I was able to pass the stomach tube without using the twitch.

"We'll be best to tie him in this corner," I suggested. The clear plastic spiral coils of the IV kit allowed him to move ten feet in any one direction, but the more he was able to move around, the more likely he'd be to tangle things up and pull out his catheter.

Ruth had dragged an extension cord from the house so I could prep Coconut's neck. I clipped the hair close over the jugular vein and scrubbed it well with surgical soap before bringing out the catheter. I blocked the vein and repeatedly stroked towards my fingers. When I could clearly define the jugular furrow, I drove the needle through the skin and into the vessel. Blood crept back around the catheter as I advanced it bit by bit through the needle. When I had passed it full-depth, I withdrew the needle from the skin and locked the protective shield around it.

"Can you hold this in place for me?"

Ruth grabbed the catheter tip while I injected the tetracycline, then hooked on the fluids and opened the valve. Electrolytes began running in a steady stream through the glass chamber.

"Do you want it running that fast?" Ruth sounded concerned.

"Yeah, I've seen them running one in each side that fast at the college. This poor guy's pretty dried out."

While she held the apparatus in place, I ran some adhesive tape around the locking device, grabbed a needle, and sutured it. I adjusted the rubber tubing to allow for plenty of slack, then taped it to Coconut's halter.

"Let the fluids run at this speed for about half an hour." I turned the metal valve on the rubber tubing to restrict the flow of fluids. "Then keep it going at about this rate."

Ruth nodded but said nothing. I was about to get into my truck when she asked, "What do I do if he pulls it out?"

"Let me know, and I'll come back and replace it. I'll drop out later this evening to see how you're making out."

All the way back to the office, I thought about my social situation. Now that I had someone to help share the workload, I needed to get on with my life. Dan and Jim and all my friends were married with families of their own. Maybe it was time for me to start thinking of doing something other than chasing around the valley looking after everyone's critters.

A few days earlier I had overheard Dan and Jim talking about taking in the Farmers Ball. It was an annual event in the fall; all the beef growers, dairymen, hay farmers, grain growers, and fruit growers got together to celebrate the harvest. The last couple of years, I had ended up tending to emergencies at the office, so I hadn't been able to show up at all. Maybe this year I should go. I wondered if Ruth would agree to go with me.

I hadn't been on an actual date since I had been in college, and even then it was hard to pry myself away from the books long enough to have some fun. I often wondered how my life would have turned out if I had been man enough to step up and ask the first woman I had fallen for to marry me my second year in vet college.

She was a down-home girl from a farm in rural Saskatchewan who was a home economics student at the university where we were both studying. We were in our first year and living in a boarding house that we all referred to as the feedlot. She and four other girls lived on the upper floors with the owners of the house, and I lived with four other guys in the basement. It was a deplorable facility with paper-thin partitions and lumpy six-foot single beds, but I was hardly ever there and didn't care much about the lack of amenities.

She and I had gotten to know one another well and had dated for the last half of our first year. We both left for summer jobs—me for a job live-trapping and tagging black bears in North Bay, Ontario, and she to a job somewhere in Nova Scotia or New Brunswick.

We returned to the same dump for our second year and took up with one another as soon as we got back to Saskatoon. In early November she took me aside, insisting she had something she had to tell me. It was right before mid-term exams, and we were both stressed out with our studies. The moment we were alone in the dining room, she burst into tears. Between sobs, she told me she was going to have a baby.

I stared at her in a state of shock as she related her story. She had worked with the baby's father back East. They had gone out a few times, and on their last date had had sex—she was now three months along in her pregnancy. I held her as she cried, and finally asked her if she loved him. She ran off to her room before I could ask her if she loved me.

I didn't see her at the breakfast table the next day before I headed off to classes. That night she didn't appear, and the landlady told me she had quit school and gone home.

I was a wreck for the next few weeks as I struggled to study while debating with myself whether or not I could marry a woman who was carrying another guy's child. When I finally finished my exams, I got her parents' phone number from the landlady. When I called, her mother told me she had moved back East. I never heard from her again.

Ruth reminded me a bit of her. There was something about their being quiet and unassuming, yet having obvious strengths of their own. And, of course, they both had rural backgrounds. I frequently wondered how my first love would have liked the house I was building now. I had always known I'd someday have a farm of my own...I guess that's why I was interested in finding a woman who could be happy as a farmer's wife.

By nine I'd had a bite to eat and finished my chores. I was apprehensive when I hopped in the truck and headed south down Canyon-Lister Road to the Boehmers. My track record with women hadn't been great to date, and I found it disconcerting that I was even considering taking another plunge into a river that was rife with concealed undertows.

I pulled into the circle of light that shone from a lone bulb dangling from one of the rafters. No one was in sight in the lean-to, so I grabbed my flashlight and got out of the vehicle. It was just as well I had made up another batch of fluids before leaving the clinic, because the bag over the horse's head was now sagging. I was focused on Coconut as I made my way into the lean-to—he was still on his feet and much more alert.

As I approached, he turned his head in my direction. "Aren't you looking brighter," I said cheerfully.

"He's doing way better."

I twirled at the sound of the voice and shone the flashlight to the other side of the manger. It was Ruth. Tossing an old woollen blanket aside, she swung her legs over the edge of some bales she had been stretched out on and got to her feet.

"He even picked at a bit of grass and carrot tops that Mom brought over for him a bit ago."

"I thought maybe you'd gone to the house to catch a few winks of sleep."

"I've been napping out here…it's quite comfortable, actually."

I was smiling as I pinched the skin over Coconut's eye and watched it slowly return to normal. I was thankful that he was rallying—it would have been hard to ask a girl out while giving the last rites to her horse.

"I brought another bag of fluids," I said. "As soon as these are gone, we'll slow them to a nice steady drip overnight."

We didn't talk as I continued my examination. I listened to his chest; his heart sounds were much better and his rate had declined to a more normal forty-four beats per minute. The tinkling sounds on his right side were diminished, as were the rumbling contractions of the caecum and colon on the right side. I inserted a thermometer. The fecal particles had dried, and the tail lifted like some kind of mosaic artifact.

"His gut has been gurgling a lot less," Ruth observed.

"It's quieted down considerably...how long since he's had a bowel movement?"

"At least an hour," she responded quietly.

I stood in silence, wondering how I could switch the conversation from horse poo to the Farmers Ball.

"Have you got other animals that have been with him?"

"My younger sisters' pony, a Jersey cow and calf and, of course, there's my mother's goats."

"You haven't noticed any problems with them?"

"They all look fine, but the moment Coconut got sick, Mom ran an electric wire to keep them away."

"What does she do with the goats?"

"We milk them," Ruth responded with a hint of disgust.

"I haven't had goat's milk since I was a kid," I said, feeling a touch of melancholy. "My dad apparently had goats when I was a baby—my mom had polio right after I was born so I think I was raised on it."

"All of us were, too," Ruth said resentfully. "I hate the taste of it now."

I laughed when she screwed up her face in obvious revulsion.

"When I was eleven or twelve a family of back-country hippies moved into Casino—where I was raised—and brought a whole herd of goats with them. I remember being so excited when they let me milk them." I shook my head. "It's funny what you remember from your childhood...being able to milk those goats seemed like such an important thing at the time."

While we sat and watched the rest of the fluids drain from the plastic carboy, our conversation wandered. I gathered she had somehow originated from the polygamous sect that referred to themselves as fundamentalist Latter-day Saints, but she was reluctant to talk about it. She did tell me that she and her sisters and brothers had picked roots and rocks from the fields of my farm when it had still been owned by the Sikoras, and that they had worked for almost all the farmers in the area. Her mother, Aloha, was apparently very proficient at keeping Ruth and her seven brothers and sisters busy to bring in a few extra dollars; they had all just finished hauling bales for the Ivanys, the farmers across the road from me.

As the night went on, I was becoming more and more convinced that she was a woman I could relate to. I was about to pop the question about next weekend's dance when she said, "I'm glad Coconut's better, because I really enjoy riding. It's too bad Amy's busy during the week, because I have to work for the next few weekends…after that, it'll probably be getting pretty cold."

"Yeah," I said with a hint of disappointment. "It is getting cold."

Chapter 17

Gonads and Other Expendable Organs

"Are you serious?"

Jim gave me a sinister smile as he watched his shapely blond client walk out the door. "Pretty nice stuff, eh, Doc?"

I looked at him with my mouth hanging open. "No one offers me trades like that."

"What can I say, Doc…some of us got it and some of us…" He didn't finish the sentence but sat down at the desk to write on his card. "I've traded a few favours myself over the years."

"Favours?" I stared at him in disbelief. Jim shrugged and peered at me as if I were a total nerd.

"For God's sake, Doc, where you been all your life? Money was tight back in Austin…I came across a few old girls with some extra change who didn't mind helping me out from time to time—it was a real lifesaver."

I gawked at him as he tossed his completed file card in the basket and headed to the kennel room. He was as nonchalant as if we had been discussing a case of ear mites.

I had given the first vaccination to this client's kitten myself, and she certainly hadn't invited me over for an evening of fun in exchange for the spaying of her cat. As a matter of fact, she had been so smitten with her new kitten that she spent the entire appointment time telling me about all Natasha's antics—how she climbed curtains and chased marbles across the apartment floor.

For the most part, things had been running pretty smoothly over the last few months. Jim and I were very different people, but we worked well together. He was good with his hands and a competent surgeon, and I had come to appreciate his ability to handle difficult clients. As Doris was wont to say, the boy was "such a schmooze."

I had definitely gotten hooked on the main benefit of having Jim in the practice—nights away from the pager. It was such a treat to start on a project at the farm with no worries of being called away before I could get it completed. Last week Father and I had accomplished several pours of cement on the walls next to the courtyard.

The house was really starting to take shape. After we had finished chipping the last pour, I had snuck off with Lug to the other side of the draw. Leaning back against a big pine tree, I sat for over an hour staring back at my home. It looked just as I had hoped it would—the stone, the logs, the cedar shakes, the surrounding trees all blended so nicely.

I tried to picture how I wanted it to appear when it was finished. What would the courtyard look like in ten or twenty years? Would there be a fountain gurgling and flowers blooming? Where would I put a hot tub? I'd have to have one somewhere; God knows with all the aches and pains I had at thirty, I'd certainly need one by the time I was forty or fifty.

Balderdash! I'd probably never live to be that age. I had always had a premonition that I'd die young.

As I sat there with Lug's head in my lap, I wondered what it would be like to have children of my own. This farm would be a great place for kids to grow up. If I had them, would they be tall like me? Heck, how likely was it that I'd even find someone to have children with? Jim was a married man with females hitting on him constantly; the same women looked on me as a guy to gush to about their pets.

I had thought several times of asking Ruth Boehmer out on a date, but I hadn't seen her again since I had removed the IV from her horse. I guess I was just destined to be Dr. Dave—when would there be time for anything more?

The telephone rang, and Doris rushed in front of me to grab it. "Oh hi, Sorina...yes, he's here...hang on a second."

She passed me the receiver. "It's Sorina Maletta. She's got a question for you."

"Good afternoon, Sorina."

"Hi, Dave. I'm sorry to take you away from something, but do you ever fix roosters?"

"I've fixed up a few roosters in my time...what's wrong with him?"

"No, I mean *fix* fix."

"You mean caponize them?"

"I guess so...if that's what it's called. I want to get him neutered."

I stood there with a dumb look on my face pondering the question. "Well, they do caponize roosters so they grow out fatter with more marbled meat, but I doubt that I'd be able to do it cheaply enough for it to be economically viable. Were you planning on trying to raise them as a specialty market?"

"Oh no, I have only one rooster I need to get fixed. He's terrible...he just won't leave Gretta alone."

"Gretta?"

"Our pet chicken."

"Oh right, I remember her." I had been checking out Sorina's horse, Corb, once at suppertime, and a huge white hen was sitting beside the table begging for scraps. Sorina's husband, Gene, had her jumping up and down on the spot pleading for handouts. "She's the one who loves eating chicken," I recalled.

Sorina laughed. "Her favourite meal is chicken and salad with French dressing—it has to be French. If you make it Italian or Thousand Island, she turns her beak up at it."

"How did she become such a pet?"

"We've had her for years, now. We raised a pair of them from chicks so they'd have company, but some pickers from the orchard next door caught one and roasted her over an open fire. I was furious when I found out about that."

"I bet you were."

"It didn't seem to bother Gretta much, though. She doesn't like other birds…I don't think she knows she is one."

"So what's with the one you want to get neutered?"

"Last summer Gretta kept nesting and sitting on her eggs. We couldn't find a rooster so I got some fertilized eggs from a neighbour and switched them for Gretta's. She sat on them through that real hot spell in August…I was so worried about her. She had settled under a piece of plywood out by the shop. I ran water over the outside to cool her down and carried food and water to her. She hatched out eight chicks—this rooster is one of them. We gave the rest of them back to the lady we got the eggs from."

"So he's over a year now?"

"Yes, and he's getting to be a real nuisance. He's constantly chasing Gretta. Yesterday when I was out in the orchard, he chased her right to the base of my ladder. She jumped up and down under me until I climbed down and picked her up."

I chuckled at the image.

"He puts the run on my poor Jeeters, too, and whenever someone pulls up to the house in a vehicle, he circles around and around it until someone gets out. If he thinks they'll run, he takes after them with his neck stretched out and wings flapping. He's terrible around kids."

"Let me have a few minutes to dig through my poultry text…I'll need to brush up on the technique. Caponizing a rooster is actually more complicated than neutering a dog or cat…their gonads are internal, and we'd have to go into his abdomen."

"Let me know what you come up with," she said and hung up.

I plucked my poultry text from the top shelf in my office and settled into my chair. After a few minutes of reading, I thought I could figure things out.

"Doris, would you please call Sorina and see if she can bring the bird in tomorrow. Have her take him off food and water overnight and pen him up right away so he can't pick up any grass or litter. We want him to have an empty gut for surgery."

Lug couldn't contain himself as we approached the Lister school. After being asked to behave all day at the office, he inevitably got worked up when we were heading home where he could run at will. He whined when I turned off 20th Street onto Sinclair.

"Sorry, old man, but the day's not done yet." My woebegone passenger continued looking up 20th where he was sure we should be going.

I glanced at my watch…it was shortly after five-thirty. It should work out just right—the Meekes boys would almost be finished milking. Bernie had requested that I stop to have a look at a cow that was giving him problems.

I continued down Sinclair through a big dip where golden trees of autumn crowded to the edge of the road. The Meekes farm was the first place on the right as I climbed back onto the bench. I turned down the long lane that ran towards their farm buildings and a pair of tall concrete bunker silos.

This was a family farm, owned and operated by John, Dora, and their three sons. I was always amazed at how everything on this property looked as if it had just been manicured. Today was no exception; the heifer lot on the right-hand side of the lane had been harrowed, and there was John in his big John Deere tractor making the last few passes over the cow lot. I waved at him as I passed by.

Lug stood up on the seat and growled as the old resident lab meandered his way from the carport by the house to greet us. Barking dutifully, he fell into step behind my vehicle as I pulled up next to the milk house.

"Perfect timing!" came a voice from inside the barn. "I just got her into the head gate."

Bernie was the oldest of the Meekes boys. Tall, handsome, and muscular, he was the definition of a perpetual motion machine—constantly on a dead run.

"I don't know what to think of this cow," he ranted, stepping forward and stopping inches from my elbow. "She's been on again, off again, since she calved two weeks ago. Yesterday, I thought we'd just stick her in for you to look at when you do herd health next week, but Paul said she was way down on milk this morning… tonight, she's almost dry."

I stuffed a thermometer, a palpation sleeve, and a bottle of ketone test tablets into my coveralls pocket and grabbed a stethoscope from the dash. Pushing Lug over to the passenger seat, I closed the door and followed Bernie into the barn.

"Paul checked her with a stud finder to see if she had a magnet this morning, and when he didn't find one, I dropped another into her just in case." Bernie entered a small holding area that housed a few stanchions and a straw-covered area where they calved out cows. He stopped beside a lanky Holstein. "She's not been right since she calved," he said with a frown. "But until today she was always out at the trough eating."

The critter stood dejectedly with her head trapped between the metal uprights of the stanchion. Her hair coat was rough and standing in disarray—she was definitely out of sorts. Although her flanks were somewhat sunken, they looked sort of puffy at the same time. Her front legs were abducted at a funny angle, and her head hung inches from an untouched flake of leafy green alfalfa hay.

"Did you check her for ketosis?" I asked.

Bernie shook his head. "Paul drenched her a couple times with Ketol, though."

"What's her temperature been?"

"I took it a couple times this week, but every time it was normal."

I moved to the back of the cow and pulled out an empty syringe case. Massaging up and down under her vulva, I waited expectantly for her to urinate. Several times she hunched slightly as if she were going to pee, then resisted. Each time she gave a slight protective grunt and dribbled a few drops of urine. After a third aborted attempt to collect a sample, I grudgingly accepted the little I had accumulated and dropped in a ketone test tablet. Unsheathing my thermometer, I slipped it into her rectum.

"She had a heck of a lactation last year," Bernie offered. "We had a hard time drying her off."

He fidgeted as I waited for the thermometer to cook, then grabbed a pitchfork and began fluffing the straw on the barn floor.

"What is it?" he asked when I wiped the thermometer on the cow's tail head and held it up to the light to read.

"Just shy of 41 Celsius," I replied wistfully.

"You're kidding! How could it have gone up so much since yesterday?"

I checked the test tablet, then passed it to Bernie. It was a bright purple colour, indicating that the cow had high levels of ketones in her urine. Bernie leaned on his pitchfork watching me as I took out my stethoscope. His brow was wrinkled; his piercing blue eyes expectant.

The cow's heart sounded normal enough, but her rate was elevated. The lung field sounded fine, but with each expiration there was a bit of a hesitation and a slight grunt. I moved my stethoscope to sit on top of the trachea, listened for a couple of breaths, then grasped the cow firmly by the withers. She reluctantly depressed her spine and released an agonizing groan.

"You don't need that thing," Bernie chirped. "I could hear her grunt from way over here."

I listened for rumen movement under the cow's left flank. That part of the stomach was completely static and as quiet as a church. I flicked my fingertip again and again over her side, searching for pockets of air under pressure—nothing. Moving to the right side, I repeated the procedure. The very first tap yielded a high-pitched ringing that sounded almost metallic. I changed the position of the stethoscope head and continued to thump. Again and again, I got the same response.

"So, do you think it's hardware?" Bernie asked. "I've never heard a cow grunt louder than she did."

"I don't think so." I rolled up my coverall sleeve and slipped on a palpation glove. "There's something amiss back here."

I squirted lube on my glove and worked my fingers into the rectum. I found a lump of hard, mucous-covered feces and dropped it to the floor at my feet. Pushing my hand forward into the distal colon, I ran head on into a hard, rounded object with an end the size of a soccer ball. It extended as far as I could reach.

"She doesn't like that," Bernie observed as I put pressure on it.

"So I hear." From where I was standing, I could hear the cow give a decisive groan. "Well, chief, looks like decision time…if you want her to live, she's definitely a cutter."

Bernie set his pitchfork aside and headed for the door. "Let's get at it…she's a heck of a cow."

By the time I got back from the truck with my surgery box, Bernie had an extension cord laid out and waiting. I plugged in my clippers and began stripping hair from the cow's right side.

Bernie rushed in from the milk house with a five-gallon bucket of warm water in each hand. "It really bugs me when something like this sneaks up on me. I spent the whole afternoon wondering how she could have gotten a hunk of metal in her gut. So, why's the temperature so high?"

"I'm not sure, Bernie…been wondering the same thing myself. I hope that the stomach hasn't been twisted long enough to cut off the blood supply. If that's the case, and we get in there and find the tissue dead, there won't be a thing we can do."

Bernie picked up his pitchfork and cleaned away the manure that I had drawn out of the cow. Breaking open a bale of barley straw, he flailed energetically at flake after flake until he was standing in a bed a foot deep. I held my breath and continued clipping as the dust from the straw filled the air. While I scrubbed the cow and blocked her in preparation for surgery, Bernie rousted calves along the edge of the room and cleaned stalls that already appeared as pristine as they could ever be.

"I need you to squirt me some soap here, Bernie."

The fair-haired dynamo expeditiously leaned his pitchfork against an adjacent stanchion and grabbed the bottle of Bridine. Waiting impatiently for me to finish my first scrub, he shot jets of the reddish-brown soap over first one arm, then the other.

By the time I had finished my third scrub, Bernie had my surgery gown unwrapped and waiting for me. He quickly tied me up, then peeled back the protective sheathing and handed me my gloves. While I was putting them on, he plunked a straw bale next to the cow, tore open the tape on my instrument pack, and stood back expectantly. When working with Bernie, I always got the feeling that if I didn't keep things moving fast enough, he'd push me aside and get on with the process himself.

"You forgot the scalpel blade," I joked. I had done enough surgeries with him that he had the procedure down pat.

"Oh, sorry." He peeled back the sides of the foil packet and dropped the blade in my instrument bowl.

Unfolding my surgery drape from the instrument pack, I cut an elongated hole in the centre of the heavy blue material, then opened the forceps and clamped the skin. I readied the scalpel and made my incision. Before I reached the bottom of the line, a bleeder from halfway down sent a jet of blood across my face and the front of my gown. I quickly grabbed a pair of mosquito forceps and clamped across it.

I incised the muscle layers, being more conscious than ever of the mass that bulged beneath my blade. Elevating the final muscle layer and the peritoneum at the bottom of the incision with a pair of thumb forceps, I stabbed through with my scalpel. Air rushed into the abdomen as I continued to pull up on the muscle.

"Why are you taking so long to open her up?" Bernie asked. I was slowly extending the incision with scissors.

"Opening a cow up on the left side is always more predictable. The rumen's the first thing we run into. On the right side, it's more of a crap shoot—I haven't a clue what we're going to find over here." I lifted the muscle layer away from the internal organs. With scissors, I extended the incision upwards to the same length as the overlying wound in the skin. "Oh oh..." I groaned as I scooped gobs of white gelatinous material from a loop of small bowel.

"What's that?" My eager assistant was peering over my shoulder.

"They're fibrinous clots...we either have a roaring infection or a major interference with circulation."

"That doesn't look good." Bernie grimaced as I manipulated the tip of a distended oblong structure through my incision.

"It sure doesn't." I flicked the greenish black structure with a fingertip.

"Is that her stomach?" Bernie asked.

"I'm not sure what it is, but whatever it is, it's dead." I motioned to the surgery box. "Pass me a fourteen-gauge needle, will you? The brown one."

He snapped off the plastic protective cap, and I grasped the hub of the needle with a pair of forceps. At the tip of the rounded protuberance, I drove the needle to the hub. The end of the needle moved back and forth as air whistled through it.

"That's rank." Bernie wrinkled his nose and took a giant step back.

For the next ten minutes, we waited for the organ to decompress.

"Is there any sense in doing more with her?" Bernie asked dejectedly. "Maybe I should just shoot her."

With the piece of bowel deflated, I was able to mobilize it better and feel to the root of the torsion. "It's the caecum," I pronounced as I rotated the structure in a counter-clockwise direction, and air gushed into the colon.

"Can she live without it?" Bernie asked.

"I really don't know," I mused. "But we can."

"We can?"

"Yeah…lots of people have their appendix removed—the appendix is our caecum."

"Where does that leave us with her?"

"Well," I said, pulling upward on the colon and caecum as hard as I could, "can you see where that greenish colour turns to pink?"

"Yeah."

"We'd have to cut all this dead stuff off down to bleeding tissue, then sew the rest together and hope she can get along without it."

"Wouldn't that cost a fortune? And what if she needs the caecum for something, and she up and croaks after we go to all that trouble?"

"Tell you what…if she doesn't make it, I'll charge you surgery time till now. If she gets better, then I'll charge it out the same as I would for a twisted stomach."

He frowned. "So we have to cut all this off?"

I nodded. "That means you'll have to dig in and get your hands dirty."

"Well, let's go for it, then."

The thought of getting involved with the surgery obviously appealed to him, and before I could even suggest he get ready, Bernie squirted surgical soap on his arms and began scrubbing madly. As he prepared himself, I tied off all the major vessels I could detect, leaving the small bowel and colon to the caecum.

I didn't want to spend too much time pondering the logic of the procedure I was about to embark on. This huge hunk of meat I was going to hack off played a big role in the production of B vitamins in many species and was the major source of fermentation in both the horse and the rabbit. I knew for a fact that neither of them would survive without it. But the cow performed those jobs in her rumen; the caecum was probably something she could live without.

"So what do you want me to do?" Bernie was standing with his freshly scrubbed hands pointed towards the ceiling.

"Well, normally I'd have you put on some gloves, but we already have a contaminated surgery area, so gloves won't likely change the outcome."

I hefted the now floppy green sac upwards and got the lay of the land. "I want you to hold tight here, and here." I indicated the portion of gut where the caecum pouched off. "This is the end of the small bowel, and this is the official beginning of the large bowel. Your job is to keep material from spilling out into the abdomen from either side." I indicated the end of the ileum. "I suspect it'll most likely try and escape at this end."

"That accounts for both of my hands," Bernie quipped. "What's going to keep the crap in the dead part?"

"I guess I'll somehow have to manage that."

The veins on Bernie's forearms bulged as he took up his position and applied pressure.

"You don't have to squeeze so hard till I start cutting."

Taking a close look at the base of the caecum where it had been twisted upon itself, I clamped across a section that appeared to be alive, then severed beneath the clamp with scissors. I slowly worked my way along the line of demarcation until, with a final snip, the organ plopped to the ground with a resounding sploosh.

"Hold it steady, Bernie."

I trimmed the wound margins back to pink tissue as quickly as possible and started suturing. Bernie's arms were shaking from the strain by the time I had finished.

"Just a few minutes more…"

Stripping my gloves, I washed away as much debris as possible with surgical scrub, then nodded to my assistant. He released his grip, and we both watched the line of sutures disappear from sight.

Jim was in the front office to greet Sorina when she arrived with the rooster the next morning. "Dave was telling me about that bird of yours. I never would have thought you could make a pet out of a chicken. Is there something special about her?"

"Her breeding, no…she's an ordinary white meat bird. But she's certainly a special chicken. Every morning she dances back and forth in front of our door until we let her in the house. She goes straight for the fridge and hops up and down until we give her something."

"Doesn't she crap on the floor?" Jim asked suspiciously.

Sorina shook her head adamantly. "She'd never poo in the house."

"And your dogs don't bother her?"

"No, they all get along. There's always a procession through the orchard when I'm out working, and she's part of it."

Jim smiled and shrugged his shoulders. "Sounds like quite a bird."

"And in the winter she sleeps with my horse, Corb, to keep warm."

"With the horse?" he blurted skeptically.

Sorina smiled. "She's too fat to fly up onto his back, so she hops up onto the bales and climbs to the top of the manger. From there, she flops onto poor old Corb's forehead and waddles her way down his neck until she can sit on his back."

"And this guy…is he trained, too?" Jim motioned to the big white rooster that stared apprehensively between the wires of the carry cage Sorina had brought him in.

"No…he's just an obnoxious rooster."

I looked anxiously at the bird as he circled the cage. Right at the moment, I was wishing I was somewhere else. I had never heard of anyone doing abdominal surgery on a rooster.

The phone rang. Doris extended the receiver in my direction. "It's Bernie Meekes returning your call."

I had called him this morning the moment I got through the door to find out how our patient was doing.

"Good morning, Bernie. What's the verdict?"

"Good decision, Dave. It looks like cows don't need their appendix any more than we do…she's eating, and her temperature's down to 39 C."

"Oh, fantastic…I needed to hear that."

"She was already picking at hay last night, and this morning she even had a few cupfuls of milk."

I glanced towards the rooster as Sorina and Jim went on with their conversation. "I'd rather be back at your place starting that surgery again instead of doing what I've got scheduled now."

"Really?" he said in disbelief. "That one was one of the hardest surgeries we've ever done…what could be worse than that?"

"Neutering a rooster."

"A rooster! Bring it out here…I'll fix him for you. While you're on the way out, I'll sharpen the axe."

He was still laughing when I hung up the phone. Farmers often came up with the most practical solutions to problems.

"I don't know why I get so worked up whenever I'm trying something new," I said to Jim as we carried the cage to the surgery room.

Sorina had gone home to await the outcome. "I'm about as confident as I was starting my first spay."

Jim chuckled. "I get first dibs on him if you screw up."

"Don't talk that way…I'm nervous enough already."

We had the anesthetic machine set up and ready when I lifted the lid to the wire cage. As soon as I threw a towel over the rooster, Jim grabbed him to hold his wings tight to his body while I got hold of his head. "Ouch! Damn, those things are sharp."

Jim scrambled to get control of the legs as the bird's spurs raked at his arm through the towel. I stuffed the critter's head into the mask and stared into his black eyes through the clear plastic of the shield. He struggled for a few seconds with eyes wide open, then closed them and lay quietly inhaling the anesthetic.

"I think we can use a cat tube on him," I said, palpating his trachea to estimate its size.

"You really think we can intubate him?" Jim sounded surprised.

"I've had no problems with hawks, owls, and eagles…I've never tried a chicken, but I can't see where they'd be much different." I had pinned the wings on a number of wild birds over the last few years, and had the satisfaction of releasing them into the wild and watching them fly away.

Within a few minutes the bird was asleep. While Jim held his beak open, I slipped a tube through his larynx and secured it in place by tying it behind his head.

"So where are we supposed to go in?" Jim asked.

I opened my poultry book to a page I had marked where the author gave a short description of a caponization.

"It would have been nice to do a dry run on a dead bird first," Jim suggested.

"I thought of that…I've got some bantams that roost in my shed and crap all over my hay. I tried catching one this morning, but they were too smart for me. I've been dying to get one of them into the stew pot."

"These guys are talking about doing birds that are two to four weeks of age," Jim said as he scanned the text.

"I noticed that…and from what I read, professional technicians do more than twenty an hour."

"Good luck on that," he groused. "We've already used up your allotted time." He read on, "The testes are located on the dorsal wall at the anterior end of the kidneys, posterior to the lungs."

"Do you remember the anatomy of a chicken any better than I do?"

He smiled. "Not very helpful, is it? I did look at my anatomy text this morning…but the answer is no."

"They talk about removing the lower or left gonad first, so that must mean they have the right side up."

"Well, we're off to a good start, then," Jim said. "He's right side up."

"It says to make a one-inch incision between the two posterior ribs, so I guess we better prepare him here." I pointed to the area on his side where the feathers thinned and his ribs ended. "You tie his wings forward, and I'll get him scrubbed."

By the time I had plucked the feathers from the area I anticipated making my incision, Jim had the bird's wings secured forward out of the way. I had my gloves on and my scalpel blade in place, when Jim interrupted. "He's not breathing, Doc."

I felt a flush of panic as I stared at the bird waiting for a movement. Jim shut off the halothane and nitrous oxide, flushed the system with straight oxygen, and compressed the bag a few times. The bird's sides began moving rhythmically again.

"There he goes," he said nervously. "Can you imagine two vets having heart failure over a five-dollar rooster?"

I took a deep breath and made my incision. "Better just keep him on one and a half." The words had no sooner left my mouth than his legs started twitching. "Better bump it up again."

I pried the ribs apart and peered down into the incision. "That must be it there." I pointed to a yellowish organ several centimetres long. "It says to remove the lower one first, though." I pried the ribs apart farther and punctured a fragile membrane that lay over the gonad. "I can't see the other one." I poked my finger deeper.

"Remember," Jim cautioned, "they're talking about doing birds that are two to four weeks—this guy's a year and a half. And it says to watch out for the large vessels located between the two testes."

"Yeah, I see them." Several large vessels were suspended in the mesentery below the gonad.

"They say that beginners should consider making incisions on both sides of the rooster to avoid causing a bleeder."

"I guess that's me."

After tying off the testes, I closed the wound with absorbable suture material. We quickly flipped the bird over and repeated the performance on the opposite side.

Thankfully, the bird was sitting up in his cage within minutes of coming off the table. Doris called Sorina to come and collect him; within half an hour I was loading him into her car.

"How'd it go?" she asked as she closed the car door.

"Not bad," I lied. "Other than a few scares with the anesthetic."

She laughed. "Well, to be honest, it wouldn't have broken Gretta's heart or mine if he hadn't made it."

I smiled meekly. Bernie's solution would certainly have been quicker, cheaper, and a heck of a lot less stressful.

Chapter 18

This Is No Bull

"I'm sorry, Doc, but I never got time to clean it up."

Jim had checked out a couple of bulls for Vern Petersen the day before, and the dials and faceplate of the new electro-ejaculator were covered with caked-on manure. I had already soaked the probe and the long cord that connected it to the control panel.

"Come on, man…we have to take care of stuff better than this. I haven't even had a chance to use the machine yet, and it looks like you dragged it through the trenches of a World War I battlefield."

"I thought Margaret would get a chance to clean it up," Jim whined in his own defence.

For some reason, he had been draggy the last couple of weeks. He had been a ball of energy all through the early winter. During the Christmas season, when things slowed down a bit, he offered to handle much of the day-to-day business at the office to give me a break. That had allowed Father and me to get some work done on the interior of my house. As the winter wore on, Jim's productivity slowed down—he had been late for work on innumerable occasions, and constantly nagged at the girls for "overbooking" him.

I shrugged and continued scrubbing the stainless steel panel. "Are you okay?" I asked.

He eyed me defensively. "What do you mean, okay?"

"You haven't been yourself the last while…How are things at home?"

"Everything's fine!" he snapped.

There was an uncomfortable silence, and Jim got up as if to leave.

"How'd the machine work?" I asked, hoping to ease the tension.

"Just like the ones we used in college," he replied with a hint of enthusiasm. "So much smoother than that other hunk of junk. It's like giving flowers and candy to your lady—the next thing you know, you have your sample."

Although I couldn't really afford to buy new equipment, I couldn't afford not to, either—the other machine was too unreliable. I had eighteen bulls to evaluate at Poganys, twenty at Dortmans, and two to do for Bob Rogers. When you threw in a few additional bulls we evaluated for individual beef producers, I convinced myself that it would bring in enough to cover the cost of the purchase.

I looked out the window and sighed—what a miserable day I had selected for doing Joe Pogany's semen testing. He had phoned in at the beginning of the week to see when I could do it, leaving the decision up to me so long as I had the paperwork ready for his opening bull sale the first week in March. I had listened to CBC Radio's weather forecast on the way to work that day; they had talked about its "warming considerably" towards the end of the week—that's why I chose Friday.

Thursday had been sunny and crisp and would have been ideal. Today the sky was overcast, and heavy, wet flakes continued to fall, adding to the layer of slush on the pavement of the parking lot. Oh well, what could you expect from the third week in February.

"Lynn Schiavon called in to make an appointment to pregnancy test Ladybug!" Doris hollered from the front. "And she says Archie's still doing fine."

"Thank God."

I had sutured Archie one last time and kept him confined in one of our kennels for six weeks until I was convinced that he wouldn't break down again. One afternoon, when Lynn brought her St. Bernards in to be vaccinated, I told her I had a kitten she should see. She reluctantly followed me to the kennel room where she was greeted by her own handsome, healthy-looking Archie. By that time, most of his hair had grown back, and he had become almost placid enough for us to handle.

I packed up my microscope to take to Joe's, and Margaret and I went over the checklist I had created, loading boxes as we went. There was nothing more aggravating than getting all set up only to discover that some necessary item was still back at the office.

The truck was already running with the heater going full bore; it was important to keep the materials that came in contact with semen warm so there was no danger of causing artefacts that would lead to erroneous evaluations in semen density and quality. Spermatozoa were designed to perform at body temperature, not at air temperatures close to or below freezing. Cold shocks could dramatically increase the incidence of a sperm cell having defects in its head and the mid-piece of its tail.

Joe was standing by the chute when I pulled up next to the corral and shut off the engine. Gigantic wet flakes continued to splotch onto the windshield and run down in the form of water. I shook my head at Margaret. "Are you ready to get wet?"

I had brought her along to expedite the setting up of equipment and to record my findings while doing the examinations. She fished a plastic head scarf from her pocket, tied it on, and zipped up her wool jacket.

"You sure picked a heck of a day!" Joe yelled as we got out of the truck. "I've got the heaters running in the cabin."

Margaret and I carried the boxes of material into the squat hut that would serve as our lab. I smiled as I stepped into the building—it hadn't changed much since I stayed here as a student. Back in 1965 when I was just seventeen, I had bunked in this very hut with several other students while picking, hauling, and stacking bales for the Poganys.

"Set the microscope up here, Margaret."

I placed several milk jugs filled with warm water on the table and settled the dropper bottle of live-dead stain between them where it would stay warm. While Margaret was setting things up in the shack, I ran an extension cord to the chute where Joe would catch the bulls.

"Are you ready for the first one?" he asked as I opened the lid of my sparkling new ejaculator and hooked on the lead that ran to the probe.

"Not quite, but it won't hurt him to stand there and settle down for a moment." I stuck my probe into a bucket of warm water, covered my shiny gadget with a garbage bag, and set it on the ledge that was used to walk on when vaccinating cattle in the chute. I headed back to see how Margaret was making out.

Joe opened the gate to the holding pen and squeezed in with the eighteen yearling bulls. Tapping one with the handle of his whip, he chased it through the opening. After closing the gate, he followed the animal down the chute, rapping on the corral rails behind him with his whip.

I went over the materials in the shack, making sure that everything was ready. I set several glass slides and wooden applicator sticks on top of the water bottles so they'd be warm when I returned with my sample. I checked the hoop and long, tapered rubber sleeve that I'd use to collect the semen, and slipped a test tube onto the end of it. Plugging in a small heater, I adjusted its flow and set it next to the microscope to keep it warm.

"Have you got all the sheets ready, Margaret?"

She nodded, then brandished the clipboard that had a couple dozen evaluation sheets clamped to it. "Just remember that I don't know what all this stuff means."

"Write what I tell you...maybe take the sheets out one at a time...and use a pencil. The way it's coming down out there, they'll be soggy wet in no time."

Margaret removed all but one of the forms and stuffed the clipboard under her jacket.

I poured warm water into a mug and settled the glass test tube inside it. "Well, I guess we're ready."

I shivered as a blast of cold, wet air burst through the opening door. Sleet pummelled my face—thank God I had chosen a white-collar job. Margaret was close behind me on the way to the chute. I walked back and forth beside the first bull, giving him a visual examination.

"His feet and legs look sound...both eyes are okay."

Margaret appeared confused until I pointed to where she was to mark the boxes. "Check them here."

I slipped a metal bar behind the animal to keep him from backing up, then raised the end gate to get better access to him. My measuring tape at the ready, I patted him on the butt and shifted his soggy tail to the side.

"His scrotal shape is good."

Once the bull realized I was there and made no attempt to kick, I squatted behind him and reached up to feel his testicles for texture and shape.

"Testicles feel normal."

My hand dropped to check the band-like structures that ended in a knob at the bottom of the testicles.

"His epididymides are normal."

I pulled both testicles to the bottom of the scrotum, then applied the tape and pulled it tight. "Thirty-four and a half centimetres." I pointed to a box on the form when Margaret was searching for the place to mark it. "Right here."

"Is that good?" she asked.

"Pretty fair for a yearling Hereford...thirty-two centimetres would usually be considered the cut-off for adequate size."

"Does size matter that much?"

"The bigger the testicular volume the bull has, the more sperm he can produce, and the less likely he'll be to shoot blanks when there are several cows in heat the same day."

I slipped on a palpation sleeve, lifted the bull's sodden tail, and pushed my hand into his rectum. My hair was already coated with a layer of slushy melting snow, and I shook my head to stem the flow of water to my eyes. I ran my hand over the base of the bull's penis to check a pair of small, firm glands that produced the clear fluid to flush and cleanse the urethra.

"The bulbourethral glands are normal."

I advanced my fingers further along to where the bladder emptied into the urethra and checked the glandular band of material there.

"The prostate's normal."

I advanced to the brim of the pelvis and examined two lobular glands, four to five inches in length, that sat on either side of the urethra—they felt something like a cluster of small grapes. This was where most of the fluid component of the semen was produced; it was also the most likely place to detect an infection in a fertility examination.

"The seminal vesicles are normal."

In preparation for collecting my sample, I began a rhythmic massage of the glands and the base of the penis. Almost immediately the penis firmed and began to pulsate.

"Give me the probe, Joe."

He grabbed the two-foot-long cylinder from the bucket of warm water and passed it to me. I slid it into the yearling's rectum as I withdrew my hand, and his anal sphincter closed around the base of the protruding wire.

I quickly pulled off my palpation sleeve, grabbed my ejaculator from the ledge, and took up my position. The bull extended his head and arched his back as I rotated the dial. I repeated the procedure four or five more times, advancing the dial a little further each time. When the very tip of the penis protruded from his prepuce, I pulled the test tube from the bucket of warm water and held it in my hand to keep it as warm as possible.

I turned the dial back and waited for him to relax, then increased the current yet another time. The bull's penis extended further; I was poised with my hoop as clear fluid dripped from the tip. I cut back the current, then once again advanced the knob. With each stimulation, the animal arched his back and extended his hind legs in a clonic contraction. The penis extended further from the sheath each time.

"His penis looks normal," I advised Margaret. Structural

abnormalities of the penis were not uncommon, and bulls with adhesions were often picked up at this stage of an evaluation. Defects such as lateral deviation, rainbow, or corkscrew formations could make it difficult for the bull to enter the cow, and therefore make him a poor breeder.

At the bull's tenth stimulation, he extended fully and deposited a creamy white sample in my test tube.

I pulled off the sleeve, deposited the tube into the mug of warm water, and rushed to the shack. Holding my head back to keep from dripping on the materials, I applied a drop of the eosin-nigrosin stain. After stirring the sample with the pair of wooden sticks I had laid out, I added a drop of semen.

"What does that tell you?" Margaret asked as I mixed the two together and smeared the sample across the glass slide.

"This stuff is often called a live-dead stain. It'll give me an idea how many of the sperm cells are alive and how many of them have abnormalities." I set the slide back on the warm water container to dry. "Any of the dead cells will take up the eosin and stain a pink colour. The healthy, live cells remain white…the nigrosin stain acts as a background so we can see the other cells more readily and pick out head and tail abnormalities."

"Are you going to do those now?"

"Nope…I'll look at them tomorrow at the office. Once they're dry, they can be done any time."

Margaret nodded and watched intently as I placed another creamy white drop of semen on a warmed slide and slipped it under the microscope. I peered through the eyepiece and smiled— no doubt about the viability of this sample. The swirls and eddies covering the slide resembled a satellite image of clouds moving across a television screen.

"Do you want to have a peek?"

Margaret's face lit up as she eagerly peered through the eyepiece.

"Just look at them all!" she exclaimed.

"See the way they go in waves…that's because there are so many of them rushing in one direction that they have to move as one, like individual animals in a herd of buffalo. When there's less density, they'll sit in one spot and vibrate."

After ticking the box under motility as "very good," I headed for the door, leaving Margaret to wash up the sleeve.

Finished with the first animal, I pulled on the cord and removed the probe. "Okay, Joe...he can go."

The moment the head gate opened, the bull tossed his head and charged down the chute, sending a shower of mud in his wake.

By the time we had tested a dozen animals, we were all soaked and miserable. The new machine had been a treat to use, and I was now thankful I had purchased it. All but two of the yearling bulls had looked great from the preliminary results.

Margaret Pogany, Joe's wife, suddenly appeared at my elbow. "You guys must be drenched through. Do you want to stop for a bite to eat?"

"Boy, do we ever," I said. "I'd love to warm up."

She had prepared a small feast with green beans, squash, potatoes, gravy, and roast beef. I ate until I was stuffed and had almost stopped shivering by the time I finished devouring a second piece of hot apple pie.

It was with a feeling of reticence that we all shuffled to the anteroom to don our wet clothing again. Margaret clucked around at her husband until Joe changed his clothes and put on a dry jacket. Margaret Berg and I were glad of the few extra minutes of warmth before going back outside.

The collection of the next two bulls went smoothly, and I was starting to think we'd be on our way back to the office in no time; however, the third bull was a different story. Although the animal was structurally sound, his testicles measured only thirty-one centimetres. His internal organs felt normal, but for some reason, he wouldn't extend his penis. Even after a long period of repeated stimulation, I got nothing more than a test tube of clear, watery fluid collected from the end of his prepuce.

When I dumped out the container and shut off the machine, the bull was panting from the exertion. "This one doesn't look good, Joe."

He grunted in disgust. "He's nominated for the first sale."

I shrugged. "We'll give him five and try him again…how old is he?"

Joe peeled a notebook from the breast pocket of his jacket and flipped through the pages. He stopped partway through the book and rolled his eyes as he contemplated. "Just over ten months."

"That's probably the reason…he's pretty young."

Joe was not at all happy about the situation. "There's so much rigmarole changing a bull once you've nominated him…and he's one of the biggest of the lot."

"He's a nice-looking animal, for sure, and his scrotal shape is good…he may simply need a bit of time to catch up in the testicle department. If we can't get a decent sample with the ejaculator, we can always try collecting him when you have a cow in heat—some bulls just won't produce with this device."

We stood shivering in silence while big white flakes fell all around us and rapidly blended into the slop at our feet. Margaret's teeth were chattering. "Why don't you go into the shack to warm up," I suggested. "I'll give you a holler when I need you."

My own teeth were rattling by the time I decided to try the bull again. I gently pulled on the cord to the probe until the bull's anal sphincter dilated enough to allow it to pop out. I slipped on a palpation sleeve, pushed into the bull's rectum, and began a rhythmic massage, focusing my attention on the base of the penis and the lobular seminal vesicles.

"He's dripping here," Joe said optimistically. "And the tip of his penis is sticking out."

"Get ready with the hoop in case I'm able to get him to ejaculate from massage—sometimes that works when nothing else does."

Joe stood ready with the hoop as I continued my efforts. "Still the same," he grumped after several minutes. "Just a bit of clear fluid."

I withdrew my arm, inserted the probe again, and quickly

manned my ejaculator. The procedure went no more smoothly this time around. After repeatedly stimulating the bull, I dumped a test tube full of clear fluid into the slop at my feet and shook my head at Joe. Setting my ejaculator on the ledge, I turned to him. "Sorry, but it's no use."

Joe was resting his hands on the latch for the head gate. "Let him go?" he asked dejectedly.

"No…not yet," I replied. I moved to the end of the chute and reached for the cord. Just then the bull lunged ahead, and the gate crashed open.

"Nooooooo!" I cried as the cord slipped from my grasp, and the bull struggled to gain his footing. I made a desperate leap for my new toy as the bull picked up momentum. "Stop him, Joe!" I hollered frantically when the machine was ripped from my fingertips. The shiny silver box flipped high in the air as it crossed over the metal bar, then landed in the mud at the front of the squeeze. The extension cord whipped through the muck like a snake as it followed the now disappearing ejaculator.

I closed my eyes when the lid of my machine hooked on the end of a wooden rail, and the probe plopped out of the bull's rectum.

"My new ejaculator…" I moaned.

Surprisingly enough, the bowels of the machine were still functional, and after stripping the mud and manure from its air vents, I was able to finish collecting the remaining samples.

All the way back to the office, I schemed how I could hide the ejaculator from Jim—at least until I could scrape it clean of manure and somehow straighten the lid.

Chapter 19

Getting Up to Speed

I had finished a long herd health session at Hanson Farms, and I was tired and hungry. I had planned on meeting my realtor friends Gordon and Ruth Veitch for lunch, but when I got back to the office, Doris had other plans for me—there were several cases that had to be attended to before I could think about eating.

"Where's Jim?"

"I don't know...he went to look at some coughing horses out in Lister at nine, and I haven't heard from him since. I paged him twice and called his house, but Mary says she hasn't heard from him either."

It had been three weeks since the Shep incident, and there was still an air of tension in the office. Jim insisted that he had simply overlooked Shep's wounds—that it never would have happened had the dog not been such an obnoxious patient. I wanted to believe him, but couldn't help feeling there was something else going on with my associate. Since Christmas, he seemed to have been in a constant state of agitation, and he hardly ever joked around like he did when he first arrived. I kept wondering if things were not going well at home, but there was no discussing it with him.

The girls had noticed the change, too, and as a result, more and more of the appointments were ending up on my side of the book.

I washed up, threw my dirty coveralls in the laundry basket, and donned a smock. Margaret and I had just inserted an intravenous catheter into a very sick old cat when the telephone rang.

I could tell from the look on Doris's face that I wasn't going to like what she had to tell me, and the furrows in her brow got deeper with each step she took towards the surgery.

"It's Agnes Spy."

I rolled my eyes and sucked in a deep breath. "What now?"

"One of her horses has been cut in barbed wire."

"Surprise, surprise." I exhaled with an exaggerated sigh. "How bad is it this time?"

"She's in tears."

"When isn't she in tears? Tell her I'll call her back in a few minutes."

I was feeling guilty about my childish reaction as I applied a few more rounds of tape to secure the catheter in Brutus's foreleg.

"Page Jim and see if he can get out there to look after her."

I adjusted the flow on my patient's intravenous and wondered why I let some clients get to me like this.

"Get him settled in his kennel, Margaret. Keep the drip going at about this rate and see if we can warm him up a bit—he's cold as ice. Put a couple of hot water bottles in with him and swaddle him with blankets."

She stroked the old cat, then folded the grey woollen blanket over his emaciated frame. She frowned. "Don't you think he'd be better off if you put him to sleep? Look at him, Dave...he's more dead than alive."

Margaret was the best assistant anyone could ask for when working on critters; I just wished there was some way of changing her attitude towards cats. In this old farmgirl's eyes, Brutus's value could only be calculated by the number of mice he'd likely eliminate from a granary.

"He'll come along...you wait and see. It wasn't his fault those kids locked him in an abandoned car. I'd agree with you if he were in this shape because his kidneys weren't working or because his heart was bad."

"Poor Mrs. Carlson was about fit to be tied," Doris chimed

in from the front desk. "She called here three or four times after Brutus went missing. She posted notices all over town."

Margaret clammed up and resolutely carried the debilitated animal to the kennel room.

"Jim's not answering the page," Doris said blandly.

"How much does Mrs. Spy still owe us?" I asked.

"A little over three hundred," she replied matter-of-factly.

"Has she paid anything on it?"

"Not for over three months…she paid fifteen dollars at the end of December."

I glared at the day page for sixty long seconds before picking up the phone; if I could magically change that three-letter name into almost any other combination of the alphabet I could think of, I wouldn't hesitate. I glanced in annoyance at my watch—where the hell was Jim? It was after one, and I dearly wanted to unload this case on him.

It was hard to believe that Agnes Spy had actually called in while it was still daylight. I couldn't remember a single other time I had worked on any of this woman's animals during office hours. If she didn't call within seconds of closing time, then she'd invariably wait until I was trying to warm something up for supper. Every time, she'd rattle on about why these things always happened to her.

"Hello?" The word came out of Mrs. Spy as an anguished plea.

"It's Dr. Perrin calling."

"Oh, thank God, it's you!" This blast was followed by a burst of sobbing and the sound of a nose being blown. "I need you out here right now…Angelica, my little Arab filly, got tangled in barbed wire and tore a huge hunk from the back of her foot."

"Is it bleeding badly?"

"Not now…there was blood all over the ground where I first found her. I'm afraid Toronado might have chased her through the fence."

I felt my blood pressure rising. What in Hades was this woman still doing with that stallion? There wasn't a fence on her place reliable enough to keep a tired plow horse in bounds, never mind that unruly critter.

"Why do these things always have to happen to me?" she went on in a whining voice. "It just isn't fair…"

Why, indeed? Each time I had suggested that she sell that wretched beast, or at least have him gelded, Mrs. Spy would spin the tale of how she'd bottle-fed Toronado for months after her cousin's mare died. Toronado may well have been adorable as a colt, but he had long since grown into an obnoxious creature that offered little to the Canadian equine gene pool.

"Will you be out right away?"

I hesitated, wishing I could say no or at least ask her for some of the money she owed me.

"I'll be out shortly."

My feet dragged as I made my way into the kennel room and grabbed a clean pair of coveralls. I slipped them on before opening the kennel for a quick look at Brutus. Nothing but the very tip of his white nose protruded through the blankets.

It was amazing that the old boy had been able to survive for so long with neither food nor water. It had been ten days since Mrs. Carlson had called in, hoping that someone had brought Brutus to us. At that point, even finding out that he'd been hit by a car would have given her some relief. Having him vanish without a trace was such a worry. If it hadn't been for the Carlsons' neighbour poking around the beehives he had stacked adjacent to the old car, Brutus's disappearance would still be a mystery.

I ran my hand over the animal's bony head and pulled back the blanket to check the catheter. Everything looked fine. I stared at the drip chamber. There was something comforting about order in the universe, something reassuring in the fact that gravity would dependably drag one drop after the other down the stainless spout and through the plastic tubing into my patient's vein. I knew with a certainty that nothing this orderly was waiting for me at the Spys.

I grudgingly left Brutus and headed through the office. "Good luck," Doris hollered as I closed the door. "See if you can get her to pay something on her bill!" Her voice trailed off as I trudged down the street.

My wipers flapped back and forth across my windshield while I waited to turn onto Canyon Street. There had been a downpour earlier in the afternoon, but now it was only drizzling. I waited for a semi-trailer and a string of cars to pass, then pulled in behind them. Normally, following a slow cavalcade like this would have had me grumbling, but not today…I was in no hurry to get where I was going.

By the time I turned onto the road that led to the Spy menagerie, I had myself convinced that it was going to be as horrendous as the last time I had visited. I was praying that her son, James, was home. I kept affirming that if I had to work with Crystal, I'd turn around and drive away. James was a handsome, strapping teen who was always willing to help and seemed blissfully unaware of how dysfunctional the rest of his family was. His twenty-five-year-old sister, Crystal, was something else.

I tensed as I turned into the yard. The moment I entered the drive, the usual pack of dogs congregated from all corners. I slowed to a crawl as a ragged poodle with hair completely covering his face darted in front of my truck. I stopped with a lurch to evaluate the situation. The dogs barked incessantly. A trio of pygmy goats bounded along the fence line…and yes, there was Jessica, the three-legged one.

There was no one near the house, and I certainly wasn't able to see a horse. That's when I spotted Mrs. Spy rushing along the barbed-wire fence to the right of the driveway, madly waving her arms. Gesturing for me to follow her, she turned and made her way up a narrow grassy confine between the fence and a series of outbuildings. I pulled off the drive and followed in the vehicle, cursing under my breath at the dogs that darted back and forth in front of me.

The filly was tied to a rail fence on the other side of a chicken run. I pulled to within twenty feet of her and shut off the truck. The moment I opened the door, the dogs rushed to check me out. I pulled off my shoes and slipped on my rubber boots while the matted poodle yapped at me. As I made my way to Mrs. Spy, he dodged back and forth in front of me, continuing his persistent tirade.

"I don't know why these things always happen to me!" the woman moaned the moment I was near enough to hear above the noise of the poodle. "Other people let their animals run higgledy-piggledy and nothing seems to happen...it's like God has something in for me."

I made my way around Angelica's back end and approached her cautiously. Even for an Arab, she was small and from the way her nostrils flared when I approached, I assumed she hadn't been handled a lot.

"Crystal's been working with her," Mrs. Spy offered, "but she's still a little flighty."

"I can see that," I replied as the filly snorted and planted all four feet in the mud to pull against the rope.

I backed off until she settled and stepped towards me to give herself some slack. I took a couple of deep breaths; I had to shake this feeling of impending disaster. The dogs continued to mill around me until I was afraid to move for fear of tripping over them.

"Untie her from the rail and pass me the halter shank."

Agnes gingerly released the animal and passed me the lead. The dogs scattered as I took the horse a few steps down the fence to drier ground. She quivered when I ran my hand down her neck but made no further attempt to back away.

"See if you can keep her steady, while I see what she's done to herself." I passed the rope back to Mrs. Spy and slowly worked my hand down the filly's front leg. "She's made quite a mess of it, hasn't she?" The wire had gotten caught under the bulb of her heel and carved off a deep chunk that was still firmly attached at the coronary band.

I grasped the horse's foot, lifting it to waist height for a better look. Angelica pulled back as I carefully prodded around the edge of the wound, and Mrs. Spy's eyes widened. Although the hoof was packed with mud, the wound itself was surprisingly clean.

"Do you think you can fix it?"

"It seems to me that the circulation's good enough for it to heal, but if I sew it up and you leave her out here in the mud, I guarantee the sutures won't hold. We'll have to bandage her…and if we put her back out in this…" I pointed to the muddy corral, "it'd be a waste of time."

Mrs. Spy screwed up her brow and wiped a long lock of grey-brown hair from her forehead. For a moment she was lost in thought. Finally, she lamented, "I really don't have anywhere I could put her inside."

"Have you any neighbours with a barn or riding arena who'd help you out?"

She shook her head and worked her face into a pout.

"Then maybe we better just trim that piece off, bandage it, and treat it as an open wound."

Mrs. Spy gave me a look of incredulity. "Angelica comes from fantastic bloodlines…I don't want her disfigured."

I watched a wave of despair sweep across my client's face. Before I could say another word, she burst into tears. "It's so unfair! I try so hard, and things like this keep happening…"

"We have to deal with this, Agnes. It'll heal eventually even if we trim it back, but no matter what, you can't leave her out here in this mud."

"Let me call around," she said, wiping her face with the sleeve of her jacket. "Maybe I can come up with something."

"Can you bring me a bucket of warm water so I can start cleaning this up?" I hollered after her as she turned and headed down the lane.

"I'll send Crystal right out with some."

"But, Mrs. Spy…" Before I could protest more, the woman was gone. "Oh Lord, why are you doing this to me? Not Crystal!"

I stood for ten minutes holding the horse, waiting for someone from the Spy family to reappear before deciding to tie her back up and get prepared for the debacle I knew was coming. Within a few minutes I had everything at the ready. My twitch and cold sterilization instruments were sitting on the hood of the truck, a six-millilitre syringe was loaded with lidocaine, my suture material was ready, and all of my bandage materials were laid out on the front seat. I had a bottle of Rompun in the top pocket of my coveralls. I'd probably have to tranquillize the horse, but if I did, she'd want to stand with her feet planted to the ground and force me to kneel in the mud to work on the wound.

I sat sidesaddle on the seat of the truck and waited. The rain had let up completely, but by the look of the black clouds in the west of the valley, the respite was temporary. Closing my eyes and focusing on my breath, I tried to settle myself down. This family seemed capable of bringing out the very worst in me— maybe it was because, like Mrs. Spy, I always anticipated a disaster, and somehow God always came through. So far things were par for the course: one moment the neurotic woman calls me in a panic insisting that I break my neck getting here, then she takes off and leaves me waiting. My stomach growled. I should have gone for lunch first…where was everyone?

The lamentation had no sooner zapped through the cortex of my brain than I caught movement out of the corner of my eye. There was Crystal struggling around the corner of the chicken house with a bucket of water. Determined to get this experience off to a better start than previous encounters, I rushed towards her with my arm outstretched.

"Can I give you a hand?" I asked with as much cheer as I could muster.

"I'm not helpless!" she snapped.

Here we go again, I thought, following meekly in her wake. "Is your brother or dad around to give us a hand?"

"I'm helping you!" she barked defensively.

Oh Lord…give me strength, I incanted, as Crystal set the bucket down and glared at me.

"I was hoping we could have another person to hold Angelica's foot up while I work on it. Of course, we'll need you to restrain her."

"Dad's sleeping in front of the television and James is at school," Crystal informed me. "Besides, you won't need to have someone holding the foot if you sedate her properly."

Every muscle in my body tensed as I replied through gritted teeth, "If I can get her restrained well enough to freeze the area without sedating her, I'd much rather."

"Sounds stupid to me," she complained.

"Have you looked at the wound?"

"Of course I have…I was the one to find it."

"Then you can appreciate that it's in a very difficult location to get at if the horse won't hold her leg up. Any sedation I give her will make her plant her leg with her foot in the mud."

"If you weren't so damned big, you wouldn't have to worry yourself so much about bending over."

I felt my face flush as we continued to glare at one another. I could only imagine how red my ears were…Crystal had to know that she'd scored a direct hit.

I stepped forward, untied Angelica's rope, and led her a few steps closer to the vehicle. "Let's get on with this."

I stroked the filly's neck for a few seconds, then ran my hand down her leg. Grasping her fetlock, I lifted her foot.

"She doesn't like her feet handled," Crystal warned.

After sawing back and forth for a few seconds, the horse stood still.

"Pass me the bucket," I instructed smugly. I'd show this snotty little twit a thing or two about handling a horse.

After a few minutes of wrestling, I had the foot washed and the wound properly examined. There was no question about the viability of the tissue—all the areas I scraped were oozing fresh blood. So long as I could get it sutured and keep it dry, it should heal.

"I can't find anywhere to put her, Dr. Perrin."

I'd been so engrossed in cleaning the wound that I hadn't noticed Mrs. Spy's return.

"Surely, you must have someplace under a roof that you can bed her down?"

The woman's lower lip quivered. Tears welled and spilled down her cheeks.

"You don't have a carport or a hay shed?" I asked.

"What about the chicken house, Mom?" Crystal suggested.

"It does have a wooden floor," her mother replied. "I could lock the chickens in the run and block them out of the house while she's in there." Her face brightened and she turned to leave.

"Can you get your husband to come and help, Mrs. Spy? I want Crystal to hold Angelica, and I'll need someone to hold the foot."

"Lyle's sleeping," she replied blandly.

"Can you wake him, or better yet, call James to come help?"

Crystal scowled at me as her mother headed in the direction of the house. Paying her as little heed as possible, I picked up the twitch, grasped Angelica's upper lip, and tightened the chain. The filly threw her head and backed up a few steps before settling and staring straight ahead.

"Hold this while I start freezing the wound," I instructed.

"I don't like those things," Crystal replied, reluctantly taking hold of the wooden handle.

"Neither do I, but they serve a purpose."

Angelica stood remarkably well as I injected the inner margins of the wound with local anesthetic. I took a new needle from my pocket and slipped it under the skin at the wound's outer side. Without warning, the horse yanked her foot away and gave a defiant toss of her head. The twitch whistled past my ear as it was yanked from Crystal's grasp.

"I told you to sedate her!" my assistant shrieked. "It wasn't my fault!"

"I never said it was," I said as pleasantly as I could manage. "Oh good, here comes your father."

As the two Spys rounded the chicken coop, there was a squeal from the other side of the yard. A bay gelding tore across the length of the corral with the horse I recognized as Toronado in hot pursuit.

"Don't you think you better catch that stallion and separate them before we have more sewing to do?"

"They'll settle down," Crystal insisted.

"Well, you have lots of help, now," Mrs. Spy interrupted, depositing another bucket of water at my feet. I watched Lyle as he shuffled towards us and gave me a lukewarm smile. Although he was a tall man with a reasonable build, Mrs. Spy's husband was not a man to immediately inspire confidence. With his belly hanging over his belt and his shoulders slouched, he looked less than happy to be drawn into this activity.

"What do you need me to do?" he grumbled in a disinterested fashion.

"I need someone to hold the foot up while I freeze it."

I applied the twitch once more and passed it to Crystal. She grudgingly took the handle, then glared defiantly at her mother.

"He doesn't want to sedate her," she hissed.

I was overpowered by the image of a Great Dane being harassed by a toothless chihuahua that didn't have the sense to know when to quit. The image wouldn't leave me as I stooped and again wrestled the foot to waist height.

"Can you hold this up for me, Lyle?"

"Good luck," Crystal muttered as her father ambled forward and bent over.

"You'll have to lean into her and get a good hold on the foot, Lyle," I suggested as the man half-heartedly reached in from as far back as possible.

The moment I released Angelica's foot, Lyle groaned and allowed it to sag to within inches of the ground. Crystal snickered as I shooed the dogs away and lowered my knee to the mud. Grabbing the foot, I inserted the needle and began injecting. Lyle backed away as the horse tried to rip free.

"Hold her still for a moment longer," I begged, as the dogs crowded close. Lyle's face flushed; his cheeks puffed out like he was blowing up a massive rubber balloon. I had one side of the wound frozen and was about to start on the other, when one of the goats began rubbing his horns on my butt.

"For God's sake, Agnes, can you get rid of some of these critters?"

Just then, there was another high-pitched squeal from the corral, and Mr. Spy jumped back from Angelica.

"Toronado!" Mrs. Spy screamed frantically.

The stallion's ears were back and his thick neck was stretched out as he relentlessly pursued the gelding down the length of the pen. The gelding squealed again as the stallion bit him savagely on the rump, then reared to strike him.

"Toronado!" Mrs. Spy screamed again. Bursting into tears, she ran towards the corral with the pack of dogs on her heels. "Why do these things always happen to me?"

Crystal tied Angelica to the fence and ran after her mother.

"Toronado!"

The gelding was cornered and obviously seeking some avenue of escape from the stallion's wrath. Crow-hopping, he struck defensively with both hind feet in Toronado's direction. I closed my eyes as he wheeled and took off towards us down the length of the corral. He was running full out when he hit the fence, with the stallion close behind.

"Toronadooooo!" Mrs. Spy wailed as three fence posts in a row broke free from the ground and followed the gelding in his forward trajectory. "Toronadooooo!"

The page wire stretched, gave way, then held, and the gelding was suddenly airborne as he was launched over backwards. He scrambled to his feet and took off in the opposite direction with the stallion following.

Lyle smiled meekly and shook his head in resignation. It was twenty minutes before Crystal and Mrs. Spy were able to get a halter on the stallion. Amazingly, the gelding had escaped with only a few nasty-looking bite wounds on his flank and rump.

"Tie him to the tree!" Mrs. Spy insisted when her daughter hitched the offending animal to a fence post. "He might break that off, too."

Crystal gave her mother a vile look. Yanking on the halter shank, she led the stallion to the old dead spruce in the centre of the corral. By the time things settled down, and Mrs. Spy and

Crystal returned, Lyle was nowhere to be seen. In my mind's eye, I could see him slumbering in front of the television. How I envied him.

The rain had started again and my coveralls were already soaked through. Mrs. Spy's infernal pack of dogs still circled underfoot, and every time I turned my back, one of the goats would rub on my pant leg.

"So you're finally going to tranquillize her?" Crystal said smugly as I fished the Rompun from my pocket.

"Yes," I replied tersely.

"'Bout time…"

The Great Dane in my mind suddenly lunged at the chihuahua. Two quick snaps of his jaw and the conflict was ended. I wondered absently as I drew the clear liquid into the syringe what the head-lines in the *National Enquirer* would read. "Seven-Foot Veterinarian Squashes Defenseless Three-Foot Woman Like a Bug!" My imagina-tion took off as I pictured myself sitting before the B.C. Veterinary Council trying to explain my way out of that one.

Mrs. Spy watched glumly as I stroked Angelica's neck to locate the jugular. Her face was wet with tears, her eyes bloodshot. Every second breath saw her sniffling uncontrollably; now and then came a pathetic little whimper. She stared vacantly as blood shot back into the syringe and I injected the drug.

"Agnes…will you please find me some cardboard."

"Cardboard?" She gave a start, as if waking from a nightmare.

"Yes…for me to kneel on, and some to put under Angelica's foot to get it up out of the mud…and please do something with these critters so I can work without tripping over them."

The woman quickly disappeared in the direction of the house. Every dozen steps, she turned to call out and rally her pack of canine followers before carrying on. Crystal and I stood silently staring in different directions while waiting for the tranquillizer to have effect. Watching the woman out of the corner of my eye, I couldn't help but think she looked rather smug—as if she had been vindicated by circumstances.

By the time Mrs. Spy returned with the cardboard, Angelica was standing in a sawhorse stance with her head hanging. I leaned against her side, struggling to lift her leg and force her to bend it.

"Now, Agnes…now!"

"Now what?" she asked in a state of confusion.

"The cardboard…" I gasped, struggling to bear the entire weight of the horse as she leaned on me. "Put the cardboard under her foot!"

As if emerging from a trance, Mrs. Spy jolted to life and slipped the flattened box under the horse's foot seconds before it hit the ground.

"You and Crystal seem to have things under control here," she sniffled. "I'm going to go shovel out the henhouse and get it ready for Angelica."

As little as I enjoyed Agnes's company, I dreaded being alone with her daughter. Struggling to keep my cool, I took the other piece of cardboard and threw it in the soggy muck at my feet. After placing my suture pack on the ground beside it, I scrubbed up, then knelt on top of it. From the expression on Crystal's face as she watched me sink to my prayer bones, I was a peasant kneeling before his queen.

Bracing myself on my elbows, I drove my needle through the edge of the wound and tacked down the inside corner. I had a half dozen sutures placed when there was a tremendous crash. I got up quickly and looked around to see what had happened. There was Toronado struggling to extricate himself from under a fallen tree.

"Mom! Mom! Come help!" Crystal screamed and took off as fast as her little legs would carry her. She was already in the corral before her mother arrived on the scene. In a state of total confusion she turned first one way, then the other, to determine the cause of the latest commotion.

"Oh my God, no!" she wailed.

Just at that moment, Toronado lunged to the side, yanking the remainder of the tree from the ground by its roots.

Bursting into tears, Mrs. Spy ran to her daughter's aid. She shook her fists defiantly at the sky and screeched, "Oh God! Why are you tormenting me? What have I done to make me deserve this?"

I watched in wonderment as the Spys tried in vain to intercept the stallion. Every time they got near enough to get hold of the rope, he backed frantically in another direction dragging the thirty-foot snag in his wake.

I was shivering with cold by the time I finished with Angelica. After giving her an injection of penicillin and a vaccination for tetanus, I started cleaning my equipment and loading it in the vehicle. The whole time, Mrs. Spy and her daughter struggled to coax the horse through the narrow door of the chicken coop. With each passing moment, Crystal's voice grew shriller. Mrs. Spy didn't stop crying the entire time. I was about to go to their assistance, when I saw Angelica's butt disappear into the ramshackle outbuilding.

I sighed as I started the truck. Although I was soaked to the skin and my coveralls were plastered with mud, I was soon going to be free of this irritating assignment. As I drove past the henhouse, I remembered Doris's final plea to demand some payment on the account—she and Marg would give me no end of grief if I didn't get at least something on the bill. One look in the Spys' direction, and I hit the gas and headed for the road home.

As I reached the end of the driveway, a pickup pulled up. James stepped out and waved to the driver before he headed off up the road. I rolled down the window as I passed by him.

"Hi, Dr. Perrin!" he called cheerfully. "Did I miss out on something exciting?"

It was after four by the time I got back to the office. Everything was quiet; the waiting room was empty and my three stalwart assistants were huddled behind the desk in consultation.

"What's happening?" I asked.

"We're pretty much caught up with things," Doris answered.

"Where's Jim?"

The girls looked at one another, then Margaret spoke up. "He had some errands to run downtown."

I shook my head in amazement, and went to my office where I kept a change of clean clothes. I was pulling on a dry sweater when the telephone rang.

"John Poznikoff's on the phone!" Doris hollered. "He's wondering about a prescription that we left there to be filled."

John Poznikoff was the pharmacist who owned and operated the local Tamblyn Drugmart. Although, as a veterinarian, I filled most of my clients' prescriptions from my own pharmacy, I had an excellent relationship with John for supplying some of the more impractical medications that I didn't carry.

I was still in my stocking feet as I headed to the front. "Have we sent a prescription to John in the last day or two?"

Doris shrugged and looked questioningly at Margaret. "Not that I can recall."

"Okay, I'll take it."

"Hi, John...Dave here."

"Hi, Dave...I called to tell you that I won't be able to fill that prescription for Dexedrine your young vet left today."

"Dexedrine?"

"Yes...we gave him the fifty last Friday, and I guess I wasn't expecting your needing more so soon—it may be in tomorrow, but for sure on Thursday." He hesitated for a moment, then went on. "It seems like you've been using an awful lot of it lately. This is the fourth refill this month. I know that you need a whopping dose to treat a cow, but..."

There was an uncomfortable silence as the realization of this new information sank in. "Can I get you to itemize all of Jim's prescriptions to date, John?"

"Is there a problem?"

"There's a problem," I replied resolutely.

Silence resumed as I stared across the counter at my three mothers. Each of them had been listening intently to my side of the conversation. Marg Rogers had her hands at her ears making the familiar circular rotations we all associated with turning up the volume on her hearing aids.

"So you won't be wanting the prescription filled?"

"No, John...we won't be wanting it filled."

I passed the receiver to Margaret, and she reverently hung it up. For some time we all just stood looking at one another.

It was Doris who broke the silence. "I guess that explains a lot."

I nodded. "I guess it does."

"What are you going to do?"

"I don't know, but something has to give..."

"What is that stuff, anyway?" Margaret interrupted.

"It's a drug that increases the levels of dopamine and norepinephrine in the brain and gives a feeling of euphoria—a potent amphetamine that's used to treat depression and narcolepsy in humans. All the druggies back in college called it speed or crank."

Margaret shook her head in disgust. "I've heard of that speed stuff. Why would Jim be using something like that?"

I shrugged. "That's a question you'll have to ask him."

"You've used it to treat cows, haven't you?" Doris asked. "I'm sure I remember seeing it on a couple of bills."

"I tried it a few times on downer cows—when critters I treated for milk fever wouldn't even try to get up. A dairy practitioner at the Coast told me he was having good luck with it. I thought it might have made a bit of difference on a couple cases, but the jury's still out...Hand me the pharmacopoeia, will you."

She opened the bottom drawer of the filing cabinet and drew out the big blue book that listed all the drugs marketed in the United States, including their indications, side effects, and contraindications. I thumbed through the pages until I came up with Dexedrine, then scanned down, reading out occasional salient features.

"It's listed as a performance-enhancement drug that is often abused as a recreational substance."

I noted the reference to dependence and the fact that the drug had been subject to substantial abuse that could lead to tolerance, extreme psychological dependence, and severe social disability.

"People who abuse the drug often increase their dosage to many times the recommended level...The drug can affect blood glucose levels and increase both heart rate and blood pressure."

"That sounds terrible!" Margaret exclaimed. "Why would a handsome young guy with so much going for him get started on something like that?"

I read on. "It suggests that the medication may disguise extreme fatigue and impair the ability to perform hazardous activities like driving or operating machinery...Side effects can include dizziness, dry mouth, unpleasant taste, diarrhea, constipation, loss of appetite, nausea or vomiting, erectile dysfunction or reduced sex drive..."

"That doesn't sound like him," Margaret chirped.

"Euphoria, irritability or mood swings, restlessness, trouble sleeping, and weight loss."

"That sure does," Doris said. "I know he's been having trouble sleeping, and just the other day he said he's lost ten pounds since he's been here."

I skipped to the bottom of the page. "Check with your doctor as soon as possible if any of the following side effects occur: abnormal thoughts or behaviour, hallucinations or delusions, jerky body movements, increased blood pressure or palpitations, symptoms of depression, thoughts of suicide."

I closed the book.

"Damn."

Chapter 20

Taking Inventory

I pulled my mask under my chin and tucked my cap into my smock pocket. Margaret was standing patiently next to the surgery table waiting for Rowena to recover enough to remove her endotracheal tube. The eight-month-old calico cat was the first of four surgeries we had booked for the morning.

I drew up Atravet and wandered into the kennel room with a bottle of atropine in hand. Randy, a normally rambunctious black Lab, was feeling the effects of his premedication. Resting with his head on his paws, he briefly opened his eyes in acknowledgement of my presence, yawned, and closed them again. His neuter was next on the book.

I was adding atropine to the syringe to administer to the next cat spay when Doris appeared. "Dan Hurford's out front," she said expectantly. "He wants to talk with you."

I stared intently at Doris. "Did he say what he wanted?"

She shook her head. I hadn't seen Dan in months. For the last while that Jim was still with me, "my new vet" had done almost all the work for Tsolum Farms. It had been three weeks since my former colleague stormed from the office.

"Can you hold Mandy for me?"

Doris cuddled the orange-coloured queen to her chest as I administered the injection. I gave her an apprehensive glance before heading to the front.

Dan was sitting on the bench in the waiting room. He appeared ill at ease.

"Hi, Dan."

"Hi, Dave…can we talk in private?" He headed to the farthest exam room. When I entered after him, he closed the sliding door.

"What's up?" I asked.

He stared at his feet for a moment, then looked me in the eye. "We've been through a lot together over the years," he started. "And I thought I knew you pretty well."

I nodded as he paused.

"The last few months have been tough for me, and when Jim told me what happened between the two of you, I didn't know what to think." He hesitated again, and I stood there in silence. "He was pretty upset that you left him high and dry, and to be honest, so was I."

"Did he tell you why he left?"

"He said you wanted to cut back on his hours, and he wouldn't go for it."

"That's what he told you?"

"Yes."

"Did he mention the amphetamines?"

Dan's face clouded as he spat out the words. "You guys and your black-eyed mollies!"

"Black-eyed mollies?"

"Yeah!" Dan rebutted angrily. "Those damned pills you're always popping."

"Us guys?"

"Yeah," he said passionately. "Jim said that taking the mollies was the only way you could keep working the hours you did."

"Dan, until now, I hadn't even heard the term 'black-eyed mollies'—I sure as hell have never swallowed them."

His eyes were fiery as he stared into mine; I could see he was struggling to determine which one of his veterinarians was telling him the truth.

"I don't even take vitamin pills. I probably should…but I don't."

He looked down at his feet. "He told me you got him started on the damned things."

"The only time I've ever had those pills in my hand was when I stuffed them into a bolus for a downer cow—even then, I've administered them maybe three or four times in my practice career. Jim told me it was his football coach at university who got him hooked—said he wanted all the guys hyped up and ready to kill before they hit the field."

Dan continued to fume. I assumed that he still didn't believe me. "So he lied about that, too," he finally said.

"I guess so, if that's what he told you."

"I thought he was a pretty good friend," he said quietly. "But after working with him for the last while I was really starting to wonder what was up with him...after he ran out of his pills, he was pretty much a lost cause."

"I wanted to get him help," I explained. "I suggested he take some time off and set up some counselling and rehab through the vet association. That's when he stomped out the door and told me where to stuff the job."

Dan took a deep breath and sighed loudly. "It's all starting to make sense now."

"If you've got any influence with him, you should talk him into getting some help. He's got the makings of a good veterinarian if he can get himself straightened out."

"I guess I'm not as magnanimous as you," Dan replied angrily. His face was flushed.

"What do you mean?"

"Last week he produced an inflated bill to Dad, giving him a song and dance that he had to have the money right away. He said Mary needed it to fly home and be with her father when he got out of the hospital." I was entranced as Dan went on with the story. "The morning after he left, Dad went out to start our new John Deere tractor, and it wouldn't even turn over. When he checked out the battery, he discovered ours was gone—replaced by an old one with a decal from some garage in Austin, Texas."

I shook my head in disbelief as Dan continued. "On Friday I found out that he took off with Bob's wife, Alyssa…I can't believe that she'd bugger off and leave the poor guy with their two kids."

"Are you serious?" I stared at him with my mouth hanging open. "What about Mary? Has someone called her?"

"Called her? Hell, I went over to see her on Saturday. He left her stranded up here all by herself…She was worried sick about him when he never came home Friday night, and she called me wondering where he was. She was pretty broken up when I told her what was going on. She hardly had enough money to buy food for her and the baby."

"What's she going to do?"

"God knows…her parents are wiring enough money to get back home, but after that, it looks like she's on her own."

"What about Bob?"

"He's taking it pretty hard, but I think he'll make out. You know what Dad always says…When the going gets tough, the tough get going."

"I can't believe this…how could a guy self-destruct so quickly?"

"There's something else."

"Else?" I wondered what else he could possibly add to what he'd already told me.

"After he started working for us, he offered to buy us drugs cheaper than what you sell them for. We figured, why not, if he could buy them wholesale—we knew you bumped yours up."

I flushed as he went on, thinking that he was insinuating I put too much mark-up on the products I sold them.

"We quit ordering stuff from him when Dad found this on a box of Orbenin mastitis ointment." He showed me a plain white sticker that had been inscribed with blue ink.

I examined it closely and wrinkled my brow. "That's Doris's handwriting."

"That's what we thought." Dan paused and stared into my eyes. "He had lots of everything we would ever need."

"I wonder how he got it all. He dropped the office keys back the day after he stormed out of here, so I never thought of changing the lock—maybe he had another one made."

"Beats me…maybe he was systematically lugging it out of here one piece at a time all the while he was working with you."

"So much for my inventory control," I muttered.

It was hard to get back to the business at hand after Dan left. I couldn't wrap my mind around how the vibrant, fun-loving guy who started his career here could have resorted to this. When he arrived, Jim had the world on a string with people tripping over themselves to befriend him. Now, it was as if he had intentionally set about hurting everyone who cared about him. The entire time I was doing surgery, my mind kept running over and over the things Dan had told me. Poor Mary—what a way to leave her.

We had settled Randy in his kennel, and Margaret was on her way to the surgery with the orange cat in her arms when Doris appeared.

"I'm sorry to bother you when you're behind schedule, Dave, but there's a woman up front who's asking to talk to you."

I glanced at my watch. "You better order me a sandwich, or I'll be going without lunch again today."

I followed Doris to the front where a petite, attractive, fair-haired woman leaned against the front counter. As I approached, she introduced herself. "Hello, Dr. Perrin, I'm Nancy Barling…My husband Chris and I run Wild West Well Drilling from here and Airdrie, Alberta. We have a farm in Airdrie and an acreage in West Creston."

"Glad to meet you, Nancy…what can I help you with?"

"I'm wondering if you'd consider neutering our raccoon."

When I hesitated, she went on. "I've tried to get him done in Airdrie and Calgary, but no one wants to do it there."

"How tame is he? Is he easy to handle?"

"I can do anything with him, but he's leery of strangers and new places. I'm sure Chris could control him long enough for you to give him a shot, though."

I was silently pondering what I would even use to anesthe-
tize a raccoon. It sounded like it would have to be a hit-and-run
proposition.

"How old is he?"

"Two years."

"Oh..." I had been picturing a cuddly little fluffball. "So you've
had him for some time?"

"We adopted Coonie when he was a baby. My family back East
found him on the highway with an injured paw. They sent him out
to me."

"So you're planning on keeping him long term..."

"Oh yes...he's welcome with us for as long as he wants
to stay. I love the little guy...he's my best friend. It's not like we
keep him locked up or anything. At the farm in Airdrie, he comes
and goes whenever he wants. Sometimes he disappears for days
at a time—that's why we waited so long to neuter him. We wanted
him to be able to survive in the wild if he chose to go out on
his own."

"Isn't he pretty destructive in the house? One of my clients
down the lake had a raccoon for a bit, and it tore up her furniture
and uprooted her plants."

"No...he's very respectful of things. I had to sort of kid-proof my
house, though—he loves to open doors and pull everything out."
She chuckled as if she had just thought of something. "You should
have seen him when I put child locks on my kitchen cupboards. He
lay on his back like a repairman under the doors, tugging on them
and staring up at them to figure out what was keeping them from
opening. You could almost hear him think, 'They opened yesterday,
why aren't they opening today?'"

"And the child locks worked?"

"For the most part...we left him his own cupboard. When he's
hungry, he climbs up and grabs a handful of nuts or a granola bar."

"Doesn't he leave a big mess behind?"

"Oh no...he'll grab one granola bar from the box and leave the
rest. He does drop the wrapper on the kitchen floor, though."

"Do you have him with other pets?"

"Yes…that's why we've decided to get him neutered. He grew up with a couple of male dogs and absolutely loved them till he was a year old. Since then, he's gotten more aggressive with them. Now, whenever they get close to the house he puts the run on them."

She paused and smiled. Her blue eyes brimmed with enthusiasm as she went on. "When a girlfriend brings a female dog over, he greets them the moment they get out of the car and welcomes them into the house. He actually strokes their faces and grooms them—as long as you're female, you're in."

"Sounds like it's not too easy being a male in your house."

"He doesn't bother my teenaged sons, but he's gotten so he puts the run on my husband and any other man who comes to the door. Chris spends most of the week up here in Creston working with the drilling rig. When he comes back to the farm for the weekend, Coonie tries chasing him off. After a day or so, he sort of gives in and lets him rejoin the family."

"That would wear a little thin on a man's ego."

"Yeah, at the start Chris would keep his steel-toed boots on, and it wouldn't hurt quite as much when Coonie attacked him. He likes to go after his feet."

I raised my eyebrows. "He'd physically attack him? Would he draw blood?"

"Yes…he's quite serious."

"I can certainly see why your husband would want to settle things down a notch or two."

"When Coonie was a kit, he slept between us on the bed…now he treats Chris like an intruder."

"He sleeps with you?" I was having a hard time concealing my amazement.

"Oh yes…when he and I are alone, he lies there on his back with his head on the pillow watching me get ready for bed. It's almost like he's saying, 'Come on, honey…what's taking you so long?'"

I was at a loss for words.

"He's such a sweetheart with me…when I get to bed he reaches over and gives me a gentle pat on the cheek."

"That's probably why he's so territorial with your husband."

"When poor Chris tries to join me at night, Coonie gets agitated and runs circles around the bed to keep him from getting in."

"And he can't very well climb into the sack with his steel-toed boots on," I quipped.

The woman laughed. "That's true…but if he spends the first night or two in the spare bedroom, he can work his way back into Coonie's good graces." She sighed. "Last weekend was really the last straw for Chris. He came into the house thinking that Coonie was outside. The poor guy was taking off his coveralls when Coonie took after him hissing and clucking…You should have seen Chris trying to run up the stairs with his coveralls all bunched up around his ankles! He fell through the bathroom door and slammed it just in time."

She hesitated, then went on with a twinkle in her eyes. "I know I shouldn't have laughed, but I couldn't help it."

By this time, Doris and Margaret were standing behind me listening as well, and we all roared with laughter.

I left Mrs. Barling with the promise that I'd call Gary Wobeser at the Western College of Veterinary Medicine as soon as I had a free moment. If there was information on anesthetizing a raccoon, he'd have it. He was their wildlife specialist.

My mind was in turmoil as I tried to focus on Mandy's surgery. Although I constantly reminded myself that worrying about the past and fretting about the future were unproductive, I couldn't help stewing about how Jim had ended up in such a mess. How would he ever extricate himself from the deep hole he had dug? Surely, if I had been more observant, I'd have found out about his drug dependence sooner.

After work, Margaret and I drove over to the little house where Mary had been living in the hope we could somehow help console her. When we got there, we peered through bare windows into empty rooms—she was already gone.

I struggled through Saturday morning appointments, plotting what I could accomplish on the rest of my day off. Feeding the cattle twice a day when working alone had become a tremendous drag. Over the last few weeks, I had accumulated all the materials to build a feed bin; that way, I could blow it full of chopped hay on the weekends and let the cattle self-feed through the week. I'd still have to check on them from time to time, but at least if I got tied up at the office, they'd not be going hungry.

When the last appointment was finished, I rushed to Creston Builders Supply for the selection of spikes and nails I'd need to complete the project.

The moment I got home, I rushed upstairs to change my clothes. I was pulling on a heavy sweater when Lug ran from the room barking madly. Before I could get to the window to see what had upset him, he was already at the door downstairs fiercely announcing his presence. I saw the green Chevy in the yard just as I heard the timid knock.

I ran downstairs and pulled Lug away from the door. When I opened it, I found Ruth Boehmer standing on my doorstep.

"Hello," I said hesitantly. "Come in."

I pulled Lug back when he tried to sniff at her. "Sit!" I warned as he emitted a low grumble.

Ruth took half a step forward and extended the jar of milk she held in her hand. "You said you wanted to taste goat's milk again."

I took the jar and smiled. "Thanks...I do."

"Sit down." I pointed to the old stuffed davenport that sat in the middle of an otherwise empty living room. "Sorry it's so cool in here, but I only heat the room I live in."

"That's not a problem," she said, settling on the edge of the sofa.

"Would you like a glass, too?" I asked, heading to the kitchen.

"No thanks..."

I grabbed a mug from my little pantry and poured it full. I took a swig of it as I was returning to Ruth. By the time I had taken a few steps, I was wishing I hadn't been so generous with the portion.

"I can't stand the aftertaste," Ruth said quietly.

"I know what you mean." I smacked my lips and set the cup on the mantel of my fireplace. "It would definitely be an acquired taste."

We sat staring at one another.

"So, how's Coconut?"

"He's fine…of course, I didn't do a lot of riding in the winter." She stared at her hands through an uncomfortable silence. "How have things been going for you?" The way she asked, I was certain she'd been filled in on most of the local gossip about Jim. After all, she worked at the hospital where the rumour mill ran twenty-four hours a day.

"Fine…" I said lamely. There was no need of spilling out the last episode in the Creston Vet Clinic drama.

"Well, I better not interfere with what you had planned." She stood up.

"Not a problem…I was just going out to pound some nails. I'm building a new feed bin to chop hay into."

Ruth contemplated for a few seconds. "Would it help to have an extra pair of hands?"

On Monday morning I smiled every time I thought about the weekend. Not only had I not been paged for the entire two days, but I now had a feeder filled to the brim with chopped hay. In addition to helping me with the construction on Saturday and Sunday, Ruth had assisted in hauling bales from the shed while I fed them into the chopper. I couldn't help thinking it was exactly something a farmer's wife might do.

I was halfway to work before I remembered we had booked Coonie's neuter for the morning. As I expected, Gary Wobeser had several references on the use of injectable anesthetics in raccoons. According to him, Ketamine, a drug we used for simple procedures in cats, was the best choice. After all, it could be used intramuscularly and would best fulfill my desires for a poke-and-run.

Nancy Barling was stressed when she came into the clinic. "I hate doing this to him…Do you think he'll ever forgive us?"

"I'm sure he will, eventually. Let me give your husband a hand."

A slender man with a dark complexion was struggling to unload a wire cage from the back of his pickup.

"He's not too happy with us," he said.

The hefty raccoon twirled in his cage and hissed at me as I approached. I grabbed one end of his carry kennel and proceeded to the clinic.

"It's all right, Coonie," Mrs. Barling crooned, holding the door open for us to pass.

Coonie circled his cage as we settled him on the floor in the corner of the examining room.

"Do you have any idea what he weighs?" I asked.

"He must be twenty-some pounds," Mr. Barling suggested.

"We better get a more accurate weight than that." We had already weighed the kennel before sending it home from the clinic, so only had to place the raccoon-filled cage on the scale for the animal's true weight. "Pretty close," I said, calculating the difference. "He's nineteen pounds."

After a quick calculation, I went to the lockbox and drew up the Ketamine. Coonie was lying on his side in the kennel holding his mother's hand when I returned. "Are we ready?" I asked, closing the exam room door.

The Barlings looked to one another, and Chris pulled on his welding gloves. Coonie cautiously stepped out and surveyed his surroundings when Nancy opened the cage and moved back. I waited with needle ready as Chris maneuvered closer to his pet. When he lunged and picked the raccoon up by the scruff, I quickly jabbed him in the hindquarters and injected the Ketamine.

Coonie was on the prod as soon as Chris released him. Huffing and puffing and hissing, he stood on his hind legs and lunged in Chris's direction.

"He thinks you did it," I said gleefully as Coonie continued his complaint against his owner.

"It's okay, Coonie…it's okay," Nancy murmured.

After several minutes of circling angrily around the room, the raccoon settled down and rested on his haunches. Nancy took her leave with a very worried expression.

"I hope this settles things down for you," I said to a distraught Chris. "I can't imagine living with a pet that was constantly attacking you."

"It's not always that bad," he said softly. "It's only the first few days we're together. Last night we spent several hours watching television. He sat right next to me on the couch sharing almonds… he'd take one and I'd take one." He looked affectionately at Coonie as he lay prostrate on the floor. "I'd never had anything to do with raccoons before him…Nancy's family has always had them around."

He watched as I prodded Coonie gently, then lifted him onto the exam table. "There's something so special when he comes up and wraps his little fingers around mine. They're a lot like kids—as much as they can be a pain in the arse at times, you still love them."

Although Coonie's surgery was pretty routine, I spent the next couple of hours watching him closely. It probably didn't take much longer for him to come around than it did for most tomcats we neutered, but I was elated when he was finally able to sit up on his tummy.

The rest of the day was hectic, and I was exhausted by the time I helped Chris load Coonie's cage into the back of the pickup truck. I returned to the office and dropped onto the bench in the waiting room. Lug bounded from the back to join me.

"Man, I'm pooped. It was a crazy day."

"You better get used to it," Doris said.

"What do you mean?"

"I never had the chance to tell you earlier, but I dropped out to visit Cory and Marcie on Sunday."

"Oh," I said as nonchalantly as I could manage. Even though I had severed ties with Cory and Marcie, Doris visited them from time to time.

"Marcie's expecting."

"Oh."

"They've got their farm up for sale and are planning to move back to Saskatchewan."

Doris and I had our coats on and were heading out the door when the phone started ringing.

We both glanced at the wall clock—quarter to six. She looked at me as if to ask whether to answer it or allow it to go to the answering service.

"Better see what it's about, or I'll be getting paged when I'm halfway home."

Doris caught the phone before the fourth ring. "Creston Veterinary Clinic…" I watched her face as she listened dispassionately. For several minutes she maintained her stony demeanour. Finally, she said, "Just hang on…"

Without changing her expression, she turned to me. "Agnes Spy wants to know if you'll come out and tranquillize Angelica. She and Crystal have been trying all week to get the horse out of the chicken coop, and she refuses to come through the door."

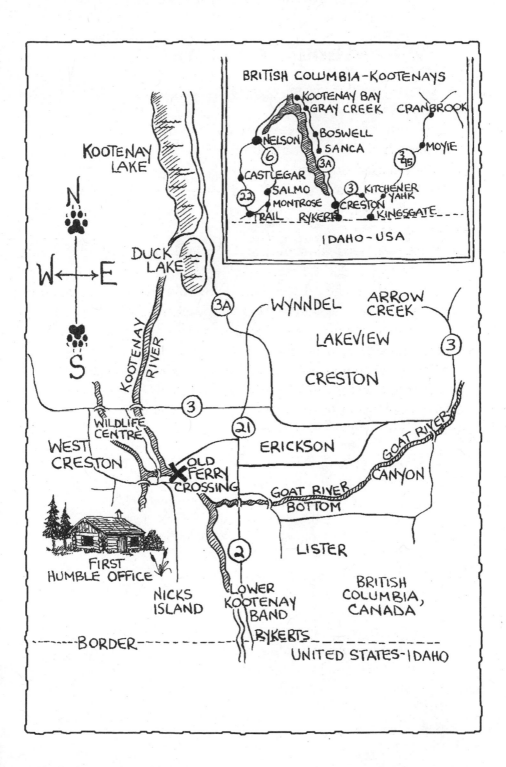

About the Author

Dave Perrin was raised in Casino, a small town near Trail, British Columbia. He attended Selkirk College in Castlegar, the University of British Columbia, and the Western College of Veterinary Medicine at Saskatoon, Saskatchewan.

He graduated as a veterinarian in 1973 and practised in the Creston Valley until 1998. After a year in Hawaii, where he began writing the first book about the profession he loved, he returned to his farm in Lister, B.C. He established Dave's Press and has published four previous books on his veterinary adventures: *Don't Turn Your Back in the Barn* (2000), *Dr. Dave's Stallside Manner* (2001), *Where Does It Hurt?* (2003), and *Never Say Die* (2006). In 2004 Dave's Press published *Keep Sweet: Children of Polygamy*, a book about a young girl growing up in the fundamentalist Mormon community of Bountiful.

Dr. Perrin lives and writes in the log home he built on his farm in the community of Lister.

Find Dr. Dave's
veterinary adventures
at your local bookstore

For more information, for comments,
or to order autographed copies of

Don't Turn Your Back in the Barn,
Dr. Dave's Stallside Manner,
Where Does It Hurt?,
Never Say Die
and
When the Going Gets Tough

or for audio MP3s and e-books
visit our Web site at:
davespress.com
Phone: 250-428-3931
E-mail: dave@davespress.com
or write to:
1521 Canyon-Lister Road
Creston, British Columbia
Canada V0B 1G2

Dave Perrin's books are distributed by
Sandhill Book Marketing Ltd. of Kelowna, B.C.